EVIDENCE-BASED

TRAINING METHODS

2ND EDITION

A Guide for Training Professionals

RUTH COLVIN CLARK

20 19 18 17   4 5 6 7

ATD Press is an internationally renowned source of insightful and practical information on workplace learning, training, and professional development.

ATD Press
1640 King Street
Alexandria, VA 22314

Ordering information: Books published by ATD Press can be purchased by visiting ATD's website at td.org/books or by calling 800.628.2783 or 703.683.8100.

Library of Congress Control Number: 2014949534

ISBN-10: 1-56286-974-4
ISBN-13: 978-1-56286-974-8
e-ISBN: 978-1-60728-506-9

ATD Press Editorial Staff
Director: Kristine Luecker
Manager: Christian Green
Community of Practice Manager, Learning and Development: Juana Llorens
Editors: Ashley McDonald and Melissa Jones
Text and Cover Design: Bey Bello

Printed by Versa Press, East Peoria, IL, www.versapress.com

CONTENTS

Acknowledgments

It bears saying that without evidence, we would not have evidence-based guidelines for practice. The evidence in this book comes from the work of hundreds of instructional research scientists located throughout the world. If you check the references at the end of the book, you will see that a large percentage of them include Richard E. Mayer and the OPWL 547 Advanced Instructional Design students, whose ongoing research program in multimedia learning is reflected throughout this book.

I owe special thanks to Steve Villachica, associate professor from Boise State University. Steve used the first edition of this book as a text and was kind enough to set up a discussion board for students to add suggestions for revisions.

Juana Llorens, former manager of ATD Learning and Development Community of Practice, has been a strong supporter of evidence-based practice in workforce learning. Among other efforts she has established a track of Research in the Learning and Instructional Sciences. Conference presentations, whitepapers, webinars, and blogs are just a few of the products of her efforts.

I wish to thank Ashley McDonald and Melissa Jones and the talented editorial and production staff at ATD Press.

Finally the support of my family is most important, including my husband Pete Sattig, daughters Kathryn Arsenault and Diane Bovy, and their always inspiring children: Joshua, Matthew, Lennon, and Luke.

Preface

WHAT PROMPTED A SECOND EDITION OF THIS BOOK?

I wrote the first edition of *Evidence-Based Training Methods* because there is a large repository of reports from research scientists in the academic literature. I believed then and today that much of this evidence remains unknown to practitioners. The academic research professionals and workforce learning practitioners constitute two quite separate communities of practice. There is little overlap in their publications and conferences. Most practitioners lack the time to search, read, and synthesize the many research reports available. Second, although many research papers do give some guidance for practitioners, guidance is not their main goal. I believe practitioners need not only guidelines, but also examples and counter examples for implementing those guidelines.

Naturally, research continues to evolve. Fortunately for me, the science of instruction and learning does not move as quickly as medical research for example. However, many of the guidelines in the first edition needed updating. I was happy to find in my research a sufficient body of evidence to warrant a new chapter on games. I am encouraged also by a continued interest in evidence-based guidelines among practitioners—especially those in the allied health professions stimulated by the focus on evidence-based medicine. Finally, what author does not look back on her previous writing and not want to improve it? A second edition has offered me the opportunity to pursue all of these goals.

What's in This Book?

The chapters are organized from smaller to larger instructional elements. Following the introductory chapters in part 1, part 2 summarizes evidence on use of the basic modes for communication, including graphics, text, and audio. Part 3 looks at evidence regarding two important instructional methods: examples and practice. Finally in part 4 I take a more macro view of lesson design with guidelines for explanations, teaching procedures, and building critical thinking skills. The book ends with a chapter on games and a short summary of some principles that go beyond the evidence discussed in individual chapters.

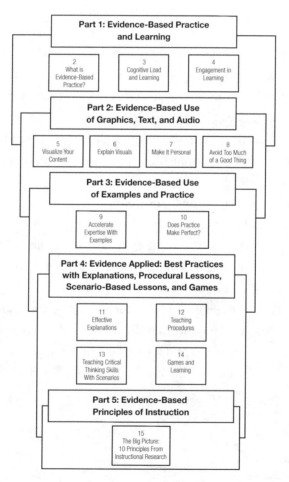

Each chapter includes questions about the instructional method, evidence to support those questions, guidelines based on the evidence, and a short checklist of best practices. If you want a quick overview, go to the Appendix to see a synopsis of guidelines and then go back to the specific chapters that discuss those guidelines in detail.

Finally, I offer you engagement opportunities through chapter lead-in questions and periodic evidence interpretation questions. Because you are in control, you can bypass these elements and go directly to the meat of the chapter.

Limits of the Book

There are many areas of interest in our field and you might wonder why certain topics are not addressed. For example, motivation is an important issue not included. My selection of topics is guided by the evidence available and by my ability to create a coherent set of guidelines around that evidence. There is in fact a great deal of material on motivation. And we are starting to see more measures of motivation in learning research. However as of this writing I did not find a clear set of guidelines to inform practice.

No one person can claim to be cognizant of all relevant evidence, so I apologize for any omissions. Nor can I claim a flawless interpretation of the evidence I do review. Some research scientists would feel that my guidelines exceed the evidence provided. In this edition I cited the evidence sources more rigorously than in the first. Intellectual integrity demands it. But the citations also provide you the opportunity to review the evidence firsthand and draw your own conclusions.

I welcome your comments.

Ruth Clark
Ruth@Clarktraining.com

TRAINING FADS AND FABLES

CHAPTER 1

Training Fads and Fables

"At any given daylight moment across America, approximately 660,000 drivers are using cell phones or manipulating electronic devices while driving, a number that has held steady since 2010."

"Engaging in visual-manual subtasks (such as reaching for a phone, dialing and texting) associated with the use of hand-held phones and other portable devices increased the risk of getting into a crash by three times." (Statistics drawn from the National Highway Traffic Safety Administration and Virginia Tech Transportation Institute, cited on distraction.gov, 2014).

Do you talk on your cell phone while driving? If yes, you are among the 66 percent of drivers who do. However, similar to seat belt use, your cell phone use may soon change. Evidence shows that even hands-free cell phones are potentially lethal distractions, putting you at four times greater risk of a crash. As of early 2009, when the first edition of this book was written, only five states had banned handheld phones while driving. No state completely banned all types of cell phone use. As of early 2014, 12 states had banned handheld cell phones and 41 had banned texting. Are you surprised that in the past five years the number of states banning cell phone use more than doubled, but still totals less than 25 percent of all states?

The journey from evidence to application of evidence is often slow and workforce learning is no exception. In this chapter we will see how applying evidence to your instructional programs and products can save your organization time and money that could be wasted on training fads that don't work.

BLOOD, PHLEGM, AND BLACK AND YELLOW BILE

Our story starts in the early 1600s—the birth years of evidence-based practice. Prior to 1628, people believed that blood was produced by the heart and liver and was continuously used up by the body. In other words, there was no accurate conception of blood circulation. William Harvey introduced the revolutionary idea that blood was not consumed by the body. Based on measures of blood volume and anatomical observations, he proposed that blood was pumped from the heart and circulated throughout the body, returning again to the heart. Harvey—along with Galileo, Descartes, and others—turned the 17th-century world upside down by advocating evidence and reason, rather than traditional wisdom and faith, as the basis for knowledge and decisions.

We've come a long way from the days when medical diagnosis and treatments were based on a balance of the four body humors of blood, phlegm, and black and yellow bile. If you were lucky, your treatment was an amulet that at least did no harm. If you were not so lucky, you were subjected to bloodletting. Although great strides were made in medical science, more than 400 years passed before health science professionals formally adopted evidence-based practice. Old habits die hard. Even though we've seen evidence about the dangers of cell phones while driving for more than 10 years, that data are just starting to be reflected in policy changes. To see the latest updates on cell phones and driving laws, visit the Governors Highway Safety Association website.

What Do You Think?

See how your current knowledge matches up with evidence. Check off each statement you think is true:

- ❏ A. To accommodate different learning styles, it's best to explain a visual with words presented in text and in audio.
- ❏ B. Instructor-led classroom training results in better learning than computer-delivered instruction.

❑ C. Courses that get higher student ratings generally produce better learning outcomes.

❑ D. Learners make accurate decisions about their instructional needs.

❑ E. Active engagement is essential to learning.

❑ F. Games are effective instructional methods.

TRAINING MYTHOLOGY AND INVESTMENTS IN LEARNING

How much do you think is invested in workforce learning? You might be surprised to learn that in 2012 the United States allocated around $164 billion to workforce learning (ASTD, 2013). No doubt the organizations you work for make large investments in training. What kind of return does your organization get on its training investment? Think of the last class that you developed or facilitated. To what extent did the content sequencing, training methods, and facilitation techniques of that class promote learning? Many common training practices are based more on fads and fables than on evidence of what works. Let's look at the facts behind six popular training myths.

TRAINING MYTH 1: LEARNING STYLES

Are you a visual or auditory learner? Has your organization invested resources in learning styles? Like the four body humors of blood, phlegm, and black and yellow bile, learning styles represent one of the more wasteful and misleading pervasive learning myths of the past 25 years. From audio learners to visual learners or from "sensors" to "intuitives," learning styles come in many varieties. And learning styles have been a profitable concept. Including books, inventories, and classes, many resources have been devoted to learning styles. For some reason, the idea of a "learning style" has a charismatic intuitive appeal. Ask almost anyone whether he or she is a visual learner or a verbal learner and you will get an immediate commitment to a specific "learning style"!

The learning style myth leads to some very unproductive training approaches contrary to the modern evidence of what works. For example, many trainers believe that visuals should be described by words in text format for visual learners and narration mode for auditory learners. To accommodate visual and auditory learners, a visual on a screen is explained with text and audio narration of that text. As we will see in chapter 6, evidence has shown this practice to depress learning.

The time and energy spent perpetuating the various learning style myths can be more wisely invested in supporting individual differences that are proven to make a difference—namely, prior knowledge of the learner. If you make one change as a result of reading this book: Give up the learning style myth!

Evidence About Learning Styles

Do we have any evidence about learning styles? Kratzig and Arbuthnott (2006) calculated the relationship among three learning style indicators. They asked a group of university students to do three things. First, participants rated their own learning style as visual, auditory, or kinesthetic. Second, the individuals took a learning style test that classified them as a visual, auditory, or kinesthetic learner. Finally, they were given three tests to measure visual memory, auditory memory, and kinesthetic memory. If the learning style concept had substance, we would expect to find some positive relationships among these measures. For example, someone who considered herself a visual learner would score higher on the visual index of a learning styles test and have better memory for visual information. However, when all of the measures were compared, there were absolutely no relationships! A person who rated himself an auditory learner was just as likely to score higher on the kinesthetic scale of the learning style test and show best memory for visual data. The research team concluded: "In contrast to learning style theory, it appears that people are able to learn effectively using all three sensory modalities" (241).

Another research study focused on sensing versus intuitive learning styles. Cook et al. (2009) compared learning of medical residents who tested as having a sensing learning style with individuals who tested as having an intuitive learning style. Each resident completed four web-based training modules. Half the lessons started with a clinical problem followed by traditional information. The other half reversed the sequence, starting with information and ending with a clinical problem. Sensing learners should learn better with a case-first approach, while intuitive learners should learn better from a traditional rule-example approach. Knowledge tests were administered at the end of each module, as well as several months later. As in the experiment described previously, there was no association between learning style and instructional method. The research team concluded: "It appears from the preponderance of evidence that sensing-intuitive styles have little impact, if any, on educational outcomes"(88).

A comprehensive review by Pashler and others (2008) concludes that while people do differ regarding aptitudes, "at present there is no adequate evidence base to justify incorporating learning-styles assessments into general educational practice. Thus limited education resources would better be devoted to adopting other educational practices that have a strong evidence base, of which there are an increasing number" (105). In short, a review by Riener and Willingham (2010) concluded: "There is no credible evidence that learning styles exist" (33).

The lack of evidence about learning styles is the basis for my first recommendation.

Fads & Fables Guideline 1:

Do not waste your training resources on any form of learning style products, including instructor training, measurement of learning styles, or books.

TRAINING MYTH 2: MEDIA PANACEAS

Only a few years ago, computer-delivered instruction incited a revolution in training. Of course computers were not the first technology to cause a stir. Decades prior to computers, radio, film, and television were hailed as having high potential to revolutionize education. The first widespread dissemination of computer-based training (CBT) was primarily delivered on mainframe computers. Soon, advances in digital memory, display hardware, programming software, and Internet distribution catalyzed the rapid evolution of CBT to recent technological panaceas, including web-based training, social media, digital games, simulations, and mobile learning to name a few. With each new technology wave, enthusiasts ride the crest with claims that finally we have the tools to really revolutionize learning. And yet, if you have been around for a few of these waves, those claims begin to sound a bit hollow. In just a few years, the latest media hype of today will fade yielding to the inexorable evolution of technology and a fresh spate of technological hyperbole.

What's wrong with a technology-centric view of instruction? Instructional scientists have learned a lot about how humans learn. Like Harvey who gave birth to the modern mental model of blood circulation, instructional psychology has revealed the strengths and limits of a human brain that is the product of thousands of years of evolution. When we plan instruction solely to leverage the latest technology, we ignore the psychology of human learning, which, as we have learned again with cell phones and driving, has severe limits. In fact, technology today can deliver far more information faster than the human brain can absorb it.

Evidence Against the Technology Panacea

For more than 70 years, instructional scientists have attempted to prove the superiority of each new technology over old-fashioned classroom instruction. One of the first media comparison studies was published in the 1940s. The U.S. Army believed it could improve instructional quality and reliability by replacing many instructors with films. To their credit, before setting policy based on this idea, the Army tested it. They compared learning a simple procedure from a lesson delivered by film, by instructor, and by print. Each version used similar words and visuals. What do you think they found?

- ❑ Instructor-led training led to the best learning.
- ❑ Paper-based, the least expensive, led to the best learning.
- ❑ Films could replace instructors, because they led to the best learning.
- ❑ Learning was the same with instructor, print, and film.

The Army discovered that participants from all three lesson versions learned the procedure equally well. In technical terms, we say that there were "no significant differences in learning" among the three groups. Since that early experiment, hundreds of studies have compared learning from classroom instruction with learning from the latest technology—the most recent being various forms of digital distance learning. In fact, so many media comparisons have been published, that a synthesis of all of the results, called a meta-analysis, found the same basic conclusion that the Army reported so many years ago: no major differences in learning from classroom lessons compared to electronic distance learning lessons (Bernard et al., 2004; U.S. Department of Education, 2010).

But wait! There is an important caveat to this conclusion. The basic instructional methods must be the same in all versions. In other words, if the classroom version includes graphics and practice exercises, the computer version must include similar graphics and practice opportunities. That's because the psychological active ingredients of your lessons are what cause people to learn, regardless of what media you are using. Rather than asking which technology is best for learning, you will find more fertile ground by using a blend of media that allows you to space out learning events, provide post-training performance support, and foster synchronous and asynchronous forms of collaboration. In fact, the U.S. Department of Education found a significant learning advantage to courses using media blends compared to pure classroom-based or pure online learning (2010).

What About Social Media?

There's a lot of buzz about social media, including wikis, blogs, multimedia shared pages, Twitter, and so on. What evidence do we have for the benefits of these web 2.0 technologies for learning? A review by Hew and Cheung (2013) concluded that actual evidence regarding the impact of web 2.0 technology on learning is fairly weak (so far). As in reviews of older media, the positive effects reported to date are not necessarily attributed to the technologies per se but rather to how those technologies are used. We need a taxonomy of web 2.0 technologies that describes best practices for each based on valid data.

The more than 70 years of media comparison research is the basis for my second recommendation.

Fads & Fables Guideline 2:

Ignore panaceas in the guise of technology solutions in favor of applying proven practices on the best use of instructional methods to all media you use to deliver training. Select a mix of media that supports core human psychological learning processes.

As a postscript to this media discussion, what were once considered distinct and separate delivery technologies are increasingly converging. For example, we now have online access to multiple instructional resources. Handheld mobile devices merge functionalities of computers, newspapers, telephones, cameras, radios, clocks, and context-sensitive performance support to name a few. Perhaps the media selection discussion will evolve into a discussion of instructional methods, most of which can be delivered via a mix of digital media and in-person instructional environments.

TRAINING MYTH 3: THE MORE THEY LIKE IT, THE MORE THEY LEARN

Do you collect student ratings at the end of your courses? More than 90 percent of all organizations use end-of-training surveys to gather participant evaluation of the quality of the course, the effectiveness of the instructor, how much was learned, and so on. These rating sheets are commonly called smile sheets or Level 1 evaluations. If you are an instructor or a course designer, chances are you have reviewed ratings sheets from your classes. You might also have a sense of how much learning occurred in that class. Based on your own experience, what do you think is the relationship between participant ratings of a class and the actual learning that occurred?

- ❑ Classes that are higher rated also yield greater learning.
- ❑ Classes that are higher rated actually yield poorer learning.
- ❑ There is no relationship between class ratings and learning from that class.

To answer this question, researchers have collected student satisfaction ratings as well as lesson test scores that measure actual learning. They then evaluated the relationships between the two. For example, they considered whether higher ratings correlated with more learning or less learning.

Evidence on Liking and Learning

A meta-analysis synthesized more than 1,400 student course ratings with student test data. Sitzmann et al. (2008) found a positive relationship between ratings and learning. But the correlation was very small. In fact, it was too small to have any practical value. Specifically, the research team concluded, "Reactions have a predictive relationship with cognitive learning outcomes, but the relationship is not strong enough to suggest reactions should be used as an indicator of learning" (289).

Do you think that learners rate lessons with graphics higher than lessons without graphics? Do you think that lessons with graphics support better learning than lessons without graphics? Sung and Mayer (2012b) compared student ratings and learning from lessons that included 1) relevant graphics, 2) distracting graphics, 3) decorative graphics, and 4) no graphics. They found that all of the lessons with graphics got better ratings than lessons lacking visuals, even though only the relevant graphics led to better learning. In other words, there was no relationship between liking and learning. We'll look at evidence on graphics and learning in more detail in the next chapter.

Besides graphics, what factors are associated with higher ratings? The two most important influencers of ratings are instructor style and human interaction. Instructors who are psychologically open and available—in other words, personable instructors—are associated with higher course ratings. In addition, the opportunity to socially interact during the learning event with the instructor as well as with other participants leads to higher ratings (Sitzmann et al., 2008).

Evidence from comparisons of hundreds of student ratings and student learning is the basis for my third recommendation.

Fads & Fables Guideline 3:

Don't rely on student ratings as indicators of learning effectiveness. Instead, use valid tests to assess the pedagogical effectiveness of any learning environment. Focus on instructional methods that support liking and learning.

TRAINING MYTH 4: LEARNERS KNOW WHAT THEY NEED

One of the potential benefits of e-learning is the opportunity to offer environments that move beyond "one size fits all" instruction typical of instructor-led training. Most e-learning courses offer learners choices—choices over which lessons they may want to take in a course, whether to study an example or complete a practice exercise, as well as the amount of time to spend on a given screen. Online asynchronous e-lessons with these options are considered high in learner control. How effective are high learner control courses? Do your learners make good decisions regarding how much to study, what to study, or which instructional methods to select?

Evidence on Learner Decisions

More than 20 years of research comparing learning from courses that are learner controlled with courses that offer fewer choices concludes that quite often, learners do not make good instructional decisions. Many learners may be overly confident in their knowledge and therefore skip elements that in fact they need. A case in point: Hegarty and her associates (2012) asked subjects to compare wind, pressure, or temperatures on either a simple or more complex weather map. The more complex map included geographic detail, as well as multiple weather variables not needed to complete the assignment. Task accuracy and efficiency was better on the simpler maps. However, about one-third of the time, the subjects chose to use the more complex maps to complete the task.

Dunlosky and Rawson (2012) provided technical term definitions and asked 158 students to judge their level of confidence in recalling the definition correctly. When participants judged their response as correct, it was actually correct only 57 percent of the time. In other words, they were overconfident in their knowledge. Participants were asked to repeat the definitions until they judged their responses correct three times. Following a recall test two days later, the researchers separated students based on their level of overconfidence and compared their final test scores. Participants who were most overconfident retained fewer than 30 percent of the definitions, whereas those who showed little overconfidence during study retained nearly all of the definitions they had practiced. The authors conclude that judgment accuracy matters a great deal for effective learning and durable retention: Overconfidence leads to the premature termination of study and to lower levels of retention. When left to their own devices many students use ineffective methods to monitor their learning, which can produce overconfidence and under achievement.

A third study focused on more advanced students, internal medicine residents. Residents predicted their overall performance one week before taking a medical knowledge exam. Residents were highly inaccurate in predicting their performance. Only 31 percent scored within 10 points of their predictions. Rather than being overly confident, most were pessimistic, with 69 percent underestimating their performance (Jones, Panda, and Desbiens, 2008). The general conclusion is that many learners do not make accurate assessments of their learning and thus do not make accurate or efficient choices regarding what and how to study.

Optimizing Learner Control in E-Learning

One way to improve learning outcomes in self-study e-learning is to make important topics and instructional methods, such as examples and practice, a default rather than an option to be selected (Schnackenberg and Sullivan, 2000). In a default lesson, the "continue" button automatically leads to important instructional methods and the learner will have to consciously choose to bypass them. In addition consider ways to guide learners at the start and throughout a course or lesson. For example, ask a few job-related questions about their experience with the task or knowledge that is the focus of the lesson. Provide advisement based on the responses to these questions. Keep in mind that many learners new to the content will not make accurate self-assessments of their own knowledge and skills and over confidence will lead to underachievement.

An exception to this guideline is pacing through a lesson. Control over pacing with forward and backward buttons should be available to all learners allowing them to manage their rate of progress. For more information on learner control, see chapter 14 in Clark and Mayer (2011) and chapter 21 in Mayer (2014a).

Fads & Fables Guideline 4:

Don't count on your learners to always make good decisions about their instructional needs. If your course builds in options, accompany those options with guidance.

TRAINING MYTH 5: ACTIVE ENGAGEMENT IS ESSENTIAL TO LEARNING

"Active learning" is one of the most cherished laws of workforce learning. As a response to the pervasive use of noninteractive lectures, the training community has pushed active learning as an essential ingredient of effective instruction. By active learning, trainers and facilitators refer to overt behavioral activities on the part of learners—activities such as making content outlines, collaborating on problems, or completing practice activities. However, the evidence points to a more nuanced definition of active learning. Engagement is essential; but it is psychological engagement rather than physical engagement that counts. And physical engagement can sometimes interfere with psychological engagement.

The Evidence on Active Engagement

Imagine two groups of learners studying a biology chapter. Group A is provided with a concept map developed by the chapter author as a support guide. Group B is provided with a blank concept map, which the learners are asked to fill in as they read. Clearly, Group B is more actively engaged in learning. However, post-tests showed that Group A learned more than Group B (Stull and Mayer, 2007). It's possible that individuals in Group B did not complete the map correctly. Alternatively, perhaps the mental activity needed to complete the concept map absorbed cognitive resources needed for learning. A similar experiment by Leopold et al. (2013) evaluated learning of a science text between learners who developed their own summaries with those who studied prepared summaries. The most effective learning occurred among those who studied the predefined summaries. The authors suggest that learners who engaged in behavioral processing may not have engaged in psychological processes. In contrast, those studying a predefined summary had more resources to invest in deeper psychological processing. We will look more closely at engagement in learning in chapter 4. For now I offer the following guideline.

Fads & Fables Guideline 5:

Behavioral activity during instruction does not necessarily lead to learning. It is psychological engagement that is most important.

TRAINING MYTH 6: GAMES, STORIES, AND SIMULATIONS PROMOTE LEARNING

Attend any training conference, look at the latest training books, or check out your favorite social media site. Chances are you will find real estate devoted to mobile learning, games, simulations, social media, or whatever is the technology or instructional method du jour. Training lore is full of claims and recommendations about the latest training methods like these. What's wrong with these kinds of recommendations?

First, we are using such broad terms for our techniques that statements about them are meaningless. Take games for instance. Do you mean puzzle games, adventure games, strategy games, or simulation games? Do you mean individual paper and pencil games, video games, or group participation games? As a category, games include so much diversity that it is nearly impossible to make any generalizations about their instructional effectiveness. I'll have more to say about games in chapter 14. (If you are especially interested in games feel free to jump to chapter 14 now.) The same critique applies to many other instructional techniques such as graphics or stories.

No Yellow Brick Road Effect

Second, even if we narrow down to a fairly specific set of criteria for any given instructional method, its effectiveness will depend on the intended learning outcome and the learners. Is your goal to build awareness, to help learners memorize content, to teach procedural skills, to motivate, or to promote critical thinking?

And what about your learners? Regarding learner differences, prior knowledge (not learning styles!) is the most important factor that moderates the effects of instructional methods. Techniques that help novice learners are not necessarily going to apply to a learner with more expertise.

The lack of universal effectiveness of most instructional techniques is the basis for what I call the No Yellow Brick Road Effect. By that I mean that there are few best practices that will work for all learners and for all learning goals. The evidence that has accumulated during years of research on general categories such as graphics and games is the basis for my sixth recommendation.

Fads & Fables Guideline 6:

Be skeptical about claims for the universal effectiveness of any instructional technique. Always ask: How is the technique defined? For whom is it useful? For what kinds of learning outcomes does it work?

As evidence accumulates, I anticipate the guidelines I offer will be refined and perhaps in some cases even superseded. However, the research efforts of the last 25 years provide a foundation for a science of instruction —one that can offer practitioners a basis for minimizing resources wasted on the myths in favor of practices proven to enhance learning.

THE BOTTOM LINE

Let's conclude by revisiting the responses you gave at the start of the chapter.

A. To accommodate different learning styles, it's best to explain a visual with words presented in text and in audio.

FALSE. The benefit of using text and audio to describe visuals is a common misconception among trainers. In chapter 6, we will examine the evidence and psychology of how to best use words to describe visuals.

B. Instructor-led classroom training results in better learning than computer-delivered instruction.

FALSE. Evidence from hundreds of media comparison studies shows that learning effectiveness does not depend on the delivery medium but rather reflects the best use of basic instructional methods. Because not all media deliver all methods, evidence suggests that blended learning environments are more effective than pure classroom or pure digital learning. We will be reviewing evidence-based best practices for instructional modes and methods in the chapters to follow.

C. Courses that get higher student ratings generally produce better learning outcomes.

TRUE, but only marginally. There is a very small positive relationship between ratings and learning. However, it is too small to draw any conclusions about the learning value of a class from student ratings of that class.

D. Learners make accurate decisions about their instructional needs.
FALSE. Many learners are poor calibrators of their knowledge and skills; in instructional environments designed with learner control they may not make optimal learning decisions. An exception is pacing control, which should be provided in all e-courses.

E. Active engagement is essential to learning.
TRUE, but. . . . What's important is psychological engagement that builds job-relevant knowledge and skills. Behavioral engagement can sometimes defeat appropriate psychological engagement and psychological engagement can occur in the absence of behavioral engagement, such as learning while reading or studying an example. See chapter 4 for more details.

F. Games are effective instructional methods.
FALSE. The effectiveness of any instructional strategy, such as a game, will depend on features of the game, the intended learning outcome, and the prior knowledge of the learners. See chapter 14 for more on games.

APPLYING EVIDENCE-BASED PRACTICE TO YOUR TRAINING

The evidence I will review in this book can guide your decisions regarding the best instructional methods to use in your training. But more importantly, I will consider the book a success if you become a more critical consumer of the various training recommendations appearing in practitioner articles, social media sites, and conferences. My hope is next time you hear or read some generalizations about the latest technology or hot training method you will ask:

- What exactly are the features of this method?
- What is the evidence that supports this method?
- How valid is that evidence ?

- For whom is the method most appropriate?
- How does the method fit with our understanding of the limits and strengths of human memory?

COMING NEXT

To move beyond training myths, I recommend taking an evidence-based approach. What is an evidence-based approach? What kind of evidence should you factor into your training decisions? What are the limits of research data? I turn to these questions in the next chapter.

FOR MORE INFORMATION

Clark, R.E., and D.F. Feldon. (2014). Six Common but Mistaken Principles of Multimedia Learning. In *Cambridge Handbook of Multimedia Learning*, 2nd edition, ed. R.E. Mayer. Boston, MA: Cambridge Press.

This handbook includes many chapters written by researchers that are relevant to workforce learning professionals.

Moos, D.C., and R. Azevedo. (2008). Self-Regulated Learning With Hypermedia: The Role of Prior Domain Knowledge. *Contemporary Educational Psychology* 33:270-298.

This is a technical report of research on the relationship between prior domain knowledge and self-regulation during learning with multimedia media. You may not be interested in the details of the study, but the literature review at the beginning and discussion at the end are very interesting.

Pashler, H., M. McDaniel, D. Rohrer, and R. Bjork. (2008). Learning Styles Concepts and Evidence. *Psychological Science in the Public Interest* 9:105-119.

A comprehensive and readable review of research on learning styles.

U.S. Department of Education. (2010). Office of Planning, Evaluation, and Policy Development, Evaluation of Evidence-Based Practices in Online Learning: A Meta-Analysis and Review of Online Learning Studies. Washington, D.C.: U.S. Department of Education.

A very readable update on media comparison research. Available free of charge online.

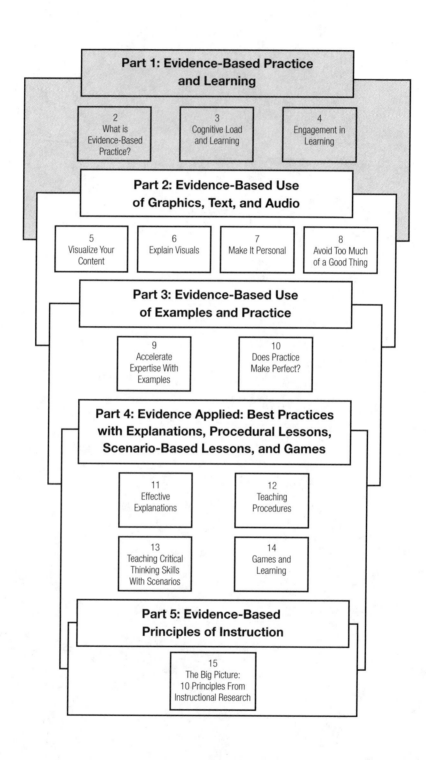

Part 1: Evidence-Based Practice and Learning

2
What is Evidence-Based Practice?

3
Cognitive Load and Learning

4
Engagement in Learning

Part 2: Evidence-Based Use of Graphics, Text, and Audio

5
Visualize Your Content

6
Explain Visuals

7
Make It Personal

8
Avoid Too Much of a Good Thing

Part 3: Evidence-Based Use of Examples and Practice

9
Accelerate Expertise With Examples

10
Does Practice Make Perfect?

Part 4: Evidence Applied: Best Practices with Explanations, Procedural Lessons, Scenario-Based Lessons, and Games

11
Effective Explanations

12
Teaching Procedures

13
Teaching Critical Thinking Skills With Scenarios

14
Games and Learning

Part 5: Evidence-Based Principles of Instruction

15
The Big Picture: 10 Principles From Instructional Research

PART 1

Evidence-Based Practice and Learning

In this section you will read about the foundational ideas that support this book. I will discuss the type of evidence included, presenting research on graphics to illustrate the different types of research you will read about throughout the book. You will also find a short summary of cognitive load theory—perhaps the most important recent explanation for how memory shapes human learning. This section of the book ends with a closer look at "active learning." Here you will distinguish between behavioral and psychological activity and find that not all activity leads to learning.

WHAT IS EVIDENCE-BASED PRACTICE?

CHAPTER 2

What Is
Evidence-Based Practice?

"An evidence-based approach offers the most helpful way to answer questions . . . because it is self-correcting. As research evidence begins to accumulate, we can reject unhelpful accounts of learning . . . and construct more useful ones" (Mayer, 2014b, 10).

In chapter 1 we reviewed six prevalent training myths. This book is written to replace myths with evidence on which to base our instructional decisions. In this chapter, I'll define evidence-based practice and look at some examples of how evidence can guide your instructional decisions. We'll look at two categories of evidence: academic research and practitioner research. Then I will focus on the types of evidence I include in this book based on academic research. I'll use research on graphics to illustrate five basic types of academic research. I could have selected a variety of instructional methods other than graphics to illustrate the ideas; however, graphics are a universal and common instructional method. From photographs to line drawings and from stills to animations, graphics populate PowerPoint slides, training manuals, and e-learning screens. In addition, there are sufficient research studies and research approaches to graphics to illustrate the main types of academic research that are the foundation for this book.

What Do You Think?

Let's start by evaluating your knowledge of evidence-based use of graphics; mark each statement you think is true.

- ❑ A. Adding visuals to text improves learning.
- ❑ B. Some learners benefit from visuals more than others.
- ❑ C. Some types of visuals are more effective than others.
- ❑ D. Learners like training materials with graphics.

EVIDENCE-BASED PRACTICE FOR INSTRUCTIONAL PROFESSIONALS

In the last part of the 20th century, the medical profession was the first applied field to formally adopt the incorporation of evidence into clinical decisions. Sackett and colleagues (1996) define evidence-based medicine as the "conscientious, explicit, and judicious use of current best evidence in making decisions about the care of individual patients" (71-72). How can performance improvement and training specialists adapt this definition to our professional practice? What kinds of evidence are most helpful and what limitations should you consider? We will answer these questions in this chapter.

I define evidence-based practice as the application of data-based guidelines as one factor when making decisions regarding the requirements, design, development, and delivery of work and instructional environments designed to optimize individual or organizational goals. Let's review this definition in more detail.

Application of Data-Based Guidelines as One Factor

When making decisions about performance support and training, you must consider many factors, including budgets, timelines, and technology, to name a few. Evidence-based practice recommends that data and guidelines based on data are weighed along with these other factors. Taken broadly, relevant data can be quantitative or qualitative and derive from many sources such as experiments, research reviews, interviews, observations, and surveys.

Decisions Regarding Requirements, Design, Development, and Delivery of Performance Environments

Workforce learning practitioners, in partnership with their clients, decide what combination of resources will optimize individual and team performance in ways that help organizations achieve operational objectives. Requirements involve gathering data that will guide the selection and specification of solutions, including training that will promote organizational goals. For example, to optimize sales, training and sales professionals may evaluate current sales metrics, interview and observe top sales performers, review social media discussions on best practices, and collect benchmarking data. The analysis of this data may suggest a solution system to include refinements to hiring criteria, training, new or revised reference and decision resources, and alignment of staff goals and incentives to organizational priorities.

Once solutions are identified, evidence is again applied to design, develop, and deliver those solutions. For example, top performers may have developed their own client management and assessment techniques that can be converted into on-demand training and mobile working aids. In the design, development, and delivery of training, research-based principles that guide content organization, communication, and engagement are applied.

ACADEMIC V. PRACTITIONER EVIDENCE

There are a number of ways to categorize evidence. In Figures 2-1 and 2-2 I summarize evidence types that best fit the goals for this book. *Academic research* refers to evidence gathered and published by research professionals using scientific methodologies to ensure validity and reliability. In contrast, *practitioner research* refers to evidence gathered and disseminated by workforce learning professionals and their clients, typically to support a specific organizational goal or problem. Practitioner research can be conducted prior to defining solutions, as in a performance assessment; during the design and development of solutions, as in prototyping tests; and after solutions are deployed, as in return-on-investment studies. Most large organizations have processes in place to assess performance needs and to design and develop solutions. There are a number of resources readily accessible to practitioners that focus on the tools and techniques to gather and analyze this type of evidence.

In contrast, although there is plentiful evidence from academic sources, it is relatively inaccessible to practitioners. Research professionals have their own communities of practice, including conferences and technical research publications. Most practitioners lack the time to gather, review, and interpret academic evidence. Therefore, my goal in this book is to help fill that void by providing guidelines derived from academic research.

Figure 2-1. Five Sources for Academic Research Evidence

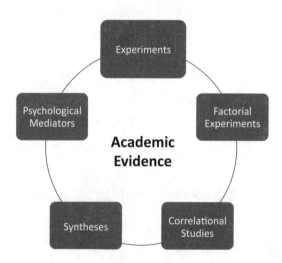

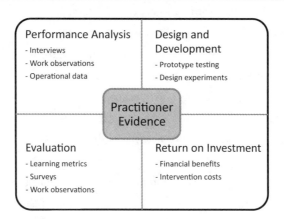

Figure 2-2. Four Sources for Practitioner Research Evidence

Types of Academic Research

For the purposes of this book, I will draw primarily on five main research genres: experimental comparisons, factorial experiments, correlational studies, qualitative research (such as analysis of talk-aloud data), and synthetic research (such as a meta-analysis). Note that these are not mutually exclusive and any given research study may include a combination of two or more of these approaches. In the remainder of this chapter I will illustrate these approaches using research on graphics in instructional materials.

DO GRAPHICS IMPROVE LEARNING? COMPARISON EXPERIMENTS

Is there evidence to support the benefits of adding graphics to your instructional materials? In a comparison experiment involving graphics, a researcher creates two lessons with the same words and adds visuals to one of them. Then she randomly assigns a group of learners to each lesson. For example, 25 may take the lesson with graphics and a different 25 take the same lesson minus the graphics. After completing their lesson version, the learners take the same test on the content. The test score averages and standard deviations from the two groups are compared using statistical tests of significance to determine whether the differences are likely due to the varying lesson formats, or more likely due to chance.

Experimental research is the foundational evidence-based method that determines whether specific instructional techniques are effective. Two critical features of experimental research are 1) random assignment of learners to different lesson versions (called treatments by researchers) and 2) comparison of learning from an experimental lesson to learning from a control lesson that does not include the instructional method being evaluated.

Take a look at Figure 2-3. The figure shows a segment from two lessons on how a bicycle pump works. The version at the top of the figure explains the content with words alone. The version below uses the same words but adds a simple diagram. Which version resulted in better learning? You are probably not surprised that Figure 2-4 shows the version with graphics was more effective.

Figure 2-3. Text v. Text Plus Graphic

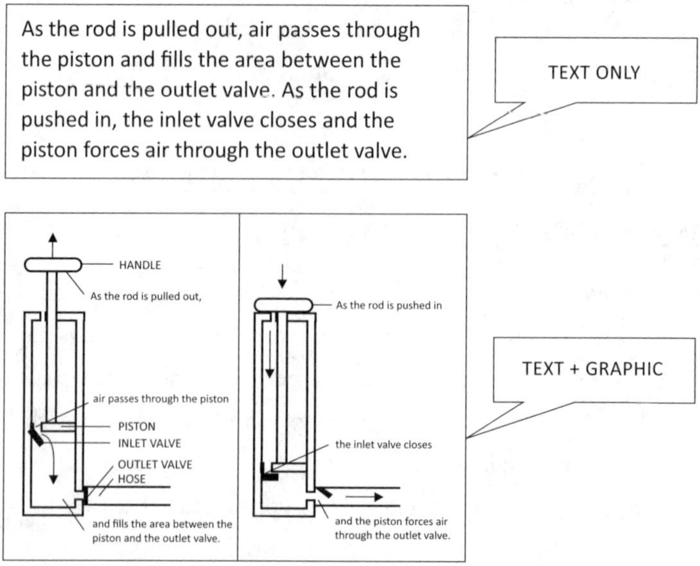

Source: Mayer and Gallini, 1990.

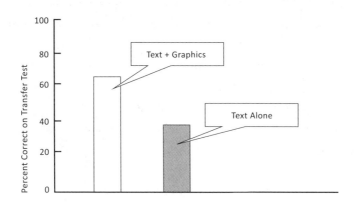

Figure 2-4. Better Learning Results From Words Plus Graphics

Source: Clark and Mayer, 2001. This material is reproduced with permission John Wiley & Sons.

How Is Learning Measured?

An important element to consider in both practitioner and experimental research is how learning is measured. For example, in the bicycle pump experiment, the test could ask learners to 1) label the parts of a bicycle pump, 2) describe from memory how a bicycle pump works, or 3) solve problems related to bicycle pumps. Tests typically measure either memory requiring the learner to recall presented content or application requiring learners to apply the content to a problem or situation. The most relevant type of test for our purposes is one that emphasizes application, as that is the goal of organizational training. I primarily rely on transfer test results as the basis for evidence-based guidelines in this book. For example, the data shown in Figure 2-4 are based on an application test on bicycle pumps with questions focusing on *how a pump could be designed to be more efficient or the effects of a defective inlet valve on the operations of the pump.* Application questions require the learner to demonstrate a deep understanding of the content. For workforce learning practitioners, application tests ask learners to apply knowledge and skills in the context of the job. For example, a test to evaluate learning in a customer-service course would include performance scenarios that would be recorded and scored by instructors using a best practices checklist.

In summary, when you hear or review claims about the learning benefits of an instructional product or method, it's always a good idea to take a look at the type of test used to measure learning.

The experimental evidence on graphics I've reviewed so far suggests the following guideline.

Evidence-Based Graphics Guideline 1:

Adding visuals to a textual description will improve learning.

ARE GRAPHICS EFFECTIVE FOR EVERYONE? FACTORIAL EXPERIMENTS

In chapter 1, we reviewed the myth of audio and visual learning styles. Although visual learning styles don't have credibility, might there be other individual differences that influence the effectiveness of graphics? To gather evidence on this type of question, researchers would conduct a factorial experiment. In a factorial experiment, two or more versions of a lesson (such as those shown in Figure 2-3) are assigned to two or more different types of learners, such as learners with and without prior knowledge of the content.

The results of this type of experiment are shown in Figure 2-5. What does the bar chart tell you about the benefits of graphics for high and low prior knowledge learners? Which of the following guidelines does the data suggest?

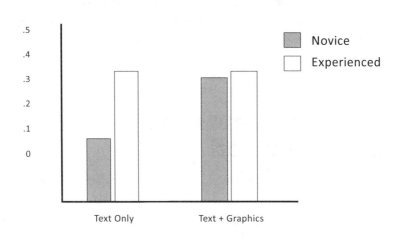

Figure 2-5. The Effects of Graphics on Novice and Experienced Learners

Source: Based on data from Mayer and Gallini, 1990.

❑ Graphics are equally beneficial for high and low prior knowledge learners.

❑ Graphics are most beneficial for low prior knowledge learners.

❑ Graphics can depress learning of high prior knowledge learners.

From the data you can see that adding a relevant graphic boosted the performance of low prior knowledge learners to that of high prior knowledge learners. High prior knowledge learners neither benefited nor were hurt by the addition of graphics. Most likely, high prior knowledge learners can form their own images when they read or hear the words. Therefore, adding a graphic does not contribute to their learning. For reasons that we will explore more in chapter 3, novice learners will often benefit from different instructional methods than learners with background in the content.

Based on data from this type of factorial experiment, I modify the previous guideline.

Evidence-Based Graphics Guideline 2:

Adding visuals to a textual description will improve learning of individuals lacking prior knowledge about the content of the lesson.

DOES THE TYPE OF GRAPHIC MAKE A DIFFERENCE?

We've seen that a simple relevant visual of a bicycle pump improved understanding of novice learners. However, there are many different types of graphics or ways to render a visual. For example, in the bicycle pump lesson, the graphic could be more realistic if it were a photograph or a more detailed sketch of a bicycle pump. Alternatively, the graphic could be an animation of how the pump works rather than a series of still visuals. Do the features of a particular graphic make a difference? To gather evidence on this question, several different versions of the graphic could be produced and given to novice learners randomly assigned to the different versions.

Testing different types of graphics has given us some clues. For example, in a lesson on mitosis (cell division in biology) Scheiter et al. assigned learners either a photograph or a line drawing of the different stages, similar to those shown in Figure 2-6. Which version do you think led to better identification of the stages and better understanding of the process of mitosis?

Figure 2-6. Photograph of Mitosis v. Schematic Drawings

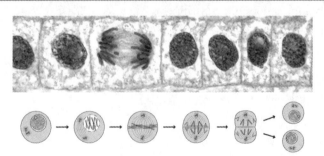

The line drawing was more effective, even for an identification test using actual photographs of the stages that learners in the line drawing group never saw (Scheiter et al., 2009). A number of experiments have shown that a simpler visual is often more effective than a more realistic or complex rendering. Naturally, the learning goal must be considered. For example, to learn about the functions of the heart, a schematic line drawing led to better understanding than a more realistic 2-D version (Butcher, 2006). However, if the goal was to teach anatomy, a more realistic rendering might be more effective. Based on these data, we will further refine our evidence-based guidelines on visuals.

Evidence-Based Graphics Guideline 3:

Use visuals in the simplest format congruent with the intended learning outcome.

DO LEARNERS LIKE LESSONS WITH GRAPHICS? A CORRELATIONAL STUDY

How learners perceive their instruction is one indicator of motivation to initiate and complete learning events. In chapter 1 I introduced research by Sung and Mayer (2012b) in which they created versions of the same lesson using different types of graphics or no graphics. Some graphics were relevant and others were distracting or decorative. They found a strong correlation between learning and relevant graphics but not distracting or decorative visuals. However, they also found a positive correlation between student ratings and any form of visual. In other words students enjoyed lessons with graphics of any type, including graphics that did not promote learning.

Correlational studies point to relationships but do not provide cause-and-effect conclusions. So what is the value in these studies? For practical, ethical, or safety reasons, sometimes experimental studies cannot be conducted. A classic example is the relationship between smoking and disease in humans. The negative effects of smoking are based primarily on correlational data in which the association between the amount of smoking and the incidence of disease has been found to be high.

In other situations, a correlational study may suggest a relationship that can be later tested in an experiment. For example, a correlational study showed a high relationship between student satisfaction ratings and social presence during the training (Sitzmann et al., 2008). A follow-up study could randomly assign learners to two versions of the same class with high and low social presence and then compare student satisfaction ratings.

HOW CONFIDENT ARE WE ABOUT THE POSITIVE EFFECTS OF VISUALS? SYNTHETIC EVIDENCE

So far we have reviewed just a few isolated experiments showing that novice learners profit from adding simple visuals to a lesson. These few studies are encouraging; however, we cannot put too much confidence in guidelines derived from just a few studies. When there are many experiments that use different topics and different visuals, we can draw conclusions using synthetic techniques—that is, research that synthesizes multiple data sets. Synthetic research can take the form of a systematic review, such as when a research team aggregates a number of experiments on a specific question and summarizes overall guidelines based on their analysis. Alternatively synthetic research can take the form of a meta-analysis in which statistical techniques are applied to data from many research studies that focus on a similar issue, such as the effects of graphics on learning.

The main output of a meta-analysis is an average effect size. An effect size is a multiplier for the amount of variation (standard deviation) found around a set of test scores. An effect size of one means that on average, a learner who uses a tested instructional method can expect a one standard deviation of improvement in their results compared to an individual who does not use that method. Table 2-1 summarizes a general guideline for interpretation of effect sizes.

Table 2-1. Effect Sizes and Practical Significance

EFFECT SIZE	PRACTICAL SIGNIFICANCE	THE INSTRUCTIONAL METHOD RESULTS IN	EXAMPLE: AVERAGE SCORE OF 70% WITH STANDARD DEVIATION OF 10 POINTS WOULD CHANGE TO
Below 0.3	Low	Less than 3/10 of a standard deviation improvement in learning	Average of less than 73%
0.3 to 0.8	Moderate	A 1/3 to 4/5 of a standard deviation improvement in learning	Average of 73% to 78%
0.8 to 1.0	High	A 4/5 to 1 standard deviation improvement in learning	Average of 78% to 83%
Above 1.0	Very High	A greater than 1 standard deviation improvement in learning	Average of more than 83%

Because many experiments have been conducted that compared learning with and without graphics, we have the benefit of effect sizes from meta-analyses of these experiments. For example, based on 11 different experiments that focused on the effects of graphics on scientific or mechanical processes, Mayer (2009) reported a median effect size of 1.5, which as you can see from Table 2-1 is very high.

A second benefit of a meta-analysis is the opportunity to define the conditions under which an instructional method is most effective. The meta-analysis team identifies a number of factors that might influence the effect size. For example, they might ask whether graphics are as effective for children as for adults. Alternatively, they may consider whether some types of content, such as mechanical processes might benefit more from graphics than other types of content, such as procedures. The research team codes each study it reviews for the variables that have been identified. For example, the researchers could aggregate all of the studies that involved children separately from those that involved adults and so on. They then determine the effect sizes of the subsets. In this way, a meta-analysis can not only give us general information on the overall benefits of an instructional method but can also give indications of the boundary conditions or situations that qualify those differences. Remember the No Yellow Brick Road theme I introduced in chapter 1? A meta-analysis can help us narrow the conditions under which a given method is most effective.

Meta-analyses are becoming so prevalent that Hattie wrote a book called *Visible Learning* (2009) that synthesized more than 800 meta-analyses on 138 factors related to students, curricula, teaching practices, home influence, and school programs. You might want to look at the 2014 version of this book called *Visible Learning and the Science of How We Learn* by Hattie and Yates, which takes a less technical approach to present the meta-analytic data of the first book.

While experimental research can tell us whether and under what conditions a given instructional method is effective, it typically has little to say about how that method works. Protocol analysis and eye tracking are two common research techniques used to get insight on the psychology of instructional methods.

THE PSYCHOLOGY OF GRAPHICS: PROTOCOL ANALYSIS

In a typical protocol analysis, learners individually vocalize their thoughts while they are studying instructional materials. The verbalizations are recorded, transcribed, and coded. The differences in codes are compared among different experimental groups or between individuals with different learning outcomes.

Butcher (2006) conducted an experiment that focused on learning the correct process of blood circulation through the heart. Her experiment compared learning from either a textual explanation or a textual explanation plus a simple diagram. While studying the lessons, learners talked aloud and the protocols were analyzed. Consistent with the results on graphics described previously, those who studied lessons with graphics learned more. To find out how graphics positively affected the learning process, the statements that learners made were coded as 1) paraphrases of the material, 2) elaborations in which the lesson content was connected to learners' background knowledge, or 3) inferences that integrated lesson information such as connecting two different concepts. She found that adding diagrams to the text increased student inferences.

From this type of data, we learn more about how graphics exert positive effects and get clues about how to optimize their effectiveness. For example, because graphics promoted inferences based on integrating information, study aids could be designed to promote such inferences through devices such as organizer visuals or questions that direct attention to corresponding elements of the graphic and text.

THE PSYCHOLOGY OF GRAPHICS: EYE-TRACKING DATA

Eye tracking has been used for many years in advertising research. Eye tracking involves tracing the subjects' duration and location of eye fixations as they view an object. By viewing the eye fixation patterns in two different displays, the research team can make inferences about how subjects allocate their attention. In chapter 1, I mentioned research by Hegarty and her colleagues (2012) showing that learners often selected more realistic, complex weather maps rather than simpler renditions to complete simple comparison tasks. The team also compared the average time performers needed to complete tasks using simpler versus more complex maps and used eye tracking to study differences in how subjects viewed simpler and more complex graphs. They found that using more complex maps slowed response times, making task completion less efficient.

As you can see in Figure 2-7, the number of eye fixations was higher and more scattered on the more realistic maps compared to the simpler versions. Eye fixation data offer clues about why a particular display is more efficient or effective than an alternative display. A conclusion from experiments such as these is that displays that are more realistic or complex than needed are frequently preferred by learners but lead to extraneous mental events and inefficient outcomes.

Figure 2-7. Eye Fixations on Simple Map (Above) v. Complex Map (Below)

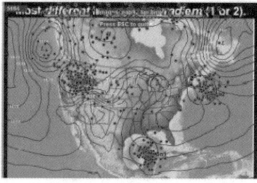

Source: Hegarty et al., 2012.

In summary, this book will draw primarily on academic evidence in the form of experiments, factorial experiments, correlational data, reviews of evidence, and qualitative methods (such as protocol analysis and eye tracking). Together, these methods can tell us 1) whether a given instructional method leads to more learning than a lesson without that method, 2) whether a given instructional method is more effective for some types of learners or some types of content, 3) whether there is a relationship between two or more sets of data, and 4) how a given instructional method may influence learning processes such as focus of attention.

READ THE FINE PRINT: LIMITS OF EVIDENCE-BASED TRAINING GUIDELINES

Most research reports include sections on experimental procedure and testing methods—often in smaller font size than the rest of the report. Although I'm an advocate of evidence-based practice, there are some constraints in that fine print that we practitioners should consider as we review academic research. Some of the more salient issues include:

- **Length of lessons**: In many experiments, lessons last one hour or less. In some cases they are only a few minutes long. To what extent can we generalize the results from short lessons to longer instructional environments typical of workforce training?

- **Immediate learning**: With a few exceptions, most experiments measure learning immediately following completion of the lesson. In workforce learning our goal is longer-term learning, ideally transferring to the job over time.

- **Learner characteristics**: Most experiments conducted in academic settings use college-aged students for subjects. The United States, Europe, and Australia are the source for much of this type of research. Therefore, most of the data reflect results from younger generation higher education Western culture populations. You will need to consider the extent to which these results will apply to your learners.

- **Instructional context**: Because experimental research attempts to control all variables other than those being tested, laboratory settings are common. There are a few studies conducted in a more naturalistic environment such as a classroom but these are the exception.

- **Learning measures**: I mentioned the role of testing measures earlier in the chapter. For quite a long time most research tested recall of content. Thankfully, this has changed over the past 20 years. Today, many experiments will use tests that tap different knowledge levels, such as a recall test and an application test. The majority of experimental outcomes I include in this book are based on application tests, as these are most relevant to workforce learning goals.

- **Learning domain**: Particular instructional methods may be more effective in some domains than in others. For example, a recent meta-analysis of games found them to be most effective in the domains of second language learning and science but not as effective in math or social studies (Wouters et al., 2013). As you review a research study, consider the extent to which the mental demands of the domain in the research are equivalent to those in the types of tasks in your training.

The solution to address some of these constraints is prototyping or design iterations with your training solutions. In other words, test out the principles in this book with your learners, your learning domains, and contexts. This brings us to the interaction between academic and practitioner research. One is not superior to the other and data from academic and practitioner research should guide your design and development decisions.

THE BOTTOM LINE

Let's conclude by reviewing the statements from the beginning of the chapter, which you considered true.

What Do You Think?

A. Adding visuals to text improves learning.

FALSE. While the evidence we have reviewed so far supports the use of visuals, we will see in chapters 5 and 8 that some visuals can actually depress learning. The benefits of a visual will depend on the type and rendering of the visual, the prior knowledge of the learner, and your instructional objective.

B. Some learners benefit from visuals more than others.

TRUE. Evidence suggests that although most learners prefer materials with visuals, novice learners benefit the most.

C. More realistic or detailed visuals are generally better for learning and performing.

FALSE. For many purposes, a simpler graphic is more effective than a more complex version. We will see the reasons for this in the next chapter on cognitive load in learning.

D. Learners like materials with graphics.

TRUE. Learners prefer materials with visuals even though a given visual may not be optimal for learning or performance.

APPLYING EVIDENCE-BASED PRACTICE

The goal of this chapter is to define evidence-based practice and to discuss some of the different types of evidence to consider. This book will focus on academic research in the form of comparison experiments, factorial experiments, correlational studies, quantitative or qualitative reviews of research, and qualitative data. In reviewing academic research, some relevant issues for you to consider include:

- Does an experimental study use random assignment to a test lesson and a control version?

- What types of research reports are used as the basis for a review?

- What are the reported effect sizes in an experiment or meta-analysis?

- What boundary conditions influence the effects of a given method?

- Are the learning outcomes of an experiment based on recall or application tests?

- Do the learning domains and contexts in an experiment reflect yours?

COMING NEXT

Now that we have looked at instructional fables and evidence-based guidelines, we will take a look at the psychology of learning with a short review of cognitive load. Understanding cognitive load will help you extend the guidelines in this book to your own instructional environments.

FOR MORE INFORMATION

Clark, R., and R.E. Mayer. (2011). *E-Learning and the Science of Instruction*, 3rd edition. San Francisco: CA: Pfeiffer. (See chapter 4.)

A chapter discussion of the evidence on the effects of visuals on learning.

Clark, R., and C. Lyons. (2011). *Graphics for Learning, 2nd Edition.* San Francisco, CA: Pfeiffer

A detailed and comprehensive review of how best to use visuals to support workforce learning goals in different media.

Van Gog, T., and K. Scheiter. (2010). Eye Tracking as a Tool to Study and Enhance Multimedia Learning. *Learning and Instruction* 20: 95-99.

This article is an introduction to a special issue of Learning and Instruction that included several research studies that used eye-tracking data to analyze multimedia learning processes.

COGNITIVE LOAD AND LEARNING

CHAPTER 3

Cognitive Load and Learning

Forty individuals drove a car in a simulator under four conditions: 1) no distractions, 2) talking on a handheld cell phone, 3) talking on a hands-free cell phone, and 4) intoxicated to 0.08 percent blood alcohol level. On a simulated freeway, a pace car braked 32 times during the 10-mile "trip." The three participants who collided into the pace car were talking on cell phones, both handheld and hands-free; none of the drunk drivers crashed (Strayer et al., 2006).

Results like these reveal the limits of the human brain. We are often deceived because we don't realize the severe processing limits that affect all mental activities including learning.

In this chapter, we look at the psychology of learning with a focus on how instructional professionals can manage cognitive load in their training events. Our understanding of learning psychology is based on two types of memory: working memory, where conscious thought occurs, and long-term memory, where knowledge and personal memories are stored. In this chapter, we will look at the relationship between the two with particular focus on working memory.

LIMITS OF HUMAN MEMORY

Let's try a short experiment. You need a pencil and paper. Spend about 30 seconds reading through the list of words in Figure 3-1. Without looking back, write down as many as you can recall. When you are done, do the same with the list in Figure 3-2.

Figure 3-1. List A

1.	House	9.	Bedroom
2.	Computer	10.	Chair
3.	Bird	11.	Calendar
4.	Cloud	12.	Pink
5.	Scissors	13.	Ocean
6.	Book	14.	Gutter
7.	Dress	15.	Flag
8.	Marker		

Figure 3-2. List B

1.	Ethics	9.	First
2.	Hire	10.	Solution
3.	Terse	11.	Color
4.	Noun	12.	Liquid
5.	Problem	13.	Pattern
6.	Manage	14.	Basic
7.	Design	15.	Account
8.	Retro		

When you have recalled as many words as you can, refer back to the figures and count the number of words you recalled in each. Which list included more memorable words? Take a look at the two lists and consider what makes them different. Which of the following differences do you notice?

❑ A. List A has shorter words than List B.

❑ B. List A has more concrete words than List B.

❑ C. List A has more verbs than List B.

Most people recall more words from List A than from List B. In comparing the two, List B has a higher proportion of abstract words. The answer to the question above is option B—List A has more concrete words.

Now look at the positions of the words you recalled in both lists. Determine whether the words you recalled came from the start of the lists, the end of the lists, or the middle. Do you see a pattern? If you reviewed the words sequentially from top to bottom, chances are you recalled more words from the start and end of each list.

The results from this little demonstration reveal three key features of our working memory—the memory that is both the engine and bottleneck of learning. The key features are summarized in Table 3-1.

Table 3-1. Three Key Features of Working Memory

FEATURE	DESCRIPTION
Active Processor	Working memory is where conscious thought takes place including problem solving, thinking, and learning.
Limited Capacity	When active, the memory capacity of working memory is about three to five chunks of information.
Dual Channel	Working memory has separate systems for storage of visual and auditory data.

Feature 1: Active Processor

First and foremost, working memory, as its name implies, is an active processor. It is the conscious part of your brain—the part that thinks, solves problems, and learns. It was the active processing of the words you read in the lists in Figures 3-1 and 3-2 that led to your recall of them later. The words you did not recall did not receive sufficient processing for learning.

Feature 2: Limited Capacity

Chances are you did not recall all of the words in either list. Working memory has pretty severe restrictions regarding how much information it can hold. And the limits are even more stringent when working memory is processing. Recent estimates set a limit of around three to five items that can be held in the working memory when it must also be actively engaged in other activities. You recalled more words in the first part of the lists because your working memory had capacity to process those initial words. As you added more words, that processing capacity was soon exceeded. As each new word entered memory, it replaced a previous word with minimal opportunity for processing. You may have recalled more of the last words in the lists if you wrote them down right away. Those words were still active in working memory when you finished and were not replaced by additional words.

Feature 3: Dual Channel

In chapter 2 we saw that adding a relevant visual to text improves learning. The benefits of visuals are based on the dual processing feature of working memory. Dual channel refers to working memory's two centers: one for storing and processing auditory information and a second for visual information. When you read a concrete word such as "flower," you are more likely to process it in two ways: as phonetic data and also as the image that your mind forms when reading the word. In contrast, a word such as "moral" is not as easy to visualize and in many cases you encode it only in a phonetic format. Concrete words that can be encoded in two ways have a greater probability of being stored in memory. This is why List A, which included more concrete words, was overall more memorable.

These three features—active processor, limited capacity, and dual channels—are the prime determinants for what works and what does not work in your training. Working memory capacity is needed to process new information for learning to occur. But when we load it up with content or irrelevant work, that processing is corrupted. We call this cognitive overload. There are a number of techniques you can use to minimize cognitive overload, which we will review throughout the book.

LONG-TERM MEMORY AND LEARNING

While working memory is the star of the learning show, we can't leave out its supporting partner, long-term memory. Take a look at the chessboard displayed in Figure 3-3. Now imagine that after you look at it for about five seconds you are asked to reconstruct it using a real chessboard and all of the pieces. How many times would you need to refer back to the original chessboard?

Figure 3-3. A Mid-Play Chessboard

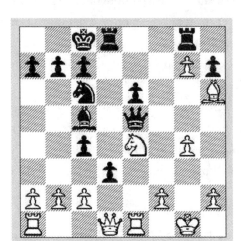

You won't be surprised that individuals like me, unfamiliar with chess, needed about seven to nine referrals to get most of the pieces correctly placed. What about a chess expert? Would she need to look back more or fewer times? Again, not surprising, chess masters got most of the pieces in place with about four tries. Why do you think that the chess masters had better memory for placement of chess pieces?

❏ A. Chess masters have better visual memory than chess novices.

❏ B. Chess masters have a higher intelligence than chess novices.

❏ C. Chess masters are more familiar with individual chess pieces than chess novices.

❏ D. Chess masters can draw on chess play patterns unavailable to chess novices.

To answer the above question, the experimenters repeated the chess experiment with a crucial difference. Instead of using a realistic mid-play chessboard, they substituted a scrambled board. The same number of pieces was placed on the board but in a random order. Again, they asked expert and novice chess players to recall the pieces. What do you think happened this time? Do you think the master players still had an advantage and needed fewer glances back at the model board? Or would the master and expert be equivalent in their memory?

The results were somewhat surprising. First, as you might expect, the novices needed about the same number of referrals as they did in the first experiment, around seven to nine repetitions. But the experts actually needed even more opportunities to refer back to the chessboard than did the novices!

These results support option D. For most novices, a chessboard like the one shown in Figure 3-3 holds about 25 chunks of information—each piece being a chunk. Since working memory can hold only around four to five chunks, naturally it takes quite a while to recall all of those pieces correctly. Psychologists have estimated that chess experts store about 50,000 chess patterns in their long-term memory. Rather than recall each piece as a single entity, they can recall whole clusters of pieces corresponding to various play patterns. However, when the pieces are placed randomly, those patterns not only don't help, they actually hinder recall performance. The chess expert looks at a world that has become topsy-turvy and the conflict with their stored mental models actually makes their recall worse than novices.

From experiments like these we learn that unlike working memory, long-term memory has a huge capacity for information. During learning—

either formal or informal—the processing in working memory produces new or expanded patterns stored in long-term memory. These patterns can be brought back into working memory when needed and thereby endow working memory with a much larger virtual capacity.

Expertise and Instruction

Recall from chapter 2 that adding relevant graphics to a text description improved learning of individuals unfamiliar with the topic; however, the graphics had no benefits for learners with topic expertise. Because experienced learners can form their own images as they read the words, instructional images add no learning value.

In some situations, expertise can get in the way of an end goal. Have you ever watched a subject matter expert teach a class? Quite often they overload the learners' working memory with too much content, unfamiliar terms, and lengthy lectures. Experts just don't realize that their memories can hold and process information much more efficiently than novices. That's why an instructional specialist who knows less about the content is a good partner for a subject matter expert; the instructor helps the expert break down the content into smaller pieces and add instructional methods that reduce cognitive overload.

BYPASSING WORKING MEMORY LIMITS WITH AUTOMATICITY

We've seen that the patterns accumulated in long-term memory over years of experience afford experts the luxury of greater virtual working memory capacity. There is a second reason behind expert proficiency. It's called automaticity. Any task—physical or mental—that is repeated hundreds of times becomes hardwired into long-term memory. Any automated task can be performed with little or no working memory capacity. As you read this paragraph, you decode the words and sentences automatically and can allocate working memory to processing the meaning. Watch any first or second grader read and you will see a very different picture. Because word decoding is still not automated, reading is a very effortful process for these young children. Only through years of reading and writing practice are the many underlying skills of reading automated, allowing fast scanning of entire paragraphs in the mature reader.

Automaticity is the other secret of expert performance in any complex domain. Over years of practice, many layers of skills have automated, allowing the expert to devote working memory to the coordination and problem solving needed to perform complex tasks. Automaticity allows multitasking. While familiar tasks such as decoding words are performed on automatic, the freed up capacity in working memory can be devoted to higher-level tasks such as comprehension of the overall meaning.

However, as we have learned from the data on cell phones and injury accidents, automaticity is a dual-edged sword. For experienced drivers, routine driving is an automated task freeing working memory to perform other tasks such as talking on a cell phone. But when the basic driving tasks suddenly require the conscious attention of working memory, the driver may not be able to switch working memory resources quickly enough to make a safe response. It is the psychological load imposed by talking on a cell phone as much as it is the physical activity of holding the phone that leads to cognitive overload. That's why a hands-free phone can be just as dangerous as a handheld set. I predict that once evidence catches up with policy, both types of mobile devices will be banned while driving.

COGNITIVE LOAD AND YOUR TRAINING

Understanding the psychology of learning will help you make informed decisions about your training. An important psychological theory of learning and instruction called cognitive load theory is based on the features of working memory and its relationship with long-term memory. According to cognitive load theory, learning requires processing in working memory, and if working memory gets overloaded, learning is disrupted. There are three forms of cognitive load: intrinsic, extraneous, and germane.

Intrinsic Cognitive Load

Intrinsic cognitive load relates to the complexity of your instructional goals and materials. Take a Spanish language lesson for example: if you are asked to write the English meaning of a vocabulary word such as "hija," the intrinsic load is relatively low. On the other hand, if you are asked to respond to a question from a native speaker, the intrinsic load is much higher. That is because you need to do several things quickly. First, you need to translate the question. Second, you need to formulate a response that is grammatically correct. Third, you need to speak your response using a reasonably correct accent. Lessons with higher intrinsic load will by definition impose greater cognitive load and require techniques to reduce cognitive load in the learning environment. Simpler lessons such as the vocabulary exercise will not require as much cognitive load management.

Extraneous Cognitive Load

As the name implies, extraneous load is work imposed on working memory that does not contribute to learning. Extraneous cognitive load is imposed by instructional design decisions that make learning more demanding. For example, take a look at Figures 3-4 and 3-5. Both screens include the same visuals and words. Put a check mark next to the example that you think imposes more extraneous cognitive load:

- ❑ Version A because the visual and text are separated on a scrolling screen.
- ❑ Version B because the text is smaller.
- ❑ Both versions impose the same load because the content is the same.

Figure 3-4. Version A Layout of Text and Graphic

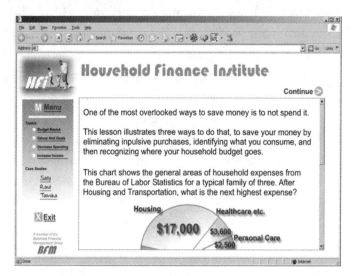

Source: Clark and Mayer, 2011. Material reproduced with permission John Wiley & Sons.

Figure 3-5. Version B Layout of Text and Graphic

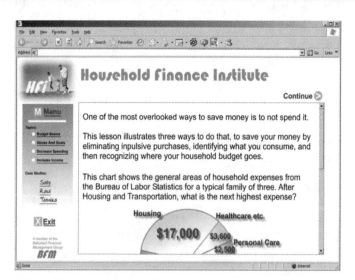

Source: Clark and Mayer, 2011. Material reproduced with permission John Wiley & Sons.

In chapter 6 we will review evidence on how best to explain graphics using either audio narration or text. In Figures 3-4 and 3-5 the designer used text to explain the pie chart. Version B imposes less extraneous cognitive load because the learner can see the graphic and the explanation together. When graphics and text explanations are separated as in Version A, extra mental effort must be devoted to integrating the two messages. First, the learner reviews and makes sense of the words. Then, while holding the words in memory, she looks at the diagram and attempts to interpret it. Working memory is being asked to hold information while reviewing and integrating the pie chart. This mental effort depletes working memory making learning less efficient. One of the main themes of this book involves evidence-based techniques to reduce extraneous cognitive load.

Germane Cognitive Load

Germane cognitive load is the good stuff. Learning requires psychological active processing in working memory that draws on limited memory resources. Instructional methods that promote effective active processing are all examples of germane cognitive load. In chapter 2, we reviewed research showing that adding a simple visual to a textual explanation of how the heart circulates blood improved mental processing by promoting more integrative inferences that resulted in better understanding. The graphic served as a form of germane cognitive load. Adding practice exercises or "clicker questions" to a lecture are common techniques that can promote germane cognitive load. In general, any productive engagement aligned to the learning goal should promote germane cognitive load.

Your Job

As a training professional, your job is to optimize these three types of cognitive load. As illustrated in Figure 3-6, when intrinsic load is high, you need to do everything you can to reduce extraneous cognitive load and promote germane cognitive load. As you read the remaining chapters, I will show evidence-based guidelines for doing just that.

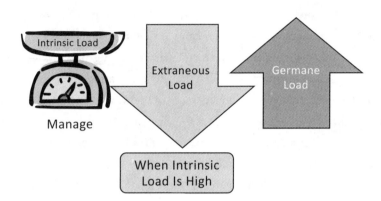

Figure 3-6. Optimizing Cognitive Load in Your Instruction

APPLYING COGNITIVE LOAD THEORY

I admit that this chapter is mostly theory. But having an understanding not only of what works in instruction, but also why it works, will help you understand and extend the guidelines in the chapters to follow. Based on the limits of working memory, its relationship with long-term memory, and cognitive load theory, you will understand the rationale of instructional methods that manage intrinsic cognitive load, reduce extraneous load, and increase germane load.

COMING NEXT

One of the essential prerequisites of all learning is active engagement—that is, active processing in working memory that will lead to encoding of new knowledge and skills in long-term memory. As mentioned in chapter 1, however, physical engagement is not equivalent to psychological engagement; in fact, it may even depress effective psychological engagement. When it comes to active learning, many training events are unbalanced. Some training is equated with lectures in which too much information is disseminated with no provision for psychological processing. In other cases, such as some games, the high level of physical activity detracts from the actual learning goal. I address the active learning balance most productive for learning in the next chapter.

FOR MORE INFORMATION

Mayer, R.E. (2014a). Cognitive Theory of Multimedia Learning. In *The Cambridge Handbook of Multimedia Learning*, 2nd edition, ed. R.E. Mayer. New York: Cambridge University Press.

Similar to the Paas and Sweller chapter, this chapter provides a slightly different perspective on cognitive load theory. Reading both chapters will give you an expanded understanding of the summary I provided in this chapter.

Paas, F., and J. Sweller. (2014). Implications of Cognitive Load Theory for Multimedia Learning. In *The Cambridge Handbook of Multimedia Learning*, 2nd edition, ed. R.E. Mayer. New York: Cambridge University Press.

Written by the researchers who have developed and tested cognitive load theory, this chapter offers a more technical and detailed account of cognitive load theory than the overview in this chapter.

ENGAGEMENT IN LEARNING

CHAPTER 4

Engagement in Learning

Consider two quite different learning environments designed to teach the same content. The instructional goal is learning basic electromechanical principles, such as how a wet cell battery works. One lesson consists of an approximately 20-minute presentation of PowerPoint slides. The alternative lesson is a narrative game shown in Figure 4-1. In the game, you assume the role of an explorer searching a World War II bunker for valuable lost art. To navigate through the bunker you will need to open doors and overcome barriers based on your understanding and application of the electromechanical concepts. The same information summarized on the Power-Point slides is available to you as you search the bunker.

Compare the slide presentation to the game. Which lesson is more engaging? Which would take longer to complete? Which would lead to better learning?

Figure 4-1. A Thematic Game to Teach Electromechanical Principles

Source: Adams et al., 2012.

In this chapter, we will take a closer look at active learning and the difference between psychological and behavioral activity. Based on research results from active learning environments that are and are not effective, we will derive a number of guidelines for the design of effective active learning events.

What Do You Think?

Mark each statement you think is true:

- ❏ Active engagement is essential for learning.
- ❏ Underlining text is an effective study strategy.
- ❏ High engagement games promote learning.
- ❏ Response clickers in classroom lectures improve learning.

WHEN ACTIVITY LEADS TO LESS LEARNING

Games are often touted as effective for learning because they elicit high learner engagement. Are all games effective? Take a look at Figure 4-2 that summarizes the results of the game versus the slide experiment described in the chapter introduction and illustrated in Figure 4-1. Then select your interpretation of that data.

Figure 4-2. Learning and Time to Complete Game and Slide Lessons

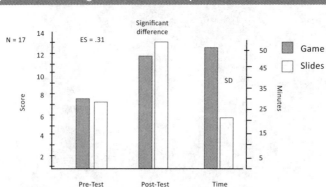

Source: Based on data from Adams et al., 2012.

Your interpretation:

- ❏ The game was more effective and efficient than the slide presentation.
- ❏ The game was more effective but less efficient than the slide presentation.
- ❏ The game was less effective and less efficient than the slide presentation.

From these results we see that a highly engaging lesson in the form of a thematic game not only took longer to complete but led to slightly less learning than a slide show that presented the same content. What are some possible reasons for this outcome? Perhaps the theme of the game was irrelevant to the learning goal and therefore imposed extraneous cognitive load. The mechanics of trying to open doors and move equipment from one area to another distracted players from learning. In contrast, learners viewing the slides could focus all of their mental resources on the content. Another possibility is that the game was only played one time. In a meta-analysis of learning games, Wouters et al. (2013) concluded that games are more effective when played multiple times. In either case, a high-engagement environment led to less learning than a "passive" slide show. Active engagement actually depressed learning. Note also that playing just one round of the game required more than double the time required to review the slides. In this experiment a narrative game was both inefficient and less effective for learning.

Similar results have been found in other comparisons of learning from high- and low-engagement learning environments. For example, in chapter 1, we saw research reported by Stull and Mayer (2007) showing that learning was more effective from a text accompanied by an author-provided organizational graphic than when the learners filled in a blank graphic. Perhaps completing the blank graphic imposed too much extraneous load. Or possibly learners entered incorrect information into the graphic. This research, as well as the game experiment, suggest that student activity alone does not necessarily lead to learning. In fact, it may even become a barrier.

THE ENGAGEMENT GRID

The grid in Figure 4-3 is a useful tool to illustrate a continuum of psychological and behavioral engagement. Along the horizontal axis I have illustrated overt behavioral activity from low to high. Along the vertical axis I graphed psychological activity that leads to learning from low to high.

Figure 4-3. The Engagement Grid

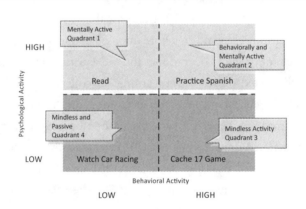

Source: Adapted from Clark and Mayer, 2008, 2011.

In the quadrants you can identify four states of engagement. For example, the narrative game described in the chapter introduction would fall into quadrant 3, high behavioral engagement but lower relevant psychological engagement. In contrast, the slide presentation would fall into quadrant 1, low behavioral engagement but high psychological engagement that led to learning.

Take a minute to fill in your own activity that would fall in each grid. For example, in quadrant 2, I put "practicing Spanish." I might respond to a question asked of me in Spanish or I might complete an exercise in which

I write in the correct tense and person of a verb. Reading can be a good quadrant 1 activity. My activity level is low, but when I am focused on the text and trying to abstract meaning, my psychological engagement is high.

Note that the upper grids shaded in a lighter hue correspond to higher or more relevant psychological activity. Basically, productive active learning methods fall into quadrants 1 or 2, both of which reflect high psychological engagement.

The Advantage of Quadrant 2

Quadrant 2 includes all environments in which learners are both behaviorally and psychologically engaged. Although learning takes place with quadrant 1 methods, the advantage of behavioral engagement is the generation of a visible product such as a response to a question, a case study solution, or a baseball pitch. A visible action or product provides a basis for feedback to correct errors or provide guidance. Although psychological engagement characteristic of quadrant 1 can generate learning, with no visible learner response, it is difficult to assess learning progress or provide feedback. Evidence derived from a comparison of high- and low-engagement environments leads to our first guideline.

Active Learning Guideline 1:

Incorporate frequent behavioral activities that promote relevant psychological processing of the content.

INSTRUCTIONAL METHODS AND THE ENGAGEMENT GRID

In this section I will summarize recent research on instructional methods that have been shown either ineffective or effective. We will interpret the results using the engagement grid and our summary of cognitive load theory from chapter 3.

Does Underlining Improve Learning?

If you look at the average college text or lecture notes, you will see plenty of markups in the form of underlining or highlighting. How effective is underlining for learning?

Underlining would definitely be considered a high behavioral activity. In spite of its popularity and high behavioral engagement, a review of many studies showed highlighting to be relatively ineffective (Dunlosky et al., 2013). Therefore I would put highlighting into quadrant 3, high behavioral but low psychological engagement. Some potential reasons for its lack of effectiveness include: 1) learners may not have enough background knowledge to underline the most important or relevant content, 2) learners may highlight too much information thus diminishing any cueing effect, or 3) while underlining draws attention to the marked sentences, it may not encourage inferences across sections of the text or promote connections between highlighted information and prior knowledge. In fact, one experiment showed that learners who underlined a history chapter scored lower on inference test questions (but not on factual test questions) on a two-month delayed test (Peterson, 1992). The Dunlosky et al. (2013) review team concluded that "In most situations that have been examined and with most participants, highlighting does little to boost performance" (21).

Active Learning Guideline 2:

Discourage the common study technique of underlining in favor of more productive activities.

Do Questions Improve Learning From Explanations?

Engagement through questions can occur in a number of contexts, including self-study, such as when learners create and study flashcards to learn facts and concepts; or in assigned exercises, such as questions posed throughout an instructional text or explanatory lecture. These instructional methods all involve behavioral activity. And evidence indicates they promote learning. Instructional psychologists refer to these kinds of activities as "practice testing" defined as exercises or learning activities completed in class or independently as low-stakes or no-stakes learning exercises.

The benefits of practice exercises have been shown for recall learning but also for inference and problem solving. McDaniel et al. (2012) assigned psychology students a weekly online practice activity. The online activity included a mix of assignments. Some of the activities involved practice questions with feedback while others assigned "restudy" of class content. Some of the course content was not included in either of the online practice assignments. Subsequent unit exams included questions presented during practice sessions as well as new questions. A summary of the results is shown in Figure 4-4. After you review the results, select your conclusions:

Figure 4-4. A Comparison of Learning From Online Activity Assignments

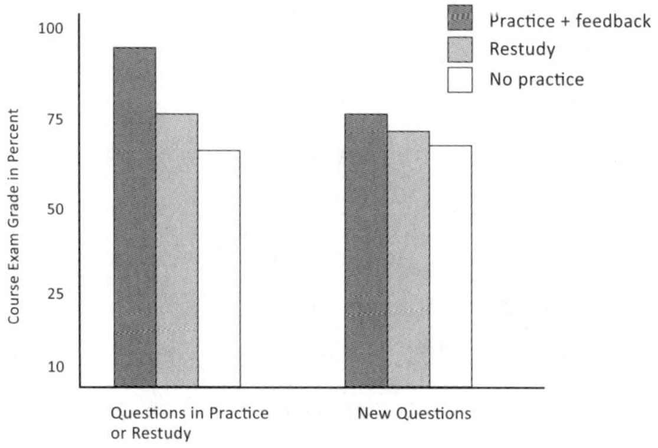

Source: Based on data from McDaniel et al. cited in Dunlosky, 2013.

Based on the data in Figure 4-4, compared to restudy, practice questions led to which result:

❏ Better exam results were achieved on the same questions practiced during study.
❏ Better exam results were achieved on new questions.

This classroom study showed the benefits of practice tests on the same questions that later appeared on the exam and also on new questions related to the content practiced. A review of multiple research studies led the Dunlosky review team to rate the utility of practice exercises as high. "Testing effects have been demonstrated across an impressive range of practice-test formats, kinds of material, learner ages, outcome measures, and retention intervals" (35). Based on the benefits of various forms of practice tests I classify them in quadrant 2, high behavioral and high psychological engagement.

Do Questions Improve Learning From Textual Explanations?

Questions placed at the end of textbook chapters or throughout online explanations represent one format for practice testing. Research from the 1970s on questions found better learning on a final test when students were required to answer questions, compared with control groups that did not answer questions. The greatest benefit occurred when questions were placed after rather than before the reading because students focused not only on questioned information but also on additional content in the chapter. Further, deeper learning was found to accrue from higher-level questions when compared with questions that asked for recognition or regurgitation of facts or verbatim text information.

Roelle and Berthold (2013) conducted a factorial experiment that compared learning of computer textual explanations on the topic of management theory among learners who answered questions in an on-screen box versus learners who could make their own notes in the box but were not asked questions. Some learners had completed pre-work that increased their prior knowledge before reading the explanations. The team found that answering questions promoted learning among low prior knowledge learners but not among those with higher prior knowledge. Perhaps individuals with more prior knowledge found the questions redundant of what they already knew, which then became an extraneous cognitive load.

Do Clicker Questions Improve Learning From Classroom Lectures?

Let's apply the research on questions added to textual explanations to large lecture settings. Mayer, Stull, and others (2009) found that learners who answered questions in a lecture with a response clicker gained on average a one-third grade-point improvement compared with learners who either answered questions on paper or who were not asked questions. Applicable to lecture formats common in higher education, some training settings and conferences use response clickers to maximize engagement. For best results, you should display a conceptual or prediction type objective question (such as multiple choice) periodically throughout a presentation. Allow learners time to respond and then project the voting results. Promote discussion of the answers and conclude with an explanation of the correct answer. Clickers have been demonstrated to have positive learning benefits by promoting psychological processing of information through this simple behavioral response and feedback mechanism.

It's important to note that although you could implement a similar technique using a show of hands, the clicker technology indicates when everyone has responded and displays the aggregated responses in a bar or pie chart on the screen, making the feedback discussion more focused. Clickers are one way to move a passive quadrant 4 environment into a quadrant 2 context. Shapiro and Gordon (2012) and Anderson et al. (2013) also report data supporting the benefits of clickers.

In summary, clickers have been shown to improve learning from lectures and to compress time when instructors are able to assess overall learning from clicker response patterns and omit further explanation. New technology allows students to use their cell phones in place of specialized response equipment. (For example: www.polleverywhere.com). Note that similar engagement techniques can be used in synchronous virtual classrooms through interactive features such as polling, whiteboard mark up, and chat.

Do Self-Explanation Questions Improve Learning?

Imagine two physics students studying a physics text—in particular, studying some example problems in the text. One student takes time to explain the example to herself by relating the specifics of the example to the principles of the lesson. The second student looks over the example but gives it only a shallow review, focusing on the specifics of the example rather than the principles it reflects. Which student would learn more?

In a classic experiment Chi et al. (1989) compared learning among physics students given problems to study. Those who spontaneously generated many self-explanations scored twice as high on the post-test compared with those who generated only a few explanations. Since then, many studies have validated the benefits of self-explaining. In fact, self-explanations will be a fundamental theme reviewed throughout this book.

Self-explanations can be promoted by asking learners to respond to questions, as discussed in the previous paragraphs. In addition, students can be trained to self-explain on their own. Ainsworth and Burcham (2007) compared understanding of blood circulation in the heart between a group of students that received self-explanation training and a group that did not. The training included examples of self-explanations that might be generated while reading a text. They found that those trained to self-explain demonstrated better learning on all post-test questions.

While some of your learners may be spontaneous self-explainers, many are not. Further, research shows that it is not the amount of self-explanation that is important so much as the quality of those explanations. For most situations, I recommend that the instructional designer or trainer promote self-explanations by adding questions to the lesson that will encourage productive self-explanations.

Active Learning Guideline 3:

Use questions throughout your training events to promote learning not only of questioned content but adjunct content as well.

Do Peer Reviews Promote Learning?

When I first taught my basic ISD class, I would review student project lessons at the end of the class. My reviews were high engagement for me but low engagement—both behavioral and psychological—for the learners. Later, I flipped my review sessions into peer reviews. In a peer review, a student is provided with a product from another participant along with some review criteria. The reviewer can provide ratings as well as written feedback to the reviewee. Do we have any evidence for the benefits of peer reviews?

Cho and MacArthur (2011) tested the value of peer reviews of the introductory section of a laboratory report as part of a science class. Three groups were formed with random assignment as follows: 1) a peer review group, 2) a reading only group, and 3) a no-treatment control group. Those in the reviewing and reading groups used previously rated writing examples to calibrate their ratings on a scoring sheet. Reviewers rated their assigned papers with a 1–7 scale and also made written comments. Readers read assigned papers but did not rate or comment. Afterward, all participants wrote their own reports on a different topic. These reports were rated by instructors.

The research team found that the average quality of reports was higher among those who had written a review than the other two groups. An analysis of the reviewer comments showed that comments reflecting detection of problems and solution suggestions were most correlated with subsequent higher writing quality.

Instructor involvement will be important to the success of peer reviews. The instructor needs to provide specific review criteria, hold calibration sessions, and monitor the reviews to assure that the feedback provided is consistent with the criteria.

Active Learning Guideline 4:

Use guided peer reviews to promote learning of the reviewer. Encourage a focus on problem identification and solution suggestions.

Does Collaboration Improve Learning?

A popular form of engagement is collaborative assignments in either classroom or asynchronous environments. There are many forms of collaboration in which groups of from two to five students are given assignments, such as to solve problems, create a product such as a marketing plan, complete a worksheet, or discuss a scenario. There is enough research on collaboration to justify a book in itself. For our purposes, I'll summarize a few recent findings on the learning value and conditions for effective collaboration during learning.

What are the trade-offs of collaboration? On the positive side, working in a small team can be synergistic with a better outcome than what an individual working solo would generate. In addition, discussing case studies, simulations, or problems can foster deeper psychological processing just through the act of articulating ideas. On the negative side, working in a group will require working memory capacity to reach a common understanding of the problem, to explain one's ideas, to listen to the ideas of others, and to make decisions based on group input. The value of collaboration will depend on the extent to which cognitive gains exceed cognitive costs.

Sears and Reagin (2013) assigned regular or advanced math students a series of "Magic Triangle" puzzles to solve either alone or with a partner. They found that the more advanced students performed significantly better on their own than with a partner. For the advanced students, collaboration was more of a hindrance than a benefit. In contrast, the regular students did better when working with a partner. For these students, the benefits of collaboration outweighed the cognitive costs.

Wouters et al. (2013) reviewed research that compared learning from serious games with learning from traditional methods. See chapter 14 for the details of this research. As part of their study, they compared games played solo with games played with a partner and found games that involved playing with another person resulted in more learning than games played solo. The research team suggests that working with a partner during a game promotes articulation of game strategy and principles, which in turn leads to more learning.

Apparently, learning from more challenging problems and cases is better in teams; whereas less challenging assignments are better completed alone. In a factorial study Kirschner et al. (2011a) created a hard and easy version of a lesson on genetics and assigned them to either individuals or groups to solve. They found that collaboration led to better learning—but only for the harder lessons.

In summary, the evidence to date suggests that when faced with challenging learning goals, collaboration leads to better products and learning than individual work. In contrast, solo work is more effective for easier assignments.

Active Learning Guideline 5:

Consider collaboration when problems or assignments are challenging and/or will benefit from group synergy.

THE BOTTOM LINE

Compare your responses from the start of the chapter with my answers below. Make a note of any instructional techniques you may want to add or edit in your learning environment.

What Do You Think?

A. Active engagement is essential for learning.

TRUE. However it is psychological engagement rather than behavioral engagement that is most important.

B. Underlining text is an effective study strategy.

FALSE. Evidence indicates that although learners are behaviorally active and believe underlining to be effective, the benefits to learning are minimal.

C. High-engagement games promote learning.

IT DEPENDS. Many games are high in behavioral engagement. However, it is important that the game design align with the psychological responses needed to achieve the target skills. See chapter 14 for more discussion on games.

D. Response clickers in classroom lectures improve learning.

TRUE. Evidence from classes that did and did not use clickers to respond to questions shows the learning advantage of clickers. Clickers can change a passive learning environment, such as a lecture, into a productive active learning event.

APPLYING ENGAGEMENT PRINCIPLES TO YOUR TRAINING

Learning relies on psychological engagement. A combination of behavioral activity that promotes appropriate psychological engagement will optimize learning provided that feedback guides responses. In chapter 10, we will review several evidence-based laws regarding practice exercises including what kind of practice to develop, how much practice is needed, where to place practice in your instruction and how to give effective feedback. Based on the evidence described in this chapter, apply the following guidelines to your training to maximize the benefits of engagement in learning:

- Early in the planning process, allow time and resources to design and deliver environments that promote behavioral and psychological engagement.

- Insert questions into explanations that will promote understanding aligned to the instructional goal.

  – Use clickers during lectures.

  – Add questions to text or computer explanations.

  – Encourage learners to self-explain during study rather than use less productive techniques such as underlining.

- Assign collaborative teams to engagement activities that are challenging.

- Ensure that engagement activities do not impose extraneous load.

COMING NEXT

This chapter completes part 1 of this book, in which we have migrated from common instructional myths reviewed in chapter 1 to the basis for evidence-based practice and the three core themes that make up the foundational ideas of this book. These include the types of evidence I will report in this book discussed in chapter 2, cognitive load theory summarized in chapter 3, and fundamental principles of engagement in learning discussed in this chapter.

All training professionals use a mix of text, graphics, and audio to communicate their content and promote engagement. In part 2, we will review evidence that will guide your best use of these communication modalities in classroom training, e-learning, and workbooks.

FOR MORE INFORMATION

Dunlosky, J., K.A. Rawson, E.J. Marsh, M.J. Nathan, and D.T. Willingham. (2013). Improving Students' Learning With Effective Learning Techniques: Promising Directions From Cognitive and Educational Psychology. *Psychological Science in the Public Interest* 14: 4-58.

I recommend this comprehensive and readable review on evidence-based active learning.

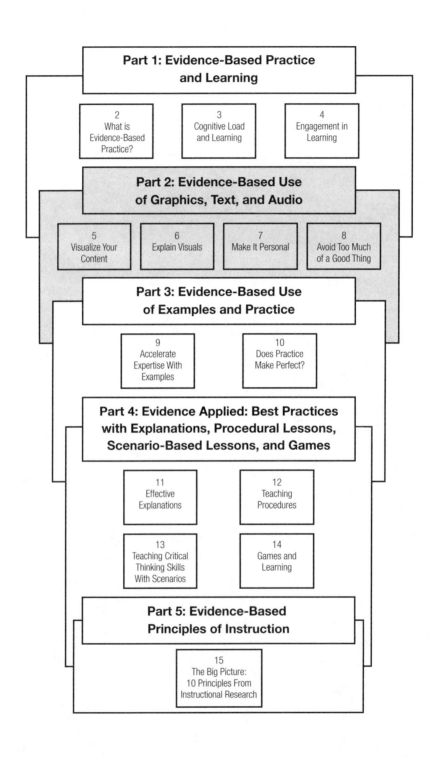

Part 1: Evidence-Based Practice and Learning

2
What is Evidence-Based Practice?

3
Cognitive Load and Learning

4
Engagement in Learning

Part 2: Evidence-Based Use of Graphics, Text, and Audio

5
Visualize Your Content

6
Explain Visuals

7
Make It Personal

8
Avoid Too Much of a Good Thing

Part 3: Evidence-Based Use of Examples and Practice

9
Accelerate Expertise With Examples

10
Does Practice Make Perfect?

Part 4: Evidence Applied: Best Practices with Explanations, Procedural Lessons, Scenario-Based Lessons, and Games

11
Effective Explanations

12
Teaching Procedures

13
Teaching Critical Thinking Skills With Scenarios

14
Games and Learning

Part 5: Evidence-Based Principles of Instruction

15
The Big Picture: 10 Principles From Instructional Research

PART 2

Evidence-Based Use of Graphics, Text, and Audio

Chapters 5 to 8 summarize evidence and guidelines on best practices with graphics and use of text and audio to describe graphics. We started our discussion of research on graphics in chapter 2. In this part of the book we will dig deeper into the evidence on visuals, including the what, when, and why of effective graphics. Most graphics need explanations and chapters 6 and 7 look at how best to explain graphics using text and audio—for example, how to exploit human social instincts by personalizing the learning environment. Finally, in chapter 8 we will unpack the theme that in learning environments, less is often more.

VISUALIZE YOUR CONTENT

CHAPTER 5

Visualize Your Content

No matter what media you use, slides or screens of text and more text make for a boring presentation. Walls of words fail to leverage one of the most powerful tools proven to boost learning: graphics!

In this chapter, I review the learning value of adding graphics to words and focus on the kinds of visuals that leverage the brain for learning. In addition, we will look at evidence on ways to use graphics to actively engage learners with your content.

THE LOST POTENTIAL OF GRAPHICS

Why do we see so many slides or screens filled with text or with decorative visuals? Chances are you will hear one of the following reasons:

- Text is much faster to create.
- I'm not an artist.
- My content does not lend itself to visuals.
- Decorative clip art is easy to find and livens up the slides.

If you are like most trainers, you are very comfortable in a world of words. Since preschool your education has focused on verbal literacy. From primary grades through college, we all devoted many hours to reading and writing. In contrast, most of us have had no training in visual literacy! We think and communicate with words rather than graphics.

What Do You Think?

Put a check next to each statement about visuals that you believe is true:

- ❑ A. Not all visuals are equally effective.
- ❑ B. Decorative visuals added for interest increase motivation and learning.
- ❑ C. Often, a simpler visual like a line drawing is more effective than a more realistic depiction, such as a photograph.
- ❑ D. Learner-generated drawings can improve learning.

WHAT IS A GRAPHIC?

For our purposes, I define a graphic as a visual representation of lesson content. I include typical iconic lesson visuals intended to directly represent the content, such as a screen capture from a software application or a line drawing of equipment. I also include more abstract visuals to illustrate lesson ideas, such as a tree diagram to show organizational relationships or a computer-generated animation to illustrate how an engine works. Graphics may be as simple as a line drawing or as complex as a photograph. They may be rendered in a still format or involve motion as in a video or animation. In addition, graphics may incorporate cues, such as arrows or highlights, to direct the learner's eye to important elements.

As you can see, graphics of various types can offer considerable visual diversity to a lesson. In most cases, adding visuals to text in your lessons will increase production time and costs of your materials. However, as we saw in chapters 1 and 2, learners prefer lessons with visuals; and, at least some types of visuals lead to increased learning—especially for novice learners. Investing resources in visuals can be a win-win—lessons that get better ratings and promote learning. An important question is: What kinds of visuals help and what kinds of visuals hinder learning?

GRAPHICS AND THE BRAIN

In chapter 2, I introduced an experiment that evaluated the effects of graphics on understanding how the heart circulates blood. In a comparison of three lesson versions, Butcher (2006) reported that the lessons with text plus simple visuals most improved understanding. To analyze the thoughts learners had while studying, she used a protocol analysis technique in which she recorded and categorized comments students made while reviewing the lessons. One category was inferential comments that connected and extended ideas stated in the lesson. For example, from text stating, "As the blood flows through the capillaries in the body, carrying its supply of oxygen, it also collects carbon dioxide. The blood that empties into the right atrium is dark colored. It has picked up carbon dioxide from the body cells," one student made the following inference: "The blood is dark because of the carbon dioxide. Oxygen probably enriches the red color of the blood" (Butcher, 2006, 196). This relationship was not explicitly stated in the text but was inferred by the learner. Figure 5-1 shows a graph of the percentage of statements that included productive inferences.

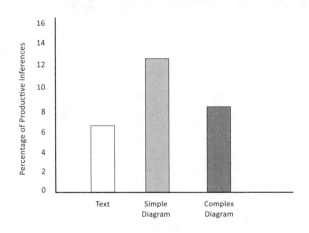

Figure 5-1. Inferences Produced in Three Lesson Versions on Blood Circulation

Source: Based on data from Butcher, 2006.

Learners studying the lessons with text and diagrams made a higher percentage of productive inferences compared to learners reviewing text alone. Although none of the lessons prompted behavioral engagement, adding diagrams stimulated deeper psychological engagement as evidenced by the higher number of inferences. In other words, adding diagrams to text promotes germane cognitive load—mental load that leads to learning.

The evidence showing the learning benefits of adding visuals to text supports my first recommendation.

Graphics Guideline 1:

Promote deeper learning by adding visuals to text.

When diagrams are added to text, learners are able to develop a more complete, more accurate mental model by making inferences about the relationships presented in the lesson. Relevant visuals work because they offer the brain an additional opportunity to build mental models.

WHO BENEFITS FROM GRAPHICS?

In chapter 2, I presented evidence comparing learning of novice versus experienced students from a diagram of a bicycle pump. The data showed that novice learners benefited from graphics more than learners with background knowledge of the content. Rather than visual or auditory learners, all learners who are new to a content domain benefit from a relevant visual.

Several other experiments have shown similar results; that is, visuals that benefit novices don't help experts. For example, Brewer and his colleagues (2004) compared understanding of judicial instructions presented with words alone (audio instructions) with instructions presented with words and visuals (audio-visual instructions). If you have ever served on a jury, you know that the judge gives a verbal explanation regarding the legal aspects of the case to consider during deliberations. Brewer's experiment included two types of mock juries: one made up of typical citizens and a second consisting of law students. The lesson included about 10 minutes of a judge's auditory instructions for a self-defense trial. The audio-visual version added a flow chart and visuals that corresponded to the judge's explanations. For example, to illustrate the requirement that the accused believes that her conduct was necessary and reasonable, animations depicted a man pointing a knife at a woman's throat and the woman kicking the man, believing she had no choice. In a second contrasting animation based on the same scenario, three other people approached and the man dropped his knife. The woman still kicked him although it was apparent that alternative action was possible. After hearing—or hearing and viewing—the instructions, all jurors were tested with a self-defense scenario. As you can see in Figure 5-2 the scores of novice jurors improved in the AV version— but the law students' scores did not. The law students had sufficient legal knowledge to understand the judge's words without the additional support of visuals.

Figure 5-2. Visuals Improve Novices' Understanding

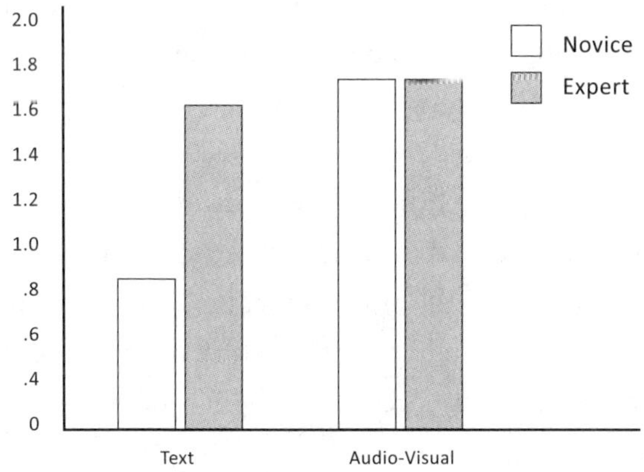

Source: Based on data from Brewer et al., 2004.

Experiments such as this one that compared the effects of visuals on learning of experts and novices are the basis for my next recommendation.

Graphics Guideline 2:

Emphasize visuals for novices more than for learners with prior knowledge of the content.

BEYOND THE PUMPKIN SLIDE

Imagine you are responsible for updating the sales force on the new printer features. Because time is short, you decide to use an explanatory presentation to be delivered through your virtual classroom. With the help of the engineering division you quickly pull together slides that summarize the features of the printer. As you review your first draft, it seems pretty boring, as most of the slides project text only. At this stage, you happen to glance at the calendar and realize it's October and that means—Halloween. Aha! You quickly do a clip art search and find some great jack-o'-lanterns and fall trees to add to your slides. Yes, your slides are more colorful, but what effect (if any) will your last-minute embellishments have on learning?

If you have used decorative art to enliven your slides, you are not alone. In an analysis of visuals used in school textbooks, Mayer, Sims, and Tajika (1995) found that pages were about evenly divided between text and illustrations. When they analyzed the type of illustrations used, the overwhelming majority served no useful instructional purpose. In other words, they were pumpkin graphics. In more formal terminology, visuals like these are called "decorative" graphics. Decorative graphics are designed to add visual interest or humor to the material.

Take a look at the visual in Figure 5-3 created for a customer service e-learning course.

Figure 5-3. Example of a Decorative Graphic

Source: Used with permission from T+D *magazine.*

The e-learning developer's organization set a standard that all e-learning use only positive image photographs for illustrations. While photographic visuals resulted in a consistent look and feel among the screens, at the same time this standard limited the visual options that could be used to support the instructional message.

Figure 5-4 shows a revision designed to summarize the concept of gift certificate access. While the revised visual may not be as "pretty," chances are it will promote learning more effectively.

Figure 5-4. A Revised Graphic That Supports the Content

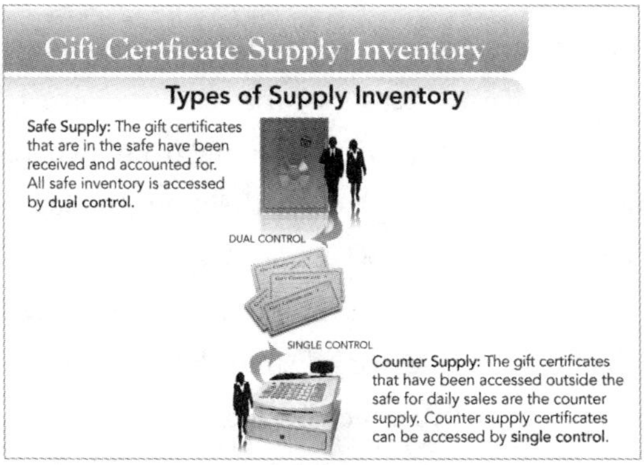

Source: With permission from T+D *magazine.*

Sometimes decorative graphics appear as overly elaborate templates that are typically irrelevant to the content and monopolize a great deal of the screen real estate. As a speaker, I have been asked more than once by the sponsoring organization to use a counterproductive template designed by the marketing department. Figure 5-5 is a slightly disguised version of a recent template I was asked to use for a national conference. Happily, when I objected to it, the conference organizers allowed me to use my own minimalist template!

Figure 5-5. An Overly Decorative Slide Template

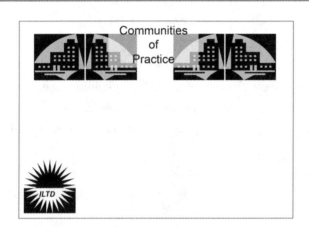

Can Decorative Visuals Defeat Learning?

You might agree that a decorative visual does not promote learning—but does it really do any harm? Let's see what the evidence tells us. Mayer, Heiser, and Lonn (2001) evaluated learning from two lessons on how lightning forms. A basic version included text and visuals that illustrated the process of lightning formation. A spiced up version added some interesting visuals and discussion about lightning. For example, a visual of an airplane struck by lightning was accompanied by a brief description of what happens to airplanes in the presence of lightning. Another visual showed the burns on a football player's uniform caused by a lightning strike. The research team added several interesting visuals like these to the basic lesson. Select the statement(s) that you think best predict the outcomes from this experiment:

❑ A. Learners found the enhanced versions more interesting.
❑ B. Learning was better from the enhanced versions.
❑ C. Learning was worse from the enhanced versions.
❑ D. Learning was the same because the core content was the same in all versions.

It's true that learners did find the versions with added anecdotes and visuals more interesting than the plain versions. Recall the research I summarized in chapter 1 showing that students gave higher ratings to all lesson versions with any form of graphic, including irrelevant and relevant visuals (Sung and Mayer, 2012b). Unfortunately, higher ratings do not correlate with better learning. Whether presented in a paper-based version or via computer, the basic lesson versions that omitted the interesting visuals led to better learning! In five experiments that compared a concise with an embellished version, the median effect size of 1.66 favored the concise versions. That means that a lesson that resulted in an average score of 75 percent with a standard deviation of 10 would boost performance to more than 91 percent when extraneous graphics are cut! The correct answers to the question above are: A and C.

Why do decorative visuals—even visuals related to the topic—defeat learning? Imagine that your brain starts to form an understanding of warm air rising and producing an updraft, then cooling and condensing into a cloud. Then on the next screen, you review some text and visuals about airplanes struck by lightning. Following the airplane story, you see that the top of the cloud extends above the freezing level leading to formation of ice crystals. Next you review some statistics and visuals about the hazards of lightning to golfers. You can see that just as you are building an understanding of lightning formation, you are distracted by an interesting but irrelevant visual. Because visuals are so powerful, graphics unrelated to your instructional goal at best do not contribute to understanding and at worst actually depress learning!

Are Decorative Visuals Ever Useful?

In lessons that are intended to build skills or teach processes, such as the lightning lesson, decorative visuals or interesting but irrelevant stories inserted into the content flow have been shown to disrupt learning. However, if the goal of the lesson is to motivate behavior or get more positive lesson ratings, a decorative visual may be a useful addition—especially if it does not distract from the content flow. We need more research on the motivational benefits of decorative visuals. For a recent review of research on motivation and graphics see Mayer (2014c).

In general, for skill-building lessons, consider the following guideline.

Graphics Guideline 3:

Minimize visuals extraneous to the instructional goal added for interest or entertainment—especially visuals that interrupt the instructional message.

WHAT KINDS OF VISUALS ARE MOST EFFECTIVE?

Because decorative visuals don't promote learning, let's review research that offers guidance as to what types of visuals are most effective.

Keep Visuals Simple

First, let's consider whether a realistic visual is more effective for learning than a simpler version. For example, is a photograph more effective than a line drawing? Recall the research on blood circulation showing that lesson versions that added a visual to text resulted in better understanding of blood circulation. That experiment compared three lesson versions. One used text alone to describe the process. The other two versions added visuals: one a simple line drawing and the other a more anatomically accurate version. You can see the two diagrams in Figure 5-6. We know that the versions with visuals resulted in better learning. Which visual do you think was more effective: the simple drawing or the more detailed drawing?

Figure 5-6. A Simple and Detailed Diagram of Blood Circulation

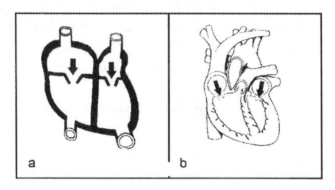

Source: From Butcher, 2006. This material is reproduced with permission of John Wiley & Sons.

You might be surprised to know that Version A in Figure 5-6 was more effective. Keep in mind that the learning goal was to understand the process of blood flow through the heart. Had the goal been to identify the parts of the heart, a more realistic rendition may have been more effective. Several experiments have shown that often a simple line drawing is more effective for learning than a more realistic graphic such as a photograph or detailed sketch. Naturally, the benefits of a simpler graphic will depend on background knowledge of the learner and the instructional goal. For novice learners and an instructional goal of understanding a process, evidence suggests simpler versions.

In addition to a simple graphic, consider visuals that depict relationships in your content. I call these types of visuals explanatory graphics. I recommend using the following four types of explanatory visuals: organizational, relational, transformational, and interpretive. Table 5-1 defines each of these. For more detail see my book, *Graphics for Learning*, co-authored with Chopeta Lyons. Evidence on learning from different types of visuals is the basis for my fourth recommendation.

Graphics Guideline 4:

Use simple, relevant visuals that depict relationships in your content in lieu of complex or decorative graphics that add extraneous cognitive load.

Table 5-1. Four Types of Explanatory Visuals

TYPE	A VISUAL THAT	EXAMPLES
Organizational	Illustrates qualitative relationships in the content	Tree diagram Concept map
Relational	Summarizes quantitative data	Pie chart Color on a map to indicate temperatures
Transformational	Depicts change in time or space	An animation of how equipment works A series of line drawings with arrows to illustrate blood flow
Interpretive	Makes abstract ideas concrete or represents principles	A simulation of feature changes by gene alterations An animation of molecular movement with changes in temperature

How to Use Explanatory Visuals

Organizational visuals are helpful to illustrate qualitative relationships among your topics. Tree diagrams and tables are both examples of organizational visuals. The chapter map graphic shown throughout this book is an organizational visual. These types of visuals are useful at the start of a lesson or course with periodic review as new topics are introduced.

McCrudden and colleagues (2007) found that adding causal diagrams—a visual display that uses boxes and arrows to summarize cause and effect relationships—resulted in better learning of a science text than the text without the diagram. In fact, they found that those who studied the diagrams alone learned more than those who read the text alone.

Relational visuals in the form of bar charts and pie graphs are commonly seen in training materials. Rather than viewing a table of numbers, seeing overall trends with graphs and charts imposes less cognitive load and makes relationships more salient. Remember to keep them simple. Although it's easy to produce graphs with 3-D appearance, research has shown faster and better comprehension from a flat version (Fischer, 2000).

Transformational visuals show changes over time or in space. Animations are commonly used to depict processes such as how equipment works. However, a number of studies have shown that a series of still visuals may be more effective than an animated version. Since the first edition of this book, there has been an explosion of research on animations, which I will discuss in chapter 8. Both the still and animated versions are examples of transformational visuals but the animation can often impose excessive mental load.

You are probably most familiar with interpretive visuals from your science lessons. An interpretive visual represents concepts or relationships that are not normally visible. Diagrams of molecules, slow motion recordings of insects in flight, and animations of genetic inheritance are common examples.

So far in this chapter we have reviewed the benefits of adding explanatory visuals to words delivered in either text or audio. Improved test scores and protocol analysis indicate that graphics are psychologically engaging. Could we get more benefit by promoting behavioral engagement with visuals? In the next section, I review research on making content-specific visuals engaging and using organizational visuals to improve content-general learning.

ENGAGING LEARNERS WITH CONTENT-SPECIFIC GRAPHICS

A content-specific graphic is a visual that depicts the core learning information. A diagram of the heart in a physiology class or a schematic of electrical circuits in a troubleshooting class are two examples.

Learning From Drawing

Rather than add visuals to text, how about asking learners to create their own diagrams while reading text? Do you think that learning from drawing would be:

- ❏ A. Better due to higher engagement with the text?
- ❏ B. Depressed due to cognitive load of having to create a drawing?
- ❏ C. Dependent on the accuracy of the drawing produced?

Schwamborn and colleagues (2010) asked students to read a scientific text explaining the chemical process of cleaning with soap and water that included the concepts of surface tension and the effects of detergent on water. Some students were directed to create drawings as they read. Rather than draw from scratch on a blank slate, learners were given elements of the drawing and the background, as shown in Figure 5-7. Learners with drawing assignments scored more than double on a problem-solving test. The research team evaluated the student drawings and divided them into high and low accuracy depictions. They found that those producing the higher accuracy drawings scored almost double with a high effect size of .99 on a problem-solving test compared to those who drew with lower accuracy. The answers to the previous question are A and C.

Figure 5-7. Support Elements Provided for a Drawing Assignment of a Chemical Process

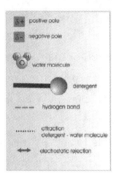

Source: From Schwamborn et al., 2010. Used with permission.

In a review of 15 research studies that compared learning from drawing textual information with learning from other activities, including reading the text, reading the text with illustrations, or writing summaries, Van Meter and Garner (2005) identified three conditions that maximize the learning benefits of drawing. First, the student-generated drawing must be accurate. To ensure accuracy, learners should get feedback on their drawings; for example, by viewing an accurate version and correcting their own drawing. Second, learners require support to manage cognitive load. In the drawing assignment illustrated in Figure 5-7, rather than draw from scratch, learners used prepared elements and background. Having access to prepared elements of the diagram reduced cognitive load that otherwise would be devoted to creating those elements. Therefore, learners can devote their working memory resources to depicting the relationships among the elements. Third, drawings benefit conceptual understanding and problem solving more than remember level performance. Most of the research reports in their review used science or mathematics content involving students ranging from kindergarten to college age.

Asking learners to assemble parts into an accurate representation may be useful in contexts that rely on understanding physical systems, such as training for allied health care professionals or mechanical technicians.

Learning by Self-Explaining Visuals

The above experiments showed ways that learners can construct graphics to promote understanding. Alternatively, you could insert short questions that prompt learners to give verbal explanations of a lesson diagram. We discussed the value of self-explanations in chapter 4. For many years, we've known that students who generate self-explanations of learning materials learn more than those who mostly paraphrase the content. Can learning from drawings be encouraged by self-explanations?

Ainsworth and Loizu (2003) compared learning the circulatory system by college-aged students who studied from a text description or from labeled diagrams that used arrows and color to illustrate blood flow.

Participants were asked to generate self-explanations as they studied either the diagram or text version. These explanations were recorded and analyzed. All students took a test that required them to draw the blood path as well as answer multiple-choice items that included factual and inference questions. Not surprisingly, those in the diagram conditions scored better on the drawing test; however, they also scored higher on the multiple-choice test. Those in the diagram condition averaged 80 percent correct on the multiple-choice test compared to 56 percent by the text students. Those studying the diagrams generated more self-explanations than those studying text even though they devoted significantly less time to studying the materials. This research showed that study of labeled and cued diagrams led to more self-explanations and better learning than study of text alone.

Cromley et al. (2013) compared learning of a genetics unit by high school students over a six-week period. They assigned students to one of three different engagement methods with graphics. A self-explanation question asked students to answer "what if" questions. For example, next to a diagram on pollination, a question asked, "What would happen if this substance did not move as shown (for example, if it was blocked)?" A drawing condition provided a drawing from the text and asked learners to draw a similar illustration. A diagram-completion condition included diagrams from the text with callouts. Students were asked to write captions in the callouts as well as a short explanation related to it. The research team found that the diagram-completion condition led to best learning with least amount of effort required of teachers.

In both of the previous experiments, the most learning resulted from assignments in which learners were required to convert a visual modality to a verbal modality—by self-explaining a diagram verbally in the first experiment and by writing short explanations in the second experiment. Perhaps having to translate ideas from one modality (visual) to a different modality (verbal) promotes deeper processing of the graphic. Based on evidence to date, I recommend the following.

Graphics Guideline 5:

Engage learners by asking them to convert verbal explanations to visuals (with help and feedback) or vice versa by generating verbal explanations of diagrams.

ENGAGING LEARNERS WITH CONTENT-GENERAL GRAPHICS

A content-general graphic is an organizational visual that can be used to organize information from a variety of domains. The graphic is not unique to the content in the lesson. A table or tree diagram that learners must complete while reading a text are typical examples.

Using Tables to Categorize Related Information

Organizing content with tables has been found to be more effective than either preparing an outline or taking freeform notes. In one experiment, a text described a number of features about various wildcats. Not into wildcats? Think product knowledge. Kauffman et al. (2011) asked learners to take online notes on the content using an open-ended text box, an outline that listed wildcat names, or a table that listed names across the top row and characteristics down the left column. The table format resulted in best learning. One benefit is that the table can offer clues as to completeness of notes. Empty cells signal missing information. Review of tabularized information also helps learners to compare and contrast a series of concepts across their features. For example, a series of products could be listed across the top row and features such as benefits, dimensions, recommended uses, and pricing could be listed along the left column.

Graphics Guideline 6:

Use graphic tools to guide the organization of content and learning.

THE BOTTOM LINE

Now that we have summarized key evidence-based guidelines for visuals that best support learning, revisit the questions below and see if you changed any of your ideas from the chapter introduction.

What Do You Think?

Put a check mark next to each statement you think is true.

❑ **Not all visuals are equally effective.**

TRUE. Recall the No Yellow Brick Road theme from chapter 1. The benefits of a visual will depend on your learning goal, the design of the visual itself, and the background knowledge of your learners.

❑ **Decorative or thematic visuals increase interest and learning.**

TRUE and *FALSE*. Evidence indicates that when used in excess, decorative visuals that are unrelated to the instructional objective at best do not improve learning and at worst can degrade learning through distraction. However, learners do like materials with visuals and current research is exploring appropriate uses for decorative visuals.

❑ **Often a simpler visual such as a line drawing is more effective than a more realistic depiction such as a photograph.**

TRUE. In general render a graphic in its simplest form congruent with the learning objective.

❑ **Learner drawings can improve learning.**

TRUE. Learner-generated graphics can improve learning if the drawings are accurate and deeper understanding is the goal of the instruction. To ensure accuracy, provide support and feedback.

APPLYING VISUALS TO YOUR TRAINING

Whether you are using slides in the classroom or preparing screens for e-learning, visuals can be one of your most powerful allies. Although you will need to invest more time and effort compared to producing materials in which words or decorative graphics predominate, when your learners are new to the content and when your goal is meaningful learning, we have ample evidence for a return on investment in relevant graphics.

Consider the following questions as you review your content:

- What relationships are important in my lesson?
- Which explanatory visuals can I use to reinforce those relationships?
- Do I have multiple topics that could benefit from an organizational graphic such as a flow chart, table, or tree diagram?

- Am I trying to illustrate a process or procedure that involves changes over time and could benefit from some type of transformational visual?

- Does my lesson include abstract ideas or concepts? If so, can I use a visual analogy to create an interpretive visual?

- Have I included visuals that will distract from the learning goal? If yes, either delete or move those visuals out of the body of the lesson.

- Have I selected or been assigned a template that is counterproductive to learning?

- How can I engage learners with visuals either by asking them to create visuals, explain visuals or use visuals as an organizational aid?

- Most trainers have historically worked primarily in text. Therefore, you may need to prime your pump to think visually with one or more of the following activities:

  - Start a collection of images—especially explanatory images that effectively communicate ideas. Remember that most images are copyrighted. However, the goal of your collection is not to use the images you find; instead, you should consider how the visual techniques can be adapted to your own content and learning goals.

  - Use your cell phone or digital camera to capture images as you do your job analysis. For example, take snapshots of sketches that subject matter experts make when explaining their ideas. Take photos of equipment or work-relevant settings.

  - Check out your organization's resources. You might be lucky to have access to a graphic artist who can help you translate your ideas into images. You might have a corporate repository of work-relevant images that you can repurpose into your lesson.

COMING NEXT

Most visuals are not self-explanatory. You will need to use words to enable learners to make sense of the message. In the next chapter we will review evidence on the best ways to explain visuals. We will consider when to use audio narration and when to use text, as well as when and how to use a combination of narration and text.

FOR MORE INFORMATION

Brewer, N., S. Harey, and S. Semmler. (2004). Improving Comprehension of Jury Instructions With Audio-Visual Presentation. *Applied Cognitive Psychology* 18: 765-776.

I liked this research because the context is an application of visuals outside of a classroom setting.

Butcher, K.R. (2006). Learning From Text With Diagrams: Promoting Mental Model Development and Inference Generation. *Journal of Educational Psychology* 98(1): 182-197.

I keep this research report in my "favorites" file because I find the study is well conceptualized, combines experimental and qualitative methods, and is clearly written.

Clark, R.C., and C. Lyons. (2011). *Graphics for Learning*, 2nd edition. San Francisco: Pfeiffer.

I recommend this book because I wrote it with my graphic design colleague, Chopeta Lyons. We blended evidence-based guidelines and practical design processes and techniques in this book.

Mayer, R.E., ed. (2014a). *The Cambridge Handbook of Multimedia Learning*, 2nd edition. New York: Cambridge University Press.

This book is a worthwhile investment. I recommend chapter 7, "The Multimedia Principle," and chapter 12, "The Coherence Principle." These chapters are written by researchers associated with their chapter theme.

Van Meter, P., and J. Garner. (2005). The Promise and Practice of Learner-Generated Drawing: Literature Review and Synthesis. *Educational Psychology Review* 17: 285-325.

I recommend this review because it drew on multiple experiments to derive major conditions for which drawing assignments will lead to effective learning. The review includes a section on classroom applications, as well as a section on empirical research.

EXPLAIN VISUALS

CHAPTER 6

Explain Visuals

The invention of written language was one of the most significant phases of human evolution. Written language made widely accessible by the invention of the printing press and later by audio recordings allows ideas to be transmitted across geography, time, and populations.

Figure 6-1. 26th Century BC Cuneiform Inscription

Imagine that you have lined up a set of visuals for your lesson. You have identified some screen captures to illustrate a computer procedure. Next you need to write the words to describe the actions in the visuals. Many trainers believe that written words plus audio narration of those words accommodate different learning styles, as well as learners with visual or auditory disabilities.

What is the best way to explain visuals: in multimedia lessons, in the classroom, or in print materials? In this chapter, we will look at evidence-based guidelines to maximize the instructional value of the words you use to explain visuals.

THE POWER OF EXPLANATIONS

We've seen in chapter 5 that relevant visuals can dramatically improve learning; however, most visuals are not self-explanatory. For meaningful learning, you need both visuals and words to communicate your content. First you need to determine if your visual needs an explanation. If it does, you need to decide whether to present words in audio, text, or both text and audio. If you decide to use text, you need to decide where to place the text in conjunction with the visuals. Whether you use text or audio, you need to decide how detailed and lengthy to make your explanation.

What Do You Think?

Look at the examples in Figures 6-2, 6-3, 6-4, and 6-5. The content is basically the same in all of the examples. What varies is how and where words are presented.

Figure 6-2. Version A: Use of On-Screen Text to Explain a Visual

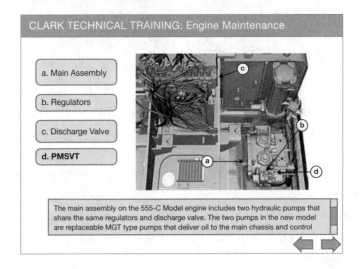

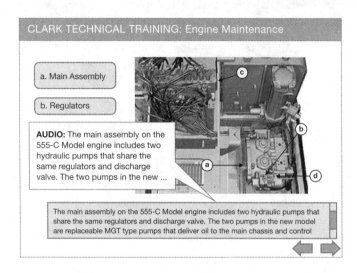

Figure 6-3. Version B: Use of On-Screen Text and Audio to Explain a Visual

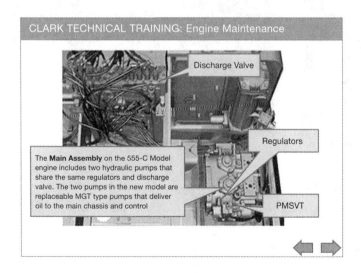

Figure 6-4. Version C: Use of On-Screen Text to Explain a Visual

Figure 6-5. Version D: Use of Audio to Explain a Visual

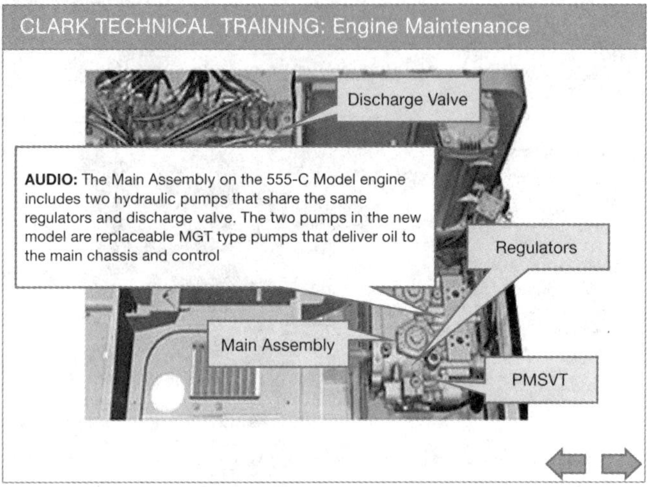

CLARK TECHNICAL TRAINING: Engine Maintenance

Discharge Valve

AUDIO: The Main Assembly on the 555-C Model engine includes two hydraulic pumps that share the same regulators and discharge valve. The two pumps in the new model are replaceable MGT type pumps that deliver oil to the main chassis and control

Regulators

Main Assembly

PMSVT

After you review the four versions, mark which presentation is the most effective.

- ❑ Version A in Figure 6-2, because the layout is the cleanest.
- ❑ Version B in Figure 6-3, because the explanations are presented in text and in audio narration of that text.
- ❑ Version C in Figure 6-4, because the explanation is presented in text that is located near the visual.
- ❑ Version D in Figure 6-5, because the explanation is presented in audio only.

In this chapter, I will review evidence that addresses the issues of when to use audio, text, or both to explain a visual and how to display text in conjunction with visuals.

WHAT ARE EXPLANATIONS?

For the purpose of this chapter I focus primarily on words used to explain visuals. The words may be presented in text and/or in audio narration.

The combination of the visual and the words should support the learning objective. For example, when teaching a procedure, your demonstration uses words to describe the actions illustrated in the visuals. When teaching a principle, such as how to defuse a tense customer situation, you debrief a video demonstration with words. When describing the parts of equipment, as in Figures 6-2 to 6-5, you use words to label the equipment and to explain how it works. In all of these instances, the combination of a relevant visual and words in text, audio, or both are used to communicate the content.

WHEN NOT TO USE WORDS

Take look at the visual in Figure 6-6. Would it be best to explain that visual with words in audio or text? The answer is neither! Research has shown that adding words to a self-explanatory visual adds extraneous cognitive load and slows down learning or performance. A couple of years ago, my grandsons were focused on LEGO. I was amazed to see the elaborate structures they built out of hundreds of small LEGO pieces. Most surprising were the directions, which rely on visuals alone, such as the example in Figure 6-7. Since LEGO are intended for younger children and international use, it makes sense to rely on self-explanatory, step-by-step visual instructions.

Figure 6-6. A Visual on Buckling Your Seatbelt

Source: Clark, Nguyen, and Sweller, 2006. Material reproduced with permission John Wiley & Sons.

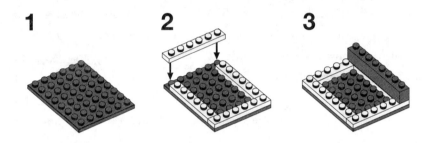

Figure 6-7. A Portion of LEGO Instructions

Adding words to a self-explanatory visual is redundant, because the meaning is already in the visual and therefore imposes extraneous cognitive load.

Explanation Guideline 1:

Do not add words in any format to a self-explanatory visual.

SHOULD YOU EXPLAIN VISUALS WITH TEXT, AUDIO, OR BOTH?

As discussed in chapter 1, it's a common misconception that some individuals are visual learners while others are auditory learners; therefore, we need to support both styles by presenting words in text as well as narration. The example shown in Figure 6-3 describes the equipment with text plus identical audio narration of that text. If the lesson is delivered online in this example, the text would appear on the screen and the audio would be delivered through narration. If the lesson is delivered in a classroom, the text would appear on the slide and the instructor would provide a verbal explanation. Is this a good idea? Or would learning be more effective if you used only text or only audio to describe the visual? Fortunately, we have evidence to guide your choice of modalities to present explanations of visuals.

When to Explain Visuals With Audio Narration

Many experiments have compared learning from visuals explained by words in audio with learning from the same visuals explained by the same words in text. In fact, enough of these studies have been done to support a meta-analysis (Ginns, 2005) and a systematic review of the data (Moreno, 2006). The experimental lessons synthesized in the meta-analysis included various content such as mathematics, electrical engineering, environmental science, and explanations of how brakes and lightning work. The meta-analysis reported that learning was consistently better when visuals were explained by audio narration with a high effect size of 0.72. This means, if a lesson that used text to explain visuals resulted in an average score of 70 percent with a standard deviation of 8, the same lesson that used audio would yield an average score of about 76 percent. The variety and amount of evidence on the use of audio leaves us with a high degree of confidence in the second recommendation.

Explanation Guideline 2:

Explain visuals with audio narration rather than text to maximize learning.

When teaching in the classroom, incorporate relevant visuals on your slides and discuss them with a verbal instructor explanation. When teaching via self-study e-learning, place relevant visuals on the screens and explain them with audio narration. Instructional scientists call this guideline the "modality principle."

MAXIMIZING THE BENEFITS OF AUDIO NARRATION

There are some exceptions to the modality principle. Audio explanations will be most effective when:

- The lesson includes a visual that requires an explanation. As mentioned, if the visual is self-explanatory, such as those shown in Figures 6-6 and 6-7, use no words at all. If there is no visual, words are better comprehended when presented in audio with key text phrases written on-screen or slide (Adesope and Nesbit, 2012).

- The narration is brief. Words presented in audio are like a mental echo—they remain in working memory for only a brief time. Therefore, in explanations of more than five sentences, the benefits of audio disappear because the initial sentences are lost to memory. Schuler et al. (2013) found no differences in learning the stages of mitosis when animations were accompanied by six paragraphs of six sentences each presented in either written text or audio. Adesope and Nesbit (2012) conclude in their meta-analysis that for longer passages, a combination of text and audio is more effective for learning than audio alone.

- The visual is complex and learners are novice to the content. A relatively simple visual does not impose much cognitive load. Therefore, an audio explanation is not as beneficial as it is with a more complex visual, such as an animation or the engine visuals shown at the beginning of this chapter.

- A complex visual incorporates visual cues directing attention to the relevant part of the visual as the narration discusses that part. For example, if complex equipment is described, the relevant part of the equipment could be highlighted as the narration describes it.

- The explanation is in the native language of the learners. Learners with a different primary language may benefit more from text and audio narration of that text than audio alone (Adesope and Nesbit, 2012).

Explanation Guideline 3:

Explain visuals with brief audio narration rather than text when the visual is complex, cues are used to draw attention to elements of the visual, learners are novice, and the words are in primary language of the learners.

WHEN TO EXPLAIN VISUALS WITH TEXT AND AUDIO

As mentioned, it's common practice to explain a visual with words in text and audio narration of that text to accommodate different learning styles or to be compliant with requirements for learners with visual or auditory disabilities. But we have quite a bit of evidence showing that in most situations, learning is depressed when you deliver the same words in identical text and audio (Adesope and Nesbit, 2012). Experiments compared learning from lessons in which visuals were explained with audio alone, as illustrated in Figure 6-5, with lessons in which visuals were explained with audio plus on-screen text that repeats the words in the audio narration, as illustrated in Figure 6-3. The results? Learners in the audio alone lessons scored higher, with a median effect size of 0.72, which is considered large (Mayer, 2009). The ample evidence we have from many experiments is the basis for the next recommendation.

Explanation Guideline 4:

Explain visuals with audio narration or text but NOT both text and narration of that text.

How can you apply this principle and accommodate learners with disabilities or perhaps individuals learning in a secondary language? I recommend that as a default, you explain a visual with brief audio, as narration in e-learning or as instructor explanations in the classroom. At the same time, provide an option for hearing impaired. In e-learning you can include an "audio control" icon. When audio is turned off, on-screen text appears. In synchronous e-learning, use closed-captioning. In a classroom, sign language or a handout with slides and text can augment the instructor's presentation.

When Text and Audio Are OK

I often see a combination of brief text and audio to explain a visual (such as the example shown in Figure 6-5). In the visual you see callouts in text that are excerpted from the audio narration. Evidence has shown that the use of limited on-screen text elaborated upon by brief audio does not hurt and can even help learning. Yue et al. (2013) tested four versions of a lesson about the life cycle of a star that included nine slides with a total of 24 sentences of explanation. The lesson versions varied as follows: 1) animated visuals explained with audio narration, 2) animated visuals explained by audio narration and identical text, 3) animated visuals explained by audio narration and shortened text, and 4) audio narration with no visuals. In Figure 6-8 you can see the results of the four versions on a transfer test. How do you interpret these results?

Learning was best from which combinations:

❑ Animation explained by audio.
❑ Animation explained by audio and identical text.
❑ Animation explained by audio and shortened text.
❑ Audio only (no visuals).

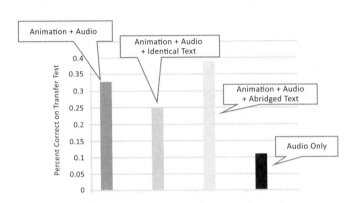

Figure 6-8. Percent Correct on Transfer Test

Source: Based on data from Yue et al. (2013).

Consistent with previous research, the audio alone version led to least learning because it lacked the benefits of relevant visuals. Also, the redundant version in which the visual was explained by text and exact audio of that text led to less learning than the other two versions. Best learning was achieved by audio elaborating on brief text explanations of the animation.

Explanation Guideline 5:

Explain visuals with brief audio narration of a slide or screen that includes a visual and short text phrases drawn from the narration.

EXPLANATIONS AND THE BRAIN

We saw in chapter 3 that working memory has two processing centers—one for auditory information and one for visual. As summarized in Figure 6-9, when you explain a complex visual with text, the visual center of working memory is overloaded.

Figure 6-9. Text and Visuals Can Overload Visual Center in Memory

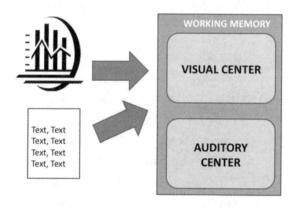

In contrast, as shown in Figure 6-10, when you explain a complex visual with brief audio, you divide the load between the visual and the auditory centers. In this way, you maximize the limited capacity of working memory to process information. This interpretation is supported by cognitive load and eye tracking evidence reported by Liu et al. (2011). In comparing visuals explained by on-screen text, on-screen text and narration of that text, or narration alone, they found that students rated cognitive load lowest in the version with audio only explanations. Compared to versions with text, visual attention was focused solely on the graphic in the audio only version. When a complex visual is explained by text, attention is generally directed to the text. In the case of an animation, the learner will miss much of the visual while reading the text explanation.

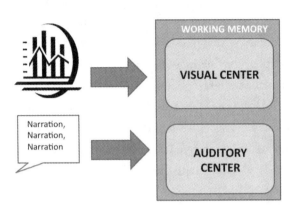

Figure 6-10. Use of Narration to Explain Visuals Balances Memory Load

Synchronization of lengthy text and narration of that text poses an additional load on the brain. Each of us reads at our own rate, which in turn is different from the rate of the narrator. Trying to synchronize our own reading rate with that of the narrator adds unnecessary mental overhead. To compensate, most of us either ignore the text and listen to the narration or turn off the narration and read the text. The bottom line is: Use brief audio to explain complex visuals and avoid a combination of text and redundant narration of that text. However, learning is not hurt and may be helped by adding a few words in text drawn from the narration on the screen.

So what about audio and visual learning styles? The reality is that novices are all visual learners; they can all profit from a relevant visual when learning unfamiliar knowledge and skills. Furthermore, novices are all auditory learners; novices can all benefit when a complex visual is described by brief audio narration rather than overloading their visual center with text. I stress the benefits for novices because they are most at risk of cognitive overload.

WHEN TO EXPLAIN VISUALS WITH TEXT ALONE

Of course there are situations in which you cannot use audio to explain a visual. A book like this one is an example. Even if you can use audio, if the content is complex and the explanation is lengthy, evidence leans in favor of giving explanations in text. Because a lengthy audio explanation is transient, by the time the last words are heard the initial words will be forgotten. In contrast, text can be read and reviewed at the learner's own pace. Of course, the best solution is to keep explanations brief or chunk complex explanations into short segments each focusing on a different element of a complex visual.

Where Should Text Be Placed on a Screen or Page?

When you use text to explain a visual, where should you position the text? For example, it could be placed at the bottom of the screen (as in Figure 6-2) or it could be integrated into the visual (as in Figure 6-4). Does the placement of text matter?

Have you ever been reading a book and find an important diagram located on the back of the page describing that diagram? To get a full understanding of the content you need to flip back and forth to read the text and then review the visual. How does that make you feel? Most of us find this annoying! That annoyance is actually your working memory complaining about the extra burden of having to hold content in its limited capacity while viewing related content and trying to integrate both elements. And this experience is not just your imagination. Researchers have measured learning from layouts like the examples in Figures 6-2 and 6-4.

For example Johnson and Mayer (2012) tracked eye movements and measured learning from three versions of a lesson on how brakes work that included words and visuals. In one version the description of the process was placed under the diagram. In a second version the words were integrated into the diagram, as shown in Figure 6-11. A third version was similar to the second but added part labels to the top diagram. They found that there were more eye movements between the text and the related portion of the diagram in versions 2 and 3 (integrated versions) than in the separated version. This division of attention between text and diagram illustrates attempts by the learners to integrate the content. In addition, learning was better in the integrated versions.

Figure 6-11. The Lesson Version That Integrated Text and Visual

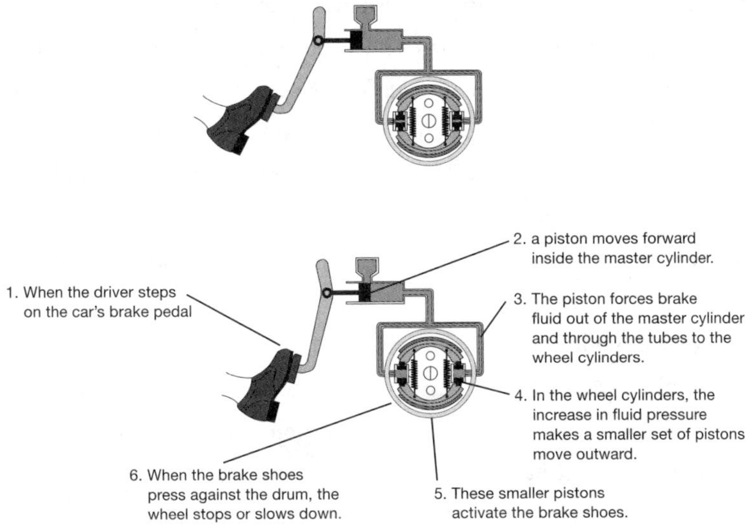

Source: From Johnson and Mayer, 2012.

Mayer (2009) reported that in five out of five experiments, learners studying from lessons that used integrated text learned more than those studying lessons with separated text. The median effect size is about one, which indicates high practical significance. Experiments like these are the basis for the sixth guideline.

Explanations Guideline 6:

Align text close to the relevant portion of the visual; at a minimum keep visuals and text visually accessible on the same spread or screen.

There are many common violations of this simple principle in all delivery media. In e-learning, a scrolling page shows a visual at the top of the page and the text underneath the visual. When you view the visual you can't see the text and vice versa. On a paper job aid, text that describes a procedure is placed under the illustration. A better solution is to insert text captions right into the relevant portion of the visual. Another common violation is to split an exercise between a workbook and a computer application. The learner reads the steps or the data in the workbook and tries to apply them on the computer. A better solution is to include all of the steps on the computer.

No matter your delivery medium, separating text and related diagrams leads to split attention and imposes unnecessary mental load on your learners. Mayer (2009) summarizes the problem: "The format of much instruction is determined by tradition, economic factors, or the whim of the instructor. Cognitive factors are rarely considered resulting in instructional designs in which split attention is common" (145).

That said, I'm hoping you won't experience too many instances of separated text and visuals in this book. In all of my books I have found that publisher templates often place text on one page and the relevant visual on the back of that page. It would be better if some figures could be reduced in size and placed on one side of a page with text wrap. Customization of layouts, however, incurs additional cost and as a result is rare. As an author, I have worked with book proofs to minimize split text and visuals by editing out text or eliminating figures so that the remaining text and figures are visible together on the same page spread. I mention this not just to make excuses but to illustrate how practical realities such as the limitations of your delivery media or budget or time will shape your products. Evidence is never the only factor to be considered in design and development of instructional environments!

THE BOTTOM LINE

What Do You Think?

Based on Figures 6-2 to 6-5, you marked the statements below indicating which presentation of words was best for learning. Try this exercise again to see if your responses have changed.

- ❑ Version A in Figure 6-2, because the layout is the cleanest.
  - This version is likely to lead to split attention because two different text segments are displayed separately from the visual.

- ❑ Version B in Figure 6-3, because the explanations are presented in text and in audio narration of that text.
  - This option will likely prove to be the worst for learning. We have seen evidence that learning is depressed when explanations are presented in text and audio narration of that text. In addition, the on-screen text is placed at the bottom of the screen leading to split attention.

- ❑ Version C in Figure 6-4, because the explanation is presented in text that is located near the visual.
  - If audio is not an option, this example is the most effective because the text is integrated into the figure.

❑ Version D in Figure 6-5, because the explanations are presented in audio only.

- – This version is the most effective because it uses audio narration to describe a complex visual. It also displays new technical terms in text callouts placed on the visual.

APPLYING THE USE OF AUDIO AND TEXT TO YOUR TRAINING EXPLANATIONS

Regardless of your delivery medium, you will generally need words to explain your visuals. Apply the following guidelines to maximize learning from those words.

If your delivery environment supports audio:

- Use brief audio narration alone to describe a complex visual on the screen.

- Use brief audio narration plus a few words in text taken from the narration placed in bullet points nearby the visual.

- Add visual cues such as highlighting or colors to your graphic to correspond with the narration.

- Avoid using text sentences and identical narration of those sentences to explain a visual.

The use of audio alone to describe visuals is not recommended under the following conditions:

- New technical terms are introduced; use text and audio.

- Learners need to refer back to the words such as directions to complete an exercise; use text.

- There are no visuals on the screen or slide; use audio and key terms in text.

- Your learners are experienced and not likely to be overloaded; use text.

- Your learners are second language; use text and audio.

- The explanation is lengthy (more than five sentences per screen or screen section); use text.

- The visual is self-explanatory; do not use any words.

If your delivery environment does not support audio:

- Enlarge the visual on the slide and integrate text into the visual.

- Use callouts to place multiple text statements nearby relevant portions of the visual.

COMING NEXT

In this chapter we focused on the modality of your explanations; that is, when to use audio or text. But modality is only one factor that will determine the effectiveness of your explanations. In the next chapter we will continue our discussion of explanations by showing how you can maximize learning by leveraging human social instincts.

FOR MORE INFORMATION

Adesope, O.O., and J.C. Nesbit. (2012). Verbal Redundancy in Multimedia Learning Environments: A Meta-Analysis. *Journal of Educational Psychology* 104. 250-263.

I found this meta-analysis that incorporated studies of explanations that were spoken-only, written-only, and spoken-written offered helpful insights regarding the conditions under which these different modalities are most effective.

Clark, R.C., and R.E. Mayer. (2011). *E-Learning & the Science of Instruction*, 3rd edition. San Francisco: Pfeiffer.

Our book includes chapters on modality, redundancy, and contiguity with illustrative examples for e-learning applications.

Kalyuga, S. (2012). Instructional Benefits of Spoken Words: A Review of Cognitive Load Factors. *Educational Research Review* 7: 145-159.

Another recent and comprehensive technical review of the use of audio in the context of cognitive load theory.

Mayer, R.E., ed. (2014a). *The Cambridge Handbook of Multimedia Learning*, 2nd edition. New York: Cambridge University Press.

This handbook includes chapters on the various issues described in this book written by the researchers. Review chapters 9 and 10 for a more detailed and technical look at the issues discussed in this chapter.

MAKE IT PERSONAL

CHAPTER 7

Make It Personal

What are your most popular computer applications outside of work? For 2014 the most popular aps are search and social connection software. Based on data from Alexa, the top four websites are Google, Facebook, YouTube, and Yahoo. The 276 million unique monthly visitors to Facebook I reported in the first edition have grown to 1.19 billion just five years later. By the way, I used Google to find this information.

The explosion of social media reflects our long-standing imperative for human-to-human communication. How can your training environments leverage social presence to improve learning? What evidence do we have about the role of "social" in learning?

In this chapter, we will look at evidence-based methods to leverage social presence—not through social media but through even more basic devices such as how you address your learners, the best use of online agents, and how to incorporate collaboration into your instructional events.

LEVERAGING SOCIAL PRESENCE

As I wrote the first draft of this chapter, the 2013 State of the Union Address had been recently delivered. Whereas there were 767K tweets during the 2012 State of the Union, in 2013 the number grew to 1.36 million! The following day I was invited on my Google page to a "Fireside Hangout" with President Obama at Google+ where he answered questions about his address. Web 2.0 has opened many opportunities to connect with friends, colleagues, and to the world, which were not previously possible. Likewise, our instructional environments offer new tools to leverage the basic human need for and response to social presence.

One of the unique outcomes of human evolution is our universal sociability. It grew from the survival need for cooperation. Cooperation relies fundamentally on communication—listening, processing, and responding to our social partners to achieve mutual goals. So embedded is this instinctive response that even self-study e-learning that incorporates some human persona can activate our social responses. We know in our heads that the computer is inanimate. But we are unconsciously compelled to process information more deeply when the lesson embeds social cues.

What Do You Think?

The content in the Excel lesson screens in Figures 7-1 and 7-2 is similar. However, the two versions differ regarding social cues. Compare them and put a check by the statements you think are true.

Figure 7-1. Version A of an Excel Lesson

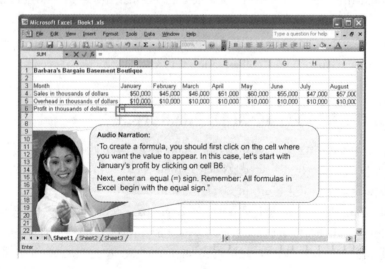

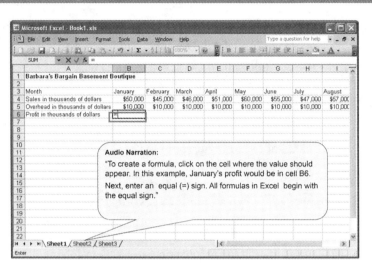

Figure 7-2. Version B of an Excel Lesson

❑ Version A will lead to better learning than Version B.

❑ Version B will lead to better learning than Version A.

❑ Versions A and B will lead to equivalent learning because the content is the same.

Both screens include instructional visuals and instructional words. Version A projects a more conversational tone, primarily through the use of first- and second-person pronouns, polite language, as well as a realistic on-screen virtual tutor. Version B is a bit more formal and does not include an on-screen tutor. You might feel that Version B is more businesslike and projects greater credibility. Alternatively, you might feel that the casual tone in Version A is more engaging. Or perhaps the most effective social treatment might depend on the content of the lesson or the cultural background of the learner. In this chapter, we will look at the evidence and psychology for how learning is affected by social cues.

WHAT IS PERSONABLE TRAINING?

By personable training I refer to instructional environments that embed social cues. Social cues can take the form of:

- use of first- and second-person language (I, you, we)
- polite phrases
- agents in e-learning
- voice quality of e-learning narration
- instructors as hosts
- a narrative rather than an expository writing approach
- responses to discussion boards
- social engagement such as collaborative problem solving during training sessions.

Although the potential for social presence is high in a face-to-face setting, often the opportunity goes unrealized. Lectures in a large classroom can be delivered in a traditional academic manner with minimal interaction between learners and instructor or among learners. Alternatively, instructors can create a more intimate environment through their tone, self-revelation, body language, and by including some collaborative interactions during the session. Personable training increases social presence. Do learners prefer higher or lower social presence? Is learning better in environments with high social presence? If so, which techniques have proven most effective? These are the questions we will consider in this chapter.

COURSE RATINGS AND SOCIAL PRESENCE

It's common practice at the end of a learning session to ask participants to rate the instruction. Typical questions ask about learners' perception of the instructor and the learning environment. Researchers have studied the correlation between student ratings and various features of the learning environment. A meta-analysis that included more than 27,000 ratings noted three main factors in the training environment associated with higher student ratings: 1) motivation to attend the training, 2) instructor style, and 3) social presence during learning (Sitzmann, 2011).

Regarding instructor style, trainers who were psychologically "available" to learners and who projected a relaxed, friendly persona received higher learner satisfaction ratings. In addition, opportunities to engage with other class members during the learning event were also correlated with higher ratings. A more recent meta-analysis found that instructional materials that were written in a conversational style were rated as more friendly and perceived by learners as being easier to process than materials written in a formal style (Ginns et al., 2013).

Although higher class ratings don't necessarily translate into more learning, by including social cues proven to increase learning, you can get better course ratings and better learning outcomes. The evidence on course ratings is the basis for my first guideline.

Personable Guideline 1:

Promote higher learner satisfaction by incorporating techniques that support social presence in your instructional environments.

PERSONALIZATION AND THE BRAIN

How do social cues promote deeper learning? The key lies in the greater attention and mental effort we invest in social interactions compared with impersonal messages. Attending to—and deeply processing—interpersonal messages likely evolved through eons, in which survival depended on mutual cooperation. Your brain is tuned to social cues and unconsciously devotes more attention and mental effort to processing associated social messages. More attention and deeper processing in working memory lead to a higher probability of encoding content into long-term memory—in other words, to better learning.

Compare your own mental state when watching TV, attending a keynote speech at a conference, and conversing with a friend. A television program often gets only cursory attention and rather shallow processing. In fact, for many, TV is a route to relaxation by shutting down effortful processing. A keynote speech may generate a bit more attention—especially if the delivery techniques are effective and content is relevant. Yet, you may find your mind wandering sometimes, as you go down your own mental rabbit trails or because you know there will be no overt response requirement from the speaker. However, when conversing with family and friends in a group or one-on-one, your level of attention and processing investment is higher because of the mutual satisfaction and unspoken conventions of social engagement.

The idea behind the personalization effect is that even in a self-study computerized study environment, the learners may feel they are in an implied conversation when the materials are written in a personal style. Let's review some techniques to build social presence, and the evidence supporting those techniques.

TECHNIQUES TO INCREASE SOCIAL PRESENCE

Whether you are teaching in an instructor-led class or developing asynchronous learning materials, building social presence into your events will improve learner satisfaction and can also enhance learning. Let's take a quick survey of six evidence-based techniques to make your learning environments more personable.

USE CONVERSATIONAL LANGUAGE

Compare the two introductions to a botany simulation game in Figure 7-3. What differences do you see? Which do you think would lead to better learning?

| Figure 7-3. Two Introductions to a Botany Simulation Game |

Version A
This program is about what type of plant survives on different planets. For each planet, a plant will be designed. The goal is to learn what type of roots, stem, and leaves allow plants to survive in each environment.

Version B
You are about to start on a journey where you will be visiting different planets. For each planet, you will need to design a plant. Your mission is to learn what type of roots, stem, and leaves will allow your plant to survive in each environment.

Source: Moreno and Mayer, 2000a.

In a series of experiments in which the words were delivered either by text or by audio narration, the more conversational versions that used first- and second-person language resulted in greater learning! In 11 experimental lessons that used different content and compared learning from first- and second-person language with learning from third-person constructions, all experiments favored use of first and second person (Mayer, 2009). All of the lessons were delivered by computer. Some were standard online tutorials and some were games. The effect sizes ranged from 0.52 to 1.93 for a median of 1.11. That means that on average, you could expect a one standard deviation improvement in lessons that speak directly to the learners using "I" and "you" statements.

A recent meta-analysis of 74 studies that compared learning from personalized materials with more formal instructional materials reports a medium effect size of 0.54 on application tests (Ginns et al., 2013). Their analysis included experiments with personalized materials in English, German, Flemish, or Turkish. They report that at least in these languages, personalization had a similar positive effect on transfer learning. Additional studies in other languages and cultures are needed to evaluate how cultural or language translations might affect the benefits of personalization. Based on their meta-analysis, Ginns et al. (2013) suggest that personalization is most effective in lessons of 30 minutes or less with diminishing effects in longer lessons.

Politeness Pays

A related form of conversational language is politeness. Wang et al., (2008) compared two versions of a lesson focusing on engineering problems through a one-hour computer game, Virtual Factory. The game included a virtual tutor who made suggestions and offered feedback in either a directive or polite manner. For example, in the direct wording version the tutor might say: "Save the factory now" compared with "Do you want to save the factory now?" The more polite version resulted in better learning. Based on strong and consistent evidence to date, I recommend the following guideline.

Personable Guideline 2:

Promote deeper learning by addressing learners in a conversational manner using first and second person and polite phrases.

BE A LEARNING HOST

In many learning environments, such as books, asynchronous digital lessons, or even traditional classroom settings, the authors or instructors remain aloof from the learners. They stick to their content and don't make any self-revelations such as how they may personally feel about the content or specific experiences they have had related to the skills. Imagine reading a text on parasitology in which the author scientifically explains the adverse effects of various parasites, including how they access their host organisms.

Now imagine reading a similar passage in which the author describes a time he was infected, even though he was very careful with what he ate and drank. He found that the hotel housekeeping staff rinsed the ashtrays in the toilet and he had laid his cigarette on one of these ashtrays. A story like this would be more memorable than the strictly informational text; but stories must be used carefully to promote the instructional goal. In addition to stories, the injection of personal opinion or reactions to content has been shown to improve learning. For example, an instructor might present two views on an issue and reveal her own personal opinion. Mayer (2009) refers to self-revealing episodes as a "visible author" technique and has found that learning improved from a visible author.

Whether writing for a textbook, for e-learning, or preparing lecture notes for an instructor-led class, you can improve learning by thinking of yourself as a "learning host." A good host makes his guests feel comfortable and engages them in the event. A good host makes himself available both physically and emotionally to his guests. In face-to-face environments, good instructors demonstrate availability in how they dress, how they greet learners, and by using diverse social cues to set an informal but productive tone throughout the event. In a similar manner, when authoring texts or e-learning courses, use hosting techniques proven to increase learning and generate better student ratings.

PROMOTE SOCIAL PRESENCE IN DISTANCE LEARNING

Sung and Mayer (2012a) identified five core elements that promote social presence in distance education courses that rely on asynchronous discussion boards:

1. **Social respect:** No one likes to feel ignored. Online learners need to feel that their postings are being read and their time and input are valued. Instructors and class participants can show social respect by responding promptly to postings and expressing appreciation for participation.

2. **Social sharing:** Online learners and instructors can exchange values, beliefs, and professional interests related to the course goals.

3. **Open mind:** All participants need to feel free to post relevant opinions about course issues and give constructive feedback to others.

4. **Social identity:** Participants value being addressed by name.

5. **Intimacy:** Social presence is increased when learners and the instructor share personal experiences relevant to the course content.

Student ratings and learning evidence are the basis for my third recommendation.

Personable Guideline 3:

When communicating instructional content in texts, online, in discussion boards, or in the classroom, adopt "hosting" techniques by using social cues that make the environment personable.

As mentioned in chapter 2, most of the research has been conducted with Western culture learners, and usually with college-aged subjects. Other cultures and other generations might respond differently to various social cues. Although I have found that workshop participants in the United States are 99 percent receptive to collaborative activities, group discussions in a workshop I led in Norway were not well received. They felt I was the expert and they did not want to "waste" their time listening to their colleagues. We will need additional research to see how findings regarding social presence are best adapted to different populations and instructional contexts.

USE ONLINE AGENTS

In the in-person classroom, the instructor's persona dictates the image and voice. However, in asynchronous e-learning courses, on-screen avatars called "pedagogical agents" have become popular, and many authoring systems offer a library of characters with easily changeable expressions. Figure 7-1 shows the use of an avatar in an Excel online class. What evidence do we have for the use of on-screen agents to promote learning in computer self-study lessons?

A recent review of the effects of on-screen agents found 15 well-controlled experiments. Of the 15, only five experiments reported a positive effect of on-screen agents on learning (Heidig and Clarebout, 2011). The research team concluded that asking whether agents improve learning is too broad a question. Instead, a closer look is needed to consider the conditions under which an agent is effective. Specific elements such as the agent's appearance, voice, and function are a few variables that might make a difference to agent effectiveness. For example, among studies that have compared different types of agents, one consistent finding is that learning is better when the agent expresses himself through audio narration rather than with on-screen text. (For more on the the benefits of audio by way of the modality principle, review chapter 6.)

Should Agents Be Realistic?

Mayer and DaPra (2012) compared the learning and motivational effects of two different agents and a no-agent control in a short slide lesson on how solar cells convert sunlight into energy. The agent was placed to the left side of the screen and the content including graphics and brief text appeared on the right. One agent projected a number of social responses, including changes in posture and facial expressions, gesturing, and eye gazes to direct attention. The other agent used the same image but remained relatively static on the screen. Both agents used audio narration to explain the information on the slide. Take a look at the learning results shown in Figure 7-4.

Which of the following conclusions are supported by this data?

- ❑ A. The rendering of the agent appearance did not affect learning.
- ❑ B. Learning was as effective with no agent as with a static agent.
- ❑ C. No agent was more effective than a static agent.

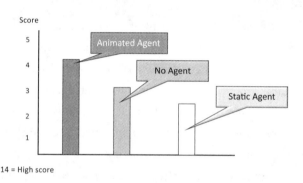

Figure 7-4. Learning From an Animated Agent, Static Agent, or No Agent

Source: Based on data from Mayer and DaPra, 2012.

The data show that the agent that exhibited human social behaviors, such as gestures and changes in facial expressions, promoted best learning. The static agent actually led to less learning than no agent. It's possible the static agent became a distractive screen element. The research team suggests that agents are most effective when they are perceived as a social partner—a response more probable in the presence of a more realistic agent. Learners rated the more realistic agent higher, supporting the idea that social cues promote social presence and in turn, learning.

Should Learners Choose Their Agents?

The Mayer and DaPra (2012) report included one experiment in which some learners were told that they were matched to an agent exhibiting features they preferred (such as outgoing or calm) while others were told they were not matched. In actuality, all agents were the expressive version described previously. No differences in learning were noted, suggesting that learner choice of agent may not be as important as ensuring that the agent exhibit the social cues described previously. Similar results were reported by Linek et al. (2010) in an experiment in which learners were given a choice of a male or female narrator. Regardless of learner choice, the female speaker led to better learning of a mathematical skill.

Many questions remain about agents. Are the effects of agents subject to cultural differences among learners? Are some accents better received than others? Should the agent be male or female? Does the content make a difference regarding the effectiveness of an agent? What are the most productive functions of an agent?

Based on evidence to date, I recommend the following guideline in relation to agents.

Personable Guideline 4:

Use on-screen agents that exhibit social cues, such as changes in expression, posture, and gestures. Ensure that the agent fulfills a valid instructional role, such as giving feedback or explanations.

CONSIDER VOICE QUALITY WHEN USING AUDIO

As mentioned, the agent should communicate with audio narration rather than on-screen text. In comparing a narration given by a native English speaker using a friendly tone with the same narration from a high-quality speech synthesizer, learning was much better from the human voice version. Linek et al. (2010) compared learning of probability theory from examples that were illustrated with narrated animations. The narrations used either a male or female voice. The versions narrated by a female speaker received higher ratings and resulted in better problem solving on the post-test, compared with the versions with male narration. However, the positive effects of female narration may have different effects depending on the content.

Accents are another element of voice quality that need more research. Rey and Steib (2013) compared learning from four versions of a lesson on computer networks. Two used conversational narration and two used formal. In addition, two used standard German and two used an Austrian dialect. Consistent with the personalization effects discussed at the start of this chapter, conversational versions led to better transfer learning. However, there was no significant effect of dialect on transfer learning. Mayer (2009) reported better learning from a standard accented voice compared to a Russian-accented voice among U.S. college-aged learners. We will need more research to verify the conditions under which voice gender or accent affect learning.

INCLUDE STRUCTURED COLLABORATIVE EXERCISES

As mentioned at the start of this chapter, classes that incorporate opportunities for learners to engage with one another as well as with the instructor get higher student ratings than classes that minimize social engagement. In chapter 4, I discussed evidence on the use of collaboration as an effective engagement technique.

One commonly used and researched collaborative technique is argumentation. In argumentation, learners work in teams to research and develop a position on a topic or issue that lends itself to multiple perspectives. Each team makes a reasoned case for their perspective and also considers counter arguments. In a final activity, arguments and counterarguments are synthesized into a final product such as a paper, presentation, or webpage. What evidence do we have for the learning benefits of argumentation?

Collaborative Argumentation

Noroozi and colleagues (2012) reviewed 15 years of research on argumentation collaborative learning in digital learning settings. The research team recommended the following guidelines:

- The topics must be debatable and neither too simplistic nor too complex for the learners' varying backgrounds.

- Some research has focused on online knowledge representation tools, such as various forms of graphic organizers. No single tool has yet emerged as most effective. A combination of synchronous and asynchronous events may give the best outcomes. Asynchronous tools allowed equal opportunity for individual participation as well as time for individual reflection while synchronous discussions resulted in more integrated arguments.

- Even with tool support, many learners will not have the skills to construct effective arguments and counter-arguments. Training with examples, practice, and feedback may be required.

- Smaller heterogeneous groups of two or three are generally more effective. For example, teams made up of learners with different background knowledge or experience may produce stronger arguments and learn more.

Roseth and colleagues (2011) compared motivation from argumentation assignments in either a face-to-face, online synchronous, or asynchronous team environment. They reported 100 percent completion in both synchronous environments (face-to-face or online) compared with 63 percent completion in the asynchronous conditions. They recommend that convergence tasks may be more effective in synchronous environments, while conveyance aspects of tasks may be more efficient in an asynchronous setting. Synchronous collaboration may also benefit new groups in order to build social presence.

Collaborative Problem Solving

Recall from chapter 4, the discussion of the trade-offs of collaboration as an engagement technique. In two separate reports Kirschner and colleagues

(2011a; 2011b) evaluated learning from problem solving in which students either worked solo or in a small collaborative team. In the experiments, they adjusted the complexity of the problems to be either relatively simple or relatively complex. In their factorial experiment they had four conditions: students working simple problems alone, students working complex problems alone, and small teams working simple or complex problems. They found that for simpler problems, individual work led to better learning; whereas for more complex problems, teams were more effective. The research team suggests that while working in a collaborative team benefits from the input of several individuals, there are also mental costs in communicating. Therefore, for simple problems, the mental load imposed by collaboration drained capacity that could have been used for learning. In contrast, more challenging tasks benefited from a sharing of the mental load imposed by the problems.

We still have many questions about the best context for optimizing learning from collaborative work. The following guidelines are based on evidence to date.

Personable Guideline 5:

A) Consider collaborative assignments when task demands are relatively high.
B) Form smaller rather than larger groups that include learners with diverse backgrounds or perspectives.
C) Blend a combination of asynchronous and synchronous collaborative events to optimize the benefits of each.
D) Use a structured form of collaboration such as argumentation.

A POSTSCRIPT ON SOCIAL MEDIA

This chapter began with a discussion on the rocketing popularity of social media. A recent review of research on Facebook was overall positive, regarding the potential of social media for learning, and recommended more research on how to use social media sites efficiently for learning purposes (Aydin, 2012). Based on what we have learned from previous research, no doubt the benefits of social media will depend on how these tools are used to support learning and knowledge management. To the extent that the applications support cognitive load and are congruent with learning goals, they should provide yet another path to extend learning by leveraging social presence. Social media should be applied in focused and deliberate ways that promote deeper processing of content.

THE BOTTOM LINE

What Do You Think?

We started with two samples from an e-learning course in Figures 7-1 and 7-2. Review those samples and see if your answers have changed.

❑ Version A will lead to better learning than Version B.

❑ Version B will lead to better learning than Version A.

❑ Versions A and B will lead to the same learning.

Based on current evidence, I would recommend Version A as incorporating more social cues and leading to better learning. The main elements that make Version A more effective are the use of first- and second-person conversational language and the social cues built into the agent. We need more research on agents to define situations in which they contribute to learning. We also need more consistent evidence on the effects of gender and accent in narration.

APPLYING PERSONALIZATION TO YOUR TRAINING

Whether you are working in a face-to-face classroom or online, leverage human unconscious instincts to deeply process information accompanied by social cues. In the classroom you can get higher student ratings and improve learning by making yourself psychologically accessible to your learners. In other words, dress and act in a manner that will make your audience feel comfortable. Note that there may be cultural differences in how you implement this principle. In most Western cultures you should greet your learners individually, use eye contact, maintain physical proximity to your learners, speak in a conversational tone, encourage and respond to comments and questions, and incorporate some collaborative activities when and where appropriate.

In synchronous e-learning as in a physical classroom, you should speak with your learners individually calling them by name, bring learners into the discussion via audio when practical, use a relaxed and conversational tone, and reveal your own experiences and opinions on the content.

In asynchronous e-learning or books, maximize social presence through the use of conversational and polite language, learning agents, and by responding to online posts in ways that generate social presence. In any learning environment, consider structured collaborative assignments such as argumentation for more challenging tasks in which you build small heterogeneous teams of two to four members.

A Personalization Checklist

❑ Use first- and second-person language in your explanations.

❑ Use a polite conversational tone.

❑ Offer your own relevant experiences and perspectives on the content.

❑ Offer relevant opportunities for social engagement among your participants.

❑ Use online agents that project social cues with gestures and eye gazes and that serve an instructionally relevant purpose.

❑ Use a friendly voice for narration; avoid narration that may seem unnatural to your learners such as machine generated.

❑ Generate social presence on discussion boards by applying techniques such as calling individuals by name, fostering an open environment, and sharing personal experiences related to course content.

❑ Make collaborative assignments for relatively challenging tasks using small heterogeneous groups.

COMING NEXT

In previous chapters we've seen the benefits of instructional methods, including graphics, learning agents, and engagement. Is it possible to overdo some of these techniques? In the next chapter we will look at evidence suggesting that when it comes to learning, less is often more.

FOR MORE INFORMATION

Clark, R.C., and R.E. Mayer. (2011). *E-Learning and the Science of Instruction*, 3rd edition. San Francisco: Pfeiffer. (See chapter 9.)

Ginns, P., A.J. Martin, and H.W. Marsh. (2013). Designing Instructional Text in a Conversational Style: A Meta-Analysis. *Educational Psychology Review* 25:445-472.

I always like to read a meta-analysis to get a good synthesis of the research on the topic. This journal is one source for reviews and meta-analyses.

Mayer, R.E. (2014a). Principles Based on Social Cues in Multimedia Learning: Personalization, Voice, Embodiment, and Image Principles. In *The Cambridge Handbook of Multimedia Learning*, 2nd edition, ed. R.E. Mayer. New York: Cambridge University Press.

This handbook provides updated research on many of the guidelines in this book. Each chapter is written by a scholar who has conducted research relevant to the chapter.

AVOID TOO MUCH OF A GOOD THING

CHAPTER 8

Avoid Too Much of a Good Thing

As instructional professionals or subject matter experts, we are often tempted to show and tell everything we know about a topic. For example, we may use animation to illustrate a topic. Or we may add technical details that go beyond the needs of the job. Alternatively, we may find our lessons a bit dry, so we spice them up to motivate learners. The "spice" can take many forms, such as games, stories, and visuals. Are these adjuncts helpful or harmful?

This is a chapter about resisting the urge to add extraneous stories, music, detailed explanations and elaborate visuals to lessons, because our brains are designed for the best learning when they're not overloaded.

WHY TRAINING IS TOO FLABBY

I believe that a lot of over-inflated training comes from good intentions on the part of instructors as a result of: 1) pressure to "cover the content" in unrealistic timeframes, 2) an instructor-centered versus a learner-centered perspective, 3) the urge to make the lessons more interesting by adding stories, or 4) the charisma of the latest training fads and technologies.

Clients often have unrealistic expectations of what can be achieved in a given time period. In an effort to accommodate, trainers pour out lots of content. Unfortunately, our brains don't soak up knowledge and skills like sponges. We have learned that content "covered" does not necessarily translate into new and desirable behaviors on the job.

Another problem that trainers often face is a stack of dry content—such as company policy on business transactions, compliance regulations, or procedural training on how to use the order-entry system. Trainers and instructional developers often look to engaging stories and visuals to spice up these lessons. They may feel that the new generation raised in an age of intensive multimedia and video games has a greater predilection for pizzazz than was the case in the past. The desire to enliven training is fueled by evolving media functionality, making animations and other visual and auditory effects easy to produce. In the end, however, these well-intended additions can have a negative effect on learning.

What Do You Think?

Imagine that you are developing a multimedia compliance lesson on information security. You prepare several visuals and write some text that summarizes the company policies. As you view your draft lesson, it seems dull and you want to make it more interesting. You do a little research on information security and discover a number of interesting factoids. For example, you find several recent news items on hacking of retail store sites for credit card information. You also see statistics on the growing business of cyber security. Armed with a number of these anecdotes, you enliven your lesson by adding visuals and text to illustrate them throughout the lesson. What is the impact of these anecdotes on student interest and on learning? Select the options you think are true:

❑ A. The lesson version with interesting text and visuals will lead to better learning because it is more engaging and motivating.

❑ B. Learners will find the lesson with added text and visuals more interesting than the basic lesson.

❑ C. The basic lesson lacking the interesting factoids will lead to better learning because it is lean and stays on target.

❏ D. Learning will be the same because both lessons include the critical core content.

WHAT IS TOO MUCH?

There are several ways lessons become bloated. Instructors commonly add stories, anecdotes, or themes to enliven a dull presentation. Music is another common addition—especially in multimedia lessons, but also in some classrooms. Along with music come visuals, which today can easily be generated as animations, three-dimensional virtual worlds, or video. These visuals can appear more polished and engaging than simple line drawings. Finally, instructors often simply provide too much explanation—too many words or too much detail on a topic. In summary, "too much" can involve stories, explanations, visuals, and music. All added with the best intentions but running the risk of depressing learning in a brain where less is often more. Let's take a look at the evidence on the benefits and risks of these additions.

WHEN STORIES DEFEAT LEARNING

A story is a true or fictitious narrative sequence of events. From war stories to jokes to anecdotes, stories are common fodder in most training programs. They are used to attract attention, generate interest, illustrate a point, dramatize a lesson or simply add some spark to dull technical material. Instructors are often encouraged to add stories as effective learning devices. Because they are concrete and often have an emotional tenor, stories are especially memorable and students like them. The concreteness and drama of stories makes them a potent psychological device, and one to be used with care. What evidence do we have on the effectiveness of stories in instruction?

Evidence on Stories

Mayer (2009) summarizes six experiments in which he compared learning from a basic lesson on lightning that included frames (similar to the one in Figure 8-1) with the same lesson, but expanded with several interesting stories and visuals about the effects of lightning.

Figure 8-1. One Frame on How Lightning Forms Using Line Diagrams and On-Screen Text

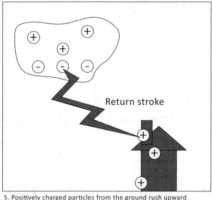

5. Positively charged particles from the ground rush upward along the same path.

Source: From Mayer and Moreno, 1998.

Early in the explanation of how lightning forms the expanded lesson adds a brief description and visual showing what happens to an airplane struck by lightning. Later, the lesson shows the uniform of a football player who had been struck by lightning. Several of these brief anecdotes are sprinkled throughout the basic lesson to create a more interesting version. You may recall the effects of these additions from my summary of this research in chapter 5.

Not surprisingly, learners rated the lessons with text and visual anecdotes as more interesting than the plain versions. However, interest did not translate into learning. In five out of six experiments, learning was dramatically depressed by the addition of interesting facts and visuals about lightning. The median effect size was 1.66 for the basic lesson version—a high effect size signaling considerable damage inflicted by the more interesting lessons. The important thing to keep in mind is that although all of the additions were about lightning, they were not relevant to the instructional goal of building an understanding of how lightning forms.

Lehman et al. (2007) repeated this experiment using a text-only basic lesson on lightning formation, with and without the interesting details. For example, a sentence rated as high in interest but low in importance is: "Golfers are prime targets for lightning strikes because they tend to stand in open grassy fields or to huddle under trees." The experiment measured reading time and learning from both versions.

Consistent with previous research, Lehman found that the comprehension scores were significantly lower among readers of the text with details added. In addition, the reading time of relevant sentences that followed the interesting (but unimportant) sentences was longer, when compared with reading time of the same sentences in the versions lacking these details. This slower pace suggests that the interesting sentences disrupted the coherence of the text, forcing readers to process the relevant sentences more slowly to make sense of the entire passage.

These experiments have shown the negative effects of adding interesting but unimportant details to expository text. Would the outcomes be similar in case-base lessons? Compared to expository text that relies primarily on a logical sequencing of content, case-based lessons use a narrative format that tells a realistic story as the basis for learning.

Abercrombie (2013) compared two case-based lessons on how to give effective written feedback to students. The participants were student teachers assigned to a narrative lesson with or without interesting details added. The test required the learners to write feedback for a draft student essay. The group that studied the version lacking interesting details scored higher.

In short, adding interesting but irrelevant details impedes learning from both expository and narrative-based lessons.

Stories and the Brain

The research by Lehman et al. (2007) suggests that irrelevant but interesting details depress learning by distracting learners from the important sentences and by disrupting the overall meaning of the paragraph. Imagine you are reading about how clouds first form and then develop ice crystals. Suddenly you are viewing some information about airplanes and lightning. Next you continue to read how negatively charged particles form and fall to the bottom of the cloud. Just as you are connecting the dots, you are seeing and reading about someone struck by lightning. You get the idea—just as you start to put two and two together, your processing is interrupted by a very distracting item that seduces your attention away from the core content. Over time, the cumulative effects of these distractions corrode learning. Mayer calls the depression of learning resulting from topic-related but goal-irrelevant details a coherence effect, as in the disruption of coherence. The evidence and psychology of adding interesting anecdotes unrelated to the learning objective to your training are the basis for my first recommendation.

Too Much Guideline 1:

Avoid adding factoids, visuals, and anecdotes that may be related to the topic but are irrelevant to the learning goal.

HOW TO MAKE LESSONS INTERESTING

We have quite a bit of evidence that adding irrelevant information to your lesson can damage learning. Are there some ways you can add interest that do not depress learning? Um et al. (2012) tested two approaches to what they call "emotional design." One approach involved inducing positive feelings prior to studying a lesson by asking students to read positive statements. Half the students read neutral statements such as, "Apples are harvested in the fall," while the other half read positive statements such as, "It's great to be alive!" Attitude measures showed that the positive statements did induce more positive feelings among learners.

A second approach involved use of color and shape design elements in a multimedia lesson on how immunization works. The emotional design version used warm colors and round shapes with eyes. You can compare the two versions in Figure 8-2. They found that both inducing positive feelings and the use of emotional design elements improved learning. Because I found only one study that focused on emotional design, it is premature to suggest any guidelines. We will look for additional research on techniques that can make lessons more interesting and at the same time avoid distracting learners from the main lesson theme.

Figure 8-2. Neutral v. Positive Emotional Design Elements

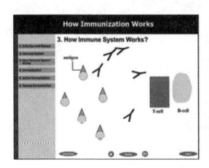
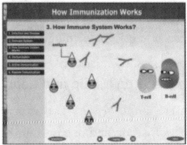

Note: The version on the right uses a pale yellow background with rounded shapes in various colors.

Source: From Um et al., 2012.

Can Stories Help?

I believe that there are situations in which stories have beneficial effects. Unfortunately, we lack research evidence to answer questions such as: What kinds of stories are most effective? Are some stories more appropriate for some kinds of learning goals? Does the number and placement of anecdotes in a lesson make a difference? For example, does a dramatic story about an injury or death told at the start of a safety lesson increase attention, learning, and transfer of safety practices? For now, I suggest that you keep stories that are relevant to your learning goal, discard stories that are tangential, and avoid placing any stories in the middle of an explanation where they might disrupt the mental processing needed for understanding.

DOES MUSIC IMPROVE LEARNING?

Do you like music playing in the background while you are working or studying? The benefits of music have been promoted in popular press articles with an emphasis on classical music. What evidence do we have on the effects of music on learning?

Evidence on Music and Learning

Mayer (2009) reports two experimental lessons—one involving lightning formation and one on how brakes work. The basic versions of each presented the process stages using narration and animations. The enhanced versions added sounds—both music and environmental sounds appropriate to the lesson topic. The sounds and music were background only and did not obscure the narration. Did music enhance or depress learning? As you can see in Figure 8-3, the auditory additions depressed learning.

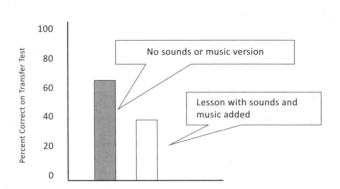

Figure 8-3. Auditory Additions Depressed Learning

Note: The average gain was 105 percent for lessons in which extraneous sounds and music were omitted.

Source: Based on data from Moreno and Mayer, 2000b.

Remember that working memory is limited in capacity and has a center for visual and auditory information. When a complex visual is explained by audio narration plus sounds and music, the audio center is overloaded and capacity for learning is depressed. I have found only a few studies on the effects of music; however, based on the evidence available and the psychology of learning I offer the following recommendation.

Too Much Guideline 2:

Avoid adding extra audio in the form of music when the goal is to help learners build understanding.

DO YOU WORK TOO HARD?

One Friday after an intense week of training I was really tired. On reflection it occurred to me that I had actually been working too hard. After all, I knew the content. I realized that the workshop participants needed to be doing much more of the work. I had been assuming that if I gave many detailed explanations presented with a lot of energy, and showed a deck of relevant slides, learning would naturally occur. From then on, I started to reverse the workload. I went from two-thirds instructor work and one-third student work to just the opposite. I cut back on explanations by presenting the bare bones followed by an exercise. When and where there was confusion on the exercise, I responded with more explanations and examples. When students experienced problems or challenges in the exercises they were more open to receive additional explanations.

When I teach e-learning design workshops, I start the session with a short case study assignment. Teams are given content to convert into a multimedia mini lesson. Later, after reviewing course content, teams return to their case lessons and make upgrades as needed. Having a product assignment as a starting exercise gives the learners a concrete context to attach the specific guidelines presented throughout workshop.

Evidence About Explanations

Using the lightning content, Mayer tested the learning effects of a very concise lesson version with a version containing a much more detailed explanation. Take a look at Figures 8-1 and 8-4 to compare the lean and inflated versions.

Figure 8-4. One Frame From an Expanded Lesson on How Lightning Forms With Additional Explanatory Text

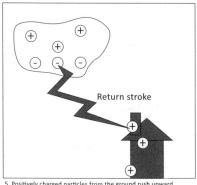

As the stepped leader nears the ground, it induces an opposite charge so positively charged particles from the ground rush upward along the same path. This upward motion of the current is the return stroke and it reaches the cloud in about 70 micro-seconds. The return stroke produces the bright light that people notice in a flash of lightning, but the current moves so quickly that its upward motion cannot be perceived. The lightning flash usually consists of an electrical potential of hundreds of millions of volts. The air along the lightning channel is heated briefly to a very high temperature. Such intense heating causes the air to expand explosively, producing a sound wave we call thunder.

5. Positively charged particles from the ground rush upward along the same path.

Source: From Mayer and Bove et al., 1996.

As you can see, the lean version consisted of a simple visual with just a few words as a caption. In total, the lean version contained about 80 words. In contrast, the detailed version added more than 500 words to the captioned figures. In three experiments, learning was better from the more concise versions with effect sizes ranging from 0.70 and 0.98.

In a different experiment that involved lessons on wave formation, Mayer and Jackson (2005) compared versions with and without technical detail. The basic lesson explained the general process of how waves form. The detailed version added technical details in the form of mathematical equations. They found better learning of the overall process of wave formation from the basic version. They suggest that when first learning a new process, learners benefit by an explanation that helps them build a qualitative understanding. Then, if relevant to the instructional goals, more details can be added in subsequent lessons.

Chunking Content

When your lesson content can't be further reduced, break it into small chunks, displaying less content on each slide or screen. In asynchronous multimedia, always include a continue button, allowing the learners to proceed at their own pace. Mayer and Chandler (2001) divided the lightning lesson into 16 segments with a continue button on each screen. They found better learning with the version that limited the amount of content presented at one time and allowed learners to control the rate at which they accessed the information.

First, the limits of working memory suggest that you provide only the amount of information needed to communicate the core content, thus leaving capacity for processing that content. When providing lean explanations, memory space would be available to read the words, look at the visual, integrate the meaning of the words and visual, and connect that meaning to the unfolding process. In other words, there would be capacity to connect the dots. Based on the evidence and the psychology of explanations I suggest the following guideline.

Too Much Guideline 3:

Keep explanations concise; use just enough words to present content. Segment content into smaller chunks that can be accessed by the learner at their preferred pace.

From photographs to 3-D drawings, from video to animations, modern technology makes production of elaborate visuals quite easy. And the ubiquitous high-end visuals in popular advertising, movies, and video games encourage us to incorporate them into training—especially multimedia training. What is the value added of complex visuals?

SIMPLE V. COMPLEX STILL VISUALS

In chapter 5 we reviewed research that focused on understanding how blood circulates through the heart. Butcher (2006) compared learning from 1) a text-only description, 2) text plus a simple line drawing image, and 3) text plus an anatomically correct drawing. Better learning was seen in both versions that included a visual; however, the simpler visual was more effective.

For the purpose of learning how something works, the details in the realistic drawing did not augment understanding and in fact may have led to confusion. Had the goal been to learn anatomical features of the heart, the more accurate drawing might have been more effective.

STILL VISUALS V. ANIMATIONS

We saw in the blood circulation experiment that a simpler visual resulted in better learning than a more complex visual. Let's look at how still visuals and animations affect learning. Imagine that you want to teach how a toilet works—a potentially very useful piece of knowledge. You could show a series of still visuals explained by text or you could play an animation with audio narration. At first glance, the animated version seems like a more effective approach, because it depicts a more realistic picture of the movement among the various flushing stages. But this is not what the experiments revealed. In four different lessons involving explanations of toilet flushing, lightning formation, how brakes work, and wave formation, the still versions led to learning that was better than or as good as the animated versions (Mayer and Hegarty et al., 2005).

An animation conveys a great deal of complex visual information that (in the experiments described) ran continuously. In contrast, the still graphics were simpler and the learners could control the rate at which they viewed them. Animated visuals can present a flood of information that quickly overloads memory capacity.

In addition to the sheer amount of information, it is also possible that learners are more actively engaged in the stills than in the animations. Often, when we view an animation, we go into "couch potato" mode—a mindset that involves little psychological engagement. In contrast, as we view a series of stills, our brains are more actively engaged to put together a story from the pieces. Ironically, what we would commonly classify as an old-fashioned display (still pictures) might engage the brain more than a modern animated illustration.

Animations for Different Learning Outcomes

Do some instructional goals warrant animations more than others? In all of the experiments summarized above, the goal was to build understanding of how something works. Understanding requires a deep level of processing to build a mental model. However, what if you are teaching someone how to perform a procedure such as tying knots, assembling equipment, or working with new software? Might animations be more effective for this type of outcome? The popularity of YouTube gives us a hint at the answer.

Animations v. Still Visuals to Learn Procedures

Ayres et al. (2009) compared learning of motor skills such as tying a knot, or solving a 3-D puzzle problem from a series of stills versus an animated demonstration. No practice was included. Learners viewed the demonstrations and then were tested without reference to the visuals. For both motor tasks, learning was about twice as good from the animated demonstrations. Researchers are postulating that working memory has another processing center in addition to the visual and phonetic centers discussed in chapter 3. It is called a mirror-neuron system and it is dedicated exclusively to human movement. The mirror-neuron system may be the basis for the advantage of animations for motor skills.

Animations v. Still Visuals v. Text Instructions as Performance Support

Most of the experiments presented focused on understanding and application as a learning goal. However, the use of performance support to guide task operations is a popular strategy in workforce environments. One form of performance support is a job aid including guided instructions to be used when needed on the job. The overall goal is accurate task completion—not necessarily learning. Performance support is especially helpful for tasks that are not routine, such as troubleshooting a copy machine.

Watson et al. (2010) compared animated, static, and text work instructions as performance support for assembling a small device. They evaluated build time over five trials with instructions presented in animation (no words), static diagrams (no words), or text. Take a look at Figure 8-5 and ask yourself which version led to fastest performance on the first and third trials.

Figure 8-5. Average Build Times in Seconds Over Five Building Trials

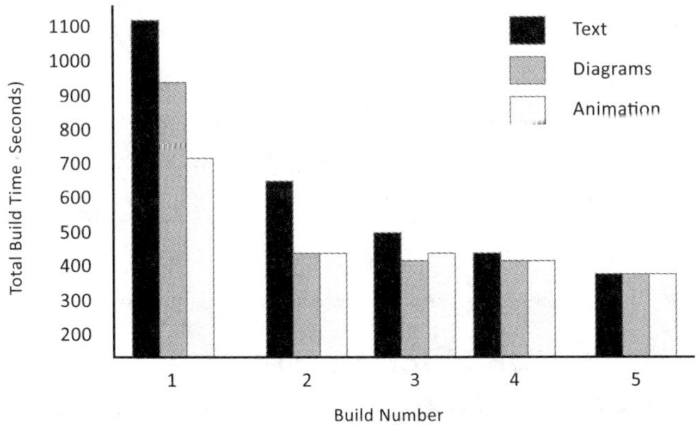

Source: Adapted from Watson et al., 2010.

The data for the first build are most relevant to a performance support application. The first build data are equivalent to one-time assembly situations. Next in importance are data from subsequent builds, which would be applicable to situations that would involve repeated performance. The correct conclusion to draw here is that after two to three builds, all instructions were equally effective. We can see that the text instructions were least efficient for the first build. Although animations led to faster build times than still diagrams, the difference was not statistically significant. In other words, the animations and still diagrams were equally effective during the first builds. Naturally, over several builds, efficiency improved in all conditions because performers learned the task.

My conclusion is that any spatial representation (still diagrams or animations) is more effective than text descriptions as guidance for a spatial procedural task that will be performed on rare occasions. For tasks that will be performed routinely, a text description will be slower initially; but after a couple of task completions, the effectiveness of a text description will not differ from visual representations as workers learn the procedures. I would opt for still visuals because they are relatively inexpensive to produce and boost performance efficiency from the start. Perhaps the best solution would involve a series of still visuals accompanied by simple text—a condition not tested in the previous experiment.

In summary, it seems that the benefits of animations will depend on the desired outcome. The evidence available at this point in time on the use of animations for different outcome goals suggests the fourth guideline.

Too Much Guideline 4:

Other than procedural learning, animations are often not as effective as a series of still visuals. A series of still visuals is recommended to depict processes and offer performance support for tasks that involve spatial assembly steps.

HOW TO MANAGE LOAD IN ANIMATIONS

Because they are transient and can display a great deal of information in a short time, animations can overload working memory capacity. Since the first edition of this book, animations have been a popular research focus. In the paragraphs to follow are some evidence-based techniques to manage the mental load imposed by animations.

1. Segment the Animation

Moreno (2007) focused her research on lessons for student teachers on seven essential teaching skills. All learners received a presentation on the essential skills. Then, some learners were randomly assigned to a video example of a teacher applying the skills. Others viewed the same video edited into seven segments. The control group simply reviewed a text summary of the presentation and did not see any example. In the follow-up test, learners viewed a different video of a teacher and identified the essential skills and critiqued how they were applied. A second experiment used animation rather than video and yielded similar results shown in Figure 8-6.

Figure 8-6. Learning From Examples Presented in Segmented Video, Video, and No Example Control

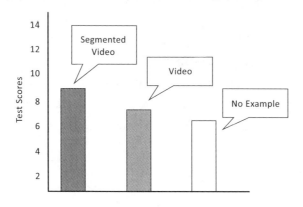

Source: Moreno, 2007.

Moreno concludes that having an example led to better learning than those who did not view an example. We will learn more about the power of examples in Chapter 9. She also recommends "segmenting instructional videos and animations into small chunks to help novice students learn from complex dynamic visualizations" (p. 778). Spanjers et al. (2011) replicated these results but contrasted the effects of segmentation of animations on novice and experienced learners. They reported that segmentation benefit- ed low prior knowledge but not high prior knowledge learners. This makes sense as the animation is likely to impose more cognitive load on novice learners than those with some background experience.

2. Add Visual Cues to Direct Attention to Relevant Portions of the Animation

Because there can be so much movement in an animation, the learners may not know where to direct their attention. The obvious movements will tend to draw the eye more than subtle movements, which might actu- ally be more relevant to the instructional goal. Several experiments have investigated the instructional benefits of adding visual cues to animations. Boucheix et al. (2013) found that color cueing led to better understanding of an animation. Color was used to illustrate the progression of movement in a mechanical process; and in a second experiment, to illustrate different elements moving at any given stage.

Another form of effective cueing involves highlighting the relevant portion of the animation, as shown in Figure 8-7. Mason et al. (2013) highlighted different parts of a heart diagram in an animated lesson on blood circulation. They reported better understanding from the lesson versions that highlighted important elements of the animations as they were discussed.

Figure 8-7. Contrast Highlighting as Cues in an Animation

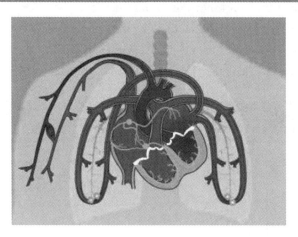

Source: de Koning et al., 2007. This material was reproduced from Graphics for Learning *with permission from John Wiley & Sons.*

3. Engage Learners in Animations

The fundamental benefits of engagement during learning were presented in chapter 4. There are a couple of recent experiments that show how engagement techniques aid learning from animations. One experiment tested the benefits of learner drawings after viewing an animation and the other evaluated the effects of self-explaining after viewing a cued animation.

Drawing Assignment

Mason et al. (2013) presented an animated demonstration of Newton's Cradle. (You're probably familiar with Newton's Cradle but did not know what it was called.) Five pendulums are hung from a string in a row. The outmost pendulum is pulled back and released and the effects of this pendulum on the movements of the others are depicted in the animation. Three different groups viewed the animation and then were asked to either: 1) sketch six drawings that depicted the initial state and the five following phases of the pendulum movement, 2) trace the given states by joining the dots on a prepared worksheet, or 3) not draw.

They tested learners immediately after the exercise and two months later. The test was scored on a 0–5 scale with a point allocated to each phase that was correctly depicted. The results are summarized in Figure 8-8.

Figure 8-8. Immediate and Delayed Learning via Drawing After an Animation

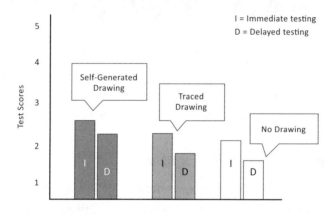

Source: Based on data from Mason et al., 2013.

As you can see, the self-generated drawings led to best understanding both upon immediate and delayed testing. In fact, there was no difference between those who traced the drawing and those who did no drawing. There is no doubt that a tracing activity did not demand much mental investment. Upon evaluating the quality of the self-generated drawings, it is not surprising that more accurate drawings were correlated with high test scores. Therefore, it will be important to give feedback on student drawings to ensure accuracy.

Self-Explanation Assignment

This chapter has reviewed the benefits of cueing animations to help draw attention to important elements. In a follow-up study, de Koning et al. (2011) combined cueing with self-explanations of an animated lesson on the circulatory system. The lesson versions were animations with and without cueing, similar to the example shown in Figure 8-8, combined with instructions for self-explaining or no assignment. First, the learners viewed a static diagram with the parts of the circulatory system labeled. Next they studied one of two versions of a five-minute animation on how the human cardiovascular system worked. Neither animation included words nor pauses, and both ran without navigational control. For each of the two animation versions, half of the learners were asked to self-explain as they viewed the animation and half were not asked to self-explain.

The inference test included open-ended questions to assess the causal relationships in heart circulation, such as: "What causes the valves of the heart to open?" Students engaged in self-explaining learned more. The combination of self-explaining and a cued animation yielded more inferences than those self-explaining with uncued animations.

Based on the evidence we have regarding management of mental load in animations I offer the following guideline.

Too Much Guideline 5:

When developing animations, manage cognitive load for novice learners with segmenting, cues, and engagement activities.

THE BOTTOM LINE

We started our discussion with a comparison of two lesson versions on information security. One lesson involved a "just the facts" approach, compared with a lesson that spiced up the content with interesting anecdotes sprinkled throughout. Let's review the statements from the beginning of the chapter.

What Do You Think?

Put a check mark next to each statement you think is true.

❏ **A. The lesson version with interesting text and visuals will lead to better learning because it is more engaging and motivating.**
FALSE. Although the lesson was more engaging based on student ratings, it actually led to less learning as a result of disruption of learning.

❏ **B. Learners will find the lesson with added text and visuals more interesting than the basic lesson.**
TRUE. However, often learner ratings are not correlated with learning.

❏ **C. The basic lesson will lead to better learning because it is lean and stays on target.**
TRUE

❏ **D. Learning will be the same because both lessons include the critical core content.**
FALSE

This is not to suggest that you never add interesting anecdotes. Rather, use care in selection and placement of stories and visuals used to add interest. A worthwhile goal is to find anecdotes and visuals that add interest and promote learning.

APPLYING LESS IS MORE TO YOUR TRAINING

We've seen that when it comes to explanations, visuals, stories, and music, in many cases learning is better when you offer learners a leaner lesson with concise explanations and simple but relevant visuals. At the same time, avoid anecdotes that don't directly contribute to the learning goal as well as extraneous audio like background music. Research is starting to emerge on ways to make lessons interesting in other ways than adding irrelevant stories. For example, one study by Um et al. (2012) found higher interest and better learning from a lesson that used graphics with warm colors and rounded shapes. I predict that we will continue to grow a research base on "emotional design."

Use the following checklist as you start to plan your lessons and when reviewing a draft lesson:

Does my lesson or presentation:
- ❑ Focus on a few topics that can be taught in a relatively short time frame.
- ❑ Include concise explanations.
- ❑ Segment content into smaller chunks.
- ❑ Use simpler visuals to illustrate content.
- ❑ Avoid anecdotes that are not relevant to the lesson goal.
- ❑ Avoid background music during episodes that require mental concentration.
- ❑ Manage cognitive load when using animations.
  - • segment animation
  - • add visual cues such as color or highlighting
- ❑ Engage learners in the animation.

COMING NEXT

In the next section we will review two of the most powerful tools in your instructor kit: examples and practice. We have a great deal of research guiding the what, when, and how of these important methods.

FOR MORE INFORMATION

Clark, R.C., and R.E. Mayer. (2011). *E-Learning & the Science of Instruction*, 3rd edition. San Francisco: Pfeiffer. (See chapter 8.)

Mayer, R.E., and L. Fiorella. (2014). Principles for Reducing Extraneous Processing in Multimedia Learning: Coherence, Signaling, Redundancy, Spatial Contiguity, and Temporal Contiguity Principles. In *Cambridge Handbook of Multimedia Learning*, 2nd edition, ed. R.E. Mayer. New York: Cambridge University Press.

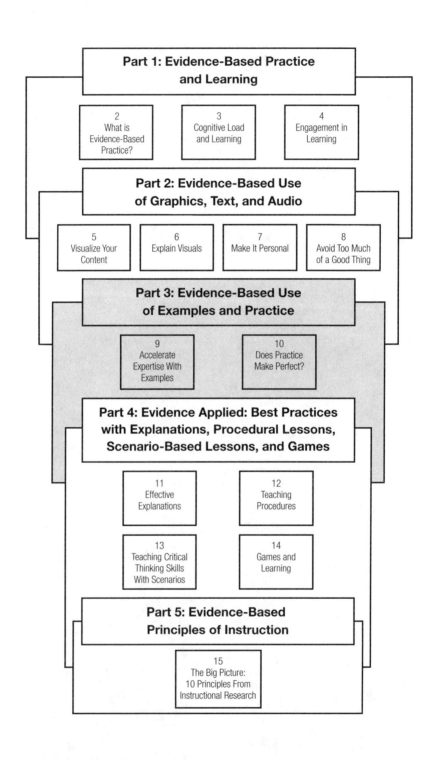

PART 3

Evidence-Based Use of Examples and Practice

In part 2 we reviewed best practices with the communication modes of graphics, text, and audio. Now we turn to two of the most powerful instructional methods associated with learning: examples and practice. Although most instructional professionals do include examples in their training, these examples are often underutilized. In chapter 9 you will learn research-based methods to boot craft and engage learners with examples. Chapter 10 focuses on practice activities. In this chapter you will read what kinds of practice activities are most effective, where to place them in your instruction, how much practice you need, as well as evidence on feedback.

ACCELERATE EXPERTISE WITH EXAMPLES

CHAPTER 9

Accelerate Expertise
With Examples

Lactose is a complex sugar found in milk. To digest lactose, you need Lactase, an enzyme that breaks lactose into two sugar molecules: glucose and galactose. Individuals lacking this enzyme have lactose intolerance. Unable to digest milk, they suffer from various gastrointestinal symptoms.

Lactase is but one of about 4,000 different enzymes that serve as catalysts of essential physiological processes. Catalysts speed up the rate of chemical reactions but are themselves unaffected.

Examples are learning catalysts. You might be able to learn without them—but adding examples to lessons has been proven to dramatically accelerate learning.

This chapter reviews evidence regarding the what, when, and how of leveraging examples to accelerate learning. We will see how examples not only improve learning outcomes but also decrease instructional time. Finally, we will continue the engagement theme introduced in chapter 4 by reviewing evidence-based engagement methods that promote processing of examples.

THE POWER OF EXAMPLES

Whether your goal is to promote awareness or to build skills, examples are useful. When you are focusing on skills, examples are an essential tool in your instructional kit. Right now, you might be thinking that you do use examples. But are you exploiting the full potential of examples to accelerate learning? Are you providing examples to the learners who most need them? Recent research has revealed techniques to help your learners get the most out of examples. With these techniques, you will extend the potential of your examples by applying evidence on the what, when, where, and for whom of examples.

What Do You Think?

Which lesson version in Figure 9-1 do you think would be most effective and efficient?

Figure 9-1. Three Lesson Versions That Differ Regarding Examples

Lesson Version A	Lesson Version B	Lesson Version C
Explanation	Explanation	Explanation
Example 1	Example 1	
Example 2	Practice 1	Practice 1
		Practice 2
Example 3	Example 2	Practice 3
Example 4	Practice 2	Practice 4
		Practice 5
Example 5	Example 3	Practice 6
Example 6	Practice 3	

As you can see, the learner reviews an equal number of problems in each lesson. In lesson Version A, all of the problems are presented in the form of examples; in lesson Version B, half the problems are in the form of examples and half in the form of practice; whereas in lesson Version C, all of the problems are solved by the learner.

Which of the following statements about these lesson versions do you think are true?

- ❑ Lesson Version A will be the most efficient because the learner does not spend time completing practice exercises.
- ❑ Lesson Version C will be the most effective because practice makes perfect.
- ❑ Lesson Version B offers the best balance for learning and efficiency.

John Sweller, one of the founding researchers of modern cognitive load theory, was the first to report the effects of examples on learning in terms of cognitive load. He took a traditional algebra lesson containing one or two examples followed by many problem assignments and converted several of the practice exercises into step-by-step examples, similar to the example in Figure 9-2. Instructional psychologists call demonstrations such as the one in Figure 9-2 worked examples. A worked example is a demonstration that illustrates a specific instance of the steps the learner must take to complete a task or solve a problem.

Figure 9-2. A Worked Example of an Algebra Problem

$$5X + 3 = 6X$$

$$1.\ 5X = 6X - 3$$
$$2.\ {-}X = {-}3$$
$$3.\ \ X\ = 3$$

Sweller and Cooper (1985) compared learning from traditional lessons containing all practice to their example-practice pairs version. You won't be surprised to learn that the traditional lesson with lots of practice problems took longer to complete. In fact, the versions that incorporated more practice took six times longer than the versions that alternated examples and practice. But did the time and effort invested in solving practice problems pay off in better learning? Surprisingly they found that learners studying the practice lesson made twice as many errors on a test than learners studying the example–practice version! A combination of examples and practice led to faster and better learning than working lots of practice problems.

Are examples followed by problems (as shown in Lesson Version B in Figure 9-1) more effective than all examples (as shown in Lesson Version A)? Recent research suggests that both designs are equally effective. Van Gog and her colleagues (2011) compared learning of the properties of electrical circuits from the three designs shown in Figure 9-1. Consistent with previous research the versions with examples led to better learning than all problems; however, there were no differences in learning from the all examples version and the example-practice pairs version.

The many experiments that have shown the benefits of worked examples support my first recommendation.

Examples Guideline 1:

Save time and improve learning by replacing practice exercises with worked examples in the form of example-practice pairs or all examples.

EXAMPLES AND THE BRAIN

How do examples work? In chapter 3 we learned that our working memory, which is our brain's active processor, has a very limited capacity. Do you remember working all those homework problems in your math class? Solving a lot of problems is hard work! When working memory capacity is tied up solving problems, there is little resource left over for learning. However, imagine that instead of working a problem, you are reviewing an example. Your working memory is free to carefully study the example and learn from it. In fact, by providing an example as a model, the student has an opportunity to build her own mental model from it. Then, by following the example with a similar practice assignment, the student can confirm that she has learned correctly!

EXAMPLES FOR ROUTINE TASKS

Two types of skills are often measured in instructional experiments: routine tasks (also known as procedures) and strategic tasks that require judgment and problem solving.

For routine tasks such as fulfilling a customer order or logging into your application, your examples should mirror the actual work environment as closely as possible. This means including the actual tools, application screens, forms, customer requests, and steps that would be used on the job. Your example should demonstrate—from the learner's perspective—how to apply steps in a realistic work context.

Examples Guideline 2:

For routine tasks, create demonstrations that mirror the context of the workplace.

EXAMPLES FOR STRATEGIC TASKS

Most of the initial research used relatively high-structure examples with clear right or wrong answers, such as the algebra problem in Figure 9-2. Only recently have researchers evaluated the benefits of examples for more strategic tasks that typically do not have a single correct answer and that require critical thinking beyond routine problem solving.

Nievelstein and colleagues (2011) evaluated the benefits of worked examples in lessons designed to teach reasoning about legal cases. In legal case reasoning, students have to read cases, formulate questions, search information sources for applicable laws, verify whether rules can be applied to the case, and provide argumentation to the questions. The research team compared learners' performance following study of four lesson versions that included: 1) worked examples and process steps that summarized the general approach to researching and responding to cases, 2) worked examples without a process summary, 3) case analysis assignments with process steps, and 4) case analysis assignments without process steps. The test consisted of a case assignment requiring learners to research and write arguments.

Consistent with previous findings, the research team found better performance among learners who had access to worked examples rather than those who were assigned case problems without examples. The process steps had no effect. We will see later in the chapter that adding explanations to worked examples is often not helpful. It is encouraging that the benefits of worked examples apply not only to routine tasks but also to less structured tasks that require critical thinking.

Use Several Worked Examples With Different Surface Features

Unlike routine tasks, strategic tasks are based on guidelines that must be adapted to a variety of work contexts. Take sales for example. Basic guidelines on effective sales techniques must be adapted to various situations depending on the product, the client, and the context. Evidence has shown that the most effective learning of strategic tasks results from two or more worked examples that reflect the same guidelines but vary regarding the surface features. Worked examples in a selling course would show how the salesperson adapts basic guidelines based on her assessment of various customer needs and diverse product specifications.

We have evidence for the benefits of varied context worked examples. Quilici and Mayer (1996) tested the learning effects of worked examples for applying statistic tests using a t-test, correlation, or chi-square. For each of these statistical tests, they created three examples. Version 1 used the same surface features for all three examples. For example, the three t-test problems used data on experience and typing speed while the three correlation examples used data on temperature and precipitation. In Version 2, the examples were varied. The t-test problems used data on experience and typing speed for one example and data on temperature and precipitation for a second example. As you can see in Figure 9-3, the lesson versions that used different context examples led to better learning.

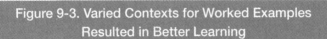

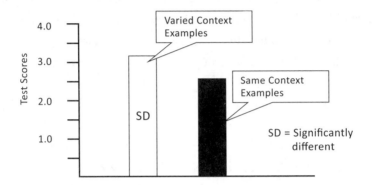

Source: From Clark and Mayer, 2011. Material reproduced with permission John Wiley & Sons.

Examples Guideline 3:

Use varied context worked examples to accelerate learning of strategic tasks.

WHEN EXAMPLES CAN HARM LEARNING

We've seen in prior chapters that some instructional techniques, such as graphics, that are powerful aids for novices, aren't much help for learners with more background knowledge.

Which of the following statements do you think is most accurate regarding who benefits the most from examples? Check all that apply:

- ❏ A. Novices benefit from examples more than experts.
- ❏ B. Novices and experts benefit equally from examples.
- ❏ C. Experts benefit from examples more than novices.
- ❏ D. Experts are better off without examples.

Kalyuga and his colleagues (2001) measured learning from lessons on how to write programs for relay circuits. The learners who were beginners were divided into two groups: an example-problem group (such as the Version B lesson in Figure 9-1) and an all problem group (such as Version C). Learning was measured at several time periods as the group gained expertise.

During the beginning stages, learners benefited greatly from studying examples. As they became more experienced, however, not only did the examples no longer help, they actually depressed learning! Based on this evidence, the correct answers are A and D.

Instructional psychologists call this an expertise reversal effect. Expertise reversal means that some methods that are useful for novices, not only don't help those with more experience, but they actually hinder their learning!

However, more recent evidence suggests that expertise reversal may not apply to worked examples that illustrate strategic tasks. Recall the experiment summarized previously, showing the benefits of worked examples in legal case reasoning. Nievelstein and colleagues (2013) tested the effects of worked examples compared with problem assignments with both novices and advanced law students and found that both groups benefitted from the examples! They concluded that the expertise reversal effect may not apply to more strategic tasks because novice and experienced learners can benefit—perhaps in different ways—from these more complex examples. We will need more studies to confirm possible exceptions to expertise reversal with examples.

Examples Guideline 4:

For routine tasks, use worked examples for novice learners. For learners with experience in the content, emphasize practice assignments more than examples. For learning strategic tasks, worked examples may benefit novice and experienced learners.

MORE ABOUT EXAMPLES AND THE BRAIN

Examples benefit learners because working memory is free to study the example and learn from it. The example serves as a learning catalyst by providing a substitute for the missing mental model of learners. However, a more experienced learner already has some relevant knowledge. For routine tasks, these learners are better off applying their own mental models to a practice assignment, rather than reviewing a demonstration that at best duplicates—and at worst might actually interfere with—their own unique approach to the task. Note that this generalization may not apply to learning of strategic tasks. Because of the complexity of worked examples of strategic tasks, both novice and experienced learners may benefit from different aspects of the examples.

HOW TO MAKE EXAMPLES ENGAGING

We've seen that examples are one of your most powerful instructional tools. But there is one problem. Many learners either skip examples completely or don't process them very deeply. Chi (2000) showed that higher-scoring physics students studied examples carefully, investing the effort to explain the examples to themselves. Poorer students, in contrast, tended to ignore examples or merely repeat the steps shown in the example.

One of the basic themes throughout this book is promotion of psychological engagement with the content. You can boost the instructional potential of your examples by encouraging your learners to study them carefully. Here we will review four methods for engagement in examples:

1) use faded worked examples, 2) add self-explanation questions, 3) assign guided example comparisons, and 4) minimize instructional explanations of examples.

Engagement Technique 1: Use Faded Worked Examples

Fading is a useful technique to increase engagement in worked examples, as well as to accommodate learners who are building expertise. You begin by providing a completely worked out example for the learner to study. You follow with a second example in which the first steps have been worked out and the learner needs to finish it. With each new example the learner completes more of it until he is completing a full problem assignment. Figure 9-4 shows a visual model for a faded worked example for a three-step task. Remember that because strategic tasks benefit from varied context, each of your examples in the faded series should use different scenarios.

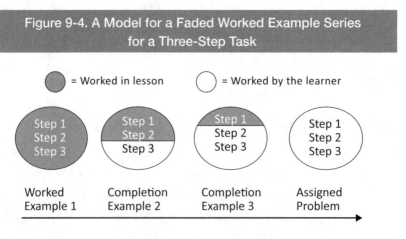

Figure 9-4. A Model for a Faded Worked Example Series for a Three-Step Task

Source: From Clark and Mayer, 2011. Material reproduced with permission John Wiley & Sons.

Research experiments reported by Atkinson and his colleagues (2003) showed that learning was better from lessons using faded worked examples than from lessons that provided example-problem pairs.

Engagement Technique 2: Add Self-Explanation Questions

As mentioned, research that compared the study habits of successful and less successful students found that more successful students explained examples to themselves. Because many learners may not spontaneously review worked examples carefully, you can encourage such review by adding questions to your worked examples. Figure 9-5 shows a simple example of a self-explanation question for a geometry worked example. Figure 9-6 shows a self-explanation question used for training of retail regional managers. The goal of the management lesson was to help regional managers identify root causes of problems in local stores. In this example, the learner must distinguish among a root cause, a symptom, an assumption, and a hypothesis.

Figure 9-5. Adding a Question Encourages Meaningful Processing of the Example

Example:
Find the area of a circle when the diameter is 8.

Step 1. Formula: $A = \pi R^2$
Step 2. Radius = 8 divided by 2 = 4
Step 3. A = 3.12 times 16
Step 4. A = 49.92

QUESTION:
In step 2, why was 8 divided by 2?

A. Because the radius must be squared
B. Because the radius is half the diameter
C. Because pi equals 4
D. Because 4 is the square root of 16

Figure 9-6. A Self-Explanation Question From a Management Training Worked Example

The regional manager (RM) has noticed a decline in commercial sales over the past six months. She meets with store manager (SM) to identify a solution.

RM: *Why are commercial sales declining?*
SM: We aren't seeing high penetration and growth in commercial sales. I think it's the economy.

The SM response reflects:

A. A root cause
B. An assumption
C. A symptom
D. A hypothesis

RM: *What are we doing to drive penetration in commercial accounts?*
SM: We've had some appreciation events . . .

RM: *What feedback did we get at those events?*

Atkinson and his colleagues (2003) compared lessons with worked examples to lessons with worked examples plus questions. They found that including the questions improved learning.

Schworm and Renkl (2007) evaluated the benefits of worked examples to illustrate principles of effective argumentation. Argumentation requires construction of reasoned positions on a question—more or less like a good editorial or debate. It involves stating a position, providing evidence for the position, considering counter-arguments, and providing rebuttals for them.

In their research, students were provided an explanation followed by video examples of argumentation. The video showing the dialog was first played completely and then replayed in short sequences. In the worked example lesson version, the video paused and a bubble appeared with a question about the techniques used in the argument. They found that adding the questions to the video examples was essential to build argumentation skills, and recommended using questions in conjunction with examples—especially for strategic tasks such as argumentation.

There are many forms of questions that could help your learners extract more value out of your examples. Try for questions that stimulate reflection on the principles or rules behind your example. It is important that learners get feedback on their responses to these questions. In e-learning, I recommend that you use an objective question format, such as multiple-choice (as shown in Figures 9-5 and 9-6), because specific feedback can be given more effectively. In classroom settings, instructor and participant discussion can provide feedback to open-ended as well as objective questions.

Engagement Technique 3: Assign Guided Example Comparisons

We've seen that strategic tasks benefit from varied worked examples that reflect the same guidelines applied in diverse contexts. One way to promote engagement in examples is to encourage learners to compare these examples in order to identify the commonalities. In other words, require learners to focus on the underlying guidelines by contrasting two or more examples.

One of my favorite research reports evaluated learning of negotiation skills by review and comparison of examples (Gentner et al., 2003). Learning was measured by a role play that followed negotiation lessons using different techniques. In the research, 158 undergraduate students studied one of four different lessons—three with examples and one without. In one example version (separate), learners were asked to analyze each negotiation example separately. In a second version (comparison), learners were asked to review two examples and list the commonalities. In a third version, students completed a guided training packet that required them to review examples displayed together (guided comparison). Which lesson do you think resulted in best learning?

❑ A. Guided comparison of examples
❑ B. Comparison of examples
❑ C. Review of each example individually

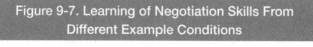

Figure 9-7. Learning of Negotiation Skills From Different Example Conditions

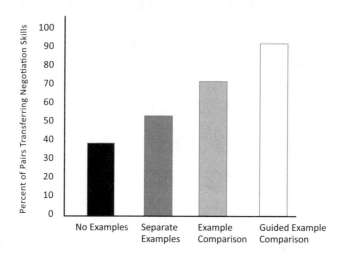

Source: Based on data from Gentner et al., 2003.

Take a look at Figure 9-7 to see the results. The guided comparison lesson led to a higher proportion of role play pairs using the trained techniques. The research team concluded that "comparing two instances of a to-be-learned principle is a powerful means of promoting rapid learning, even for novices" (Gentner et al., 2003, 402).

Engagement Technique 4: Minimize Instructional Explanations of Examples

As instructors, it's instinctive to provide learners with explanations related to a worked example. Surprisingly, research shows that learners provided with explanations of worked examples often learn less than those provided with examples alone. When faced with detailed explanations about a worked example, learners may be less likely to self-explain and are therefore less engaged.

In three experiments that used explanations of electricity and electrical circuit problems, Richey and Nokes-Malach (2013) studied the benefits of providing explanations for each step of a worked example and compared their results to examples without explanations. Figure 9-8 shows an example similar to the examples in their two lesson versions. The test included definitions (factual knowledge), problem solving, and conceptual knowledge. They found no effect on definitions or problem solving; however, regarding conceptual knowledge, learners in the withholding condition (Version A) scored higher. Although learners were not given adjunct questions, the research team suggests that in the absence of explanations, learners automatically generated their own questions and processed the examples more deeply; whereas those provided with explanations, "may have suppressed their tendencies to self-explain because explicit explanations were readily available" (116).

Figure 9-8. Worked Example Without (Version A) and With (Version B) Explanations

Worked Example Version A

1. A train travelling 70 mph leaves City A at 10:00 a.m. and arrives at City B at 1:30 p.m. What is the distance between City A and B?

Worked Example Version B

1. A train travelling 70 mph leaves City A at 10:00 a.m. and arrives at City B at 1:30 p.m. What is the distance between City A and B?

Solution

Write formula: D = R x T
We must solve for the distance in this problem.
Time = 3.5 hours
Distance = 70 x 3.5 = 245 miles

Description of Principle	Application to Problem
General principle applied: This is an example of a distance, rate, and time problem expressed with formula D = R x T. With any two values, you can calculate the third.	Write the formula: D = R x T.
Define equivalent values: Since the rate is given in miles per hour, the time must be expressed in hours.	The number of hours between 10:00 a.m. and 1:30 p.m. is 3.5.
Adjust formula for the unknown.	D = 70 x 3.5 = 245 miles

In a meta-analysis of 21 studies that reviewed the benefits of explanations of worked examples, Wittwer and Renkl (2010) concluded that when learners are encouraged to engage in self-explaining of the examples, instructional explanations resulted in no learning benefits. However, in the absence of student self-questioning, adding instructional explanations did benefit acquisition of conceptual knowledge—but not other types of knowledge. Second, their data suggest that adding explanations in mathematical domains was helpful for learning (but not in other domains). The team concluded that "maximizing the instructional guidance in example-based learning by providing instructional explanations might not be beneficial in all situations" (407). Rather, the optimal design of example-based instructions might depend on the learning outcomes goals or instructional domains.

We need to learn more about when and how to add explanations to worked examples. Based on mixed results to date, I recommend that in most situations you use one of the first three engagement methods in lieu of detailed explanations of worked examples. An exception might apply to technical domains where learners do not have the background to generate accurate self-explanations without instructional support.

In summary, learners who are encouraged to process examples deeply learn more than learners reviewing examples on their own—especially for learning strategic skills such as negotiation or argumentation. The evidence to date suggests three effective techniques: fading of a series of examples, asking questions about the example accompanied by feedback, or guided example comparisons. To maximize learner engagement, in general, minimize the amount of instructional explanation provided. We will look to future research for clearer guidelines regarding when to add instructional explanations to worked examples.

Examples Guideline 5:

Encourage engagement with examples by fading, adjunct questions (with feedback), or guided comparison of examples.

FORMATTING EXAMPLES

This section summarizes two guidelines regarding the formatting of your examples: segmentation and contiguity of examples.

Segment Example Steps

In chapter 8, we reviewed evidence showing the benefits of breaking content into chunks and allowing control over those chunks with a "continue" button in an e-learning lesson. A similar principle is recommended by Spanjers et al. (2011). They compared the benefits of four worked examples illustrating probability calculations displayed in two formats: 1) a segmented version in which blank lines were inserted to visually isolate the six different sections in the problem solution and 2) an unsegmented version that displayed all of the steps together without any separating lines. They found that the learning in the segmented and unsegmented versions was equivalent, although learners rated the segmented version as lower in mental effort. Thus, the segmented versions were more efficient. In the same study, one group was asked to segment the worked examples themselves. The actively segmenting group rated their mental load as highest and did not learn more than the other groups. Here we see another example where learner physical engagement does not always foster learning. Based on this evidence, I recommend segmenting important elements of a worked example by using line spacing in written materials, or overlays in slides and screens.

Display Examples Together to Promote Comparisons

In chapter 6 we saw the benefits of displaying visuals and explanatory text together, allowing the learner easy integration to make sense of the combined visual and text. This technique is an application of the contiguity principle. Contiguity also applies to situations in which you want learners to compare two or more examples illustrating strategic tasks. For example, Gentner et al. (2003) found better learning when examples were displayed together using a diagrammatic summary of the first solution, visible to learners as they compared the second example to the first. Learners who studied each example separately learned much less. Comparison of examples will be easier when the learner can review them together. For example, you could put each example on the same sheet of paper or on facing sheets. Online you could display one example on one screen and a second example on a second screen, next to a summary of the first example.

Likewise, if your example involves a combination of a visual and words, such as a geometry example with a diagram and text or a demonstration of how to use software, it's important to ensure simultaneous access to the words (text or audio) and to the visuals. See chapter 6 for more details on the contiguity effect. Sweller and Chandler (1994) found that when diagrams and words were separated, the benefits of worked examples disappeared. That is because the additional cognitive load imposed by split attention negated the cognitive load benefits of worked examples.

THE BOTTOM LINE

We began the chapter comparing three lesson plans shown in Figure 9-1. Research showed that lessons that used worked examples led to better and faster learning of novice learners than lessons that relied primarily on problem solving. Recent research has shown equal learning from lessons that provided all examples as from lessons that included example-problem pairs. We have also reviewed evidence showing that techniques to engage learners in the examples will increase their benefits.

APPLYING EXAMPLES TO YOUR TRAINING

The checklists are divided into hints for examples that best illustrate routine tasks, strategic tasks, and all tasks.

Examples for Routine (Procedural) Tasks

- ❏ Provide demonstrations that incorporate the tools and techniques of the job.
- ❏ Use animation for procedural tasks involving motion.
- ❏ If using animation, incorporate controls and cueing to help learners manage cognitive load.
- ❏ Explain an animated demonstration with brief audio narration.
- ❏ Minimize worked examples for experienced learners; instead rely mostly on problem assignments.

Examples for Strategic (Problem-Solving) Tasks

- ❏ Provide two or more varied context worked examples.
- ❏ Promote engagement in strategic worked examples by assigning a guided comparison task.
- ❏ Ensure that learners can see two or more worked examples together to aid in comparison.
- ❏ Limited evidence recommends you use worked examples for novice and more advanced learners.

For All Examples

❑ Encourage engagement in your examples through fading, adjunct questions with feedback, or guided comparisons.

❑ Segment complex examples into small pieces.

❑ For examples that include a diagram, ensure that both the diagram and words are visible together (contiguity principle).

Tips for Examples

In classroom training, it is difficult to spontaneously come up with several useful examples to illustrate how to perform a task. I recommend that the lesson developer (who may be the instructor) prepare these examples ahead in a student handout, in video or computer animation, or as an in-class instructor demonstration. A handout or online help that documents the worked example will serve as a useful reference on the job. Along with the example, insert questions about the example either in the handout or in the instructor guide.

Gather examples by analyzing work samples. For example, most call centers keep recordings that can provide a rich repository of examples. In other situations, you may have to rely on your subject matter experts to provide examples. Ask them to bring examples to a meeting. If confidentiality is an issue, revise the samples using different names, screenshots, and so on.

Remember that often you do not need to provide much in the way of explanation of your worked examples. If the example is quite complex and you provide additional explanations, use audio to explain them—either instructor audio or narration in e-learning. For faded examples or examples that will include questions, display the steps in text; or, pause an animated visual periodically to allow the learner ample opportunity to review the worked out steps prior to finishing the example themselves or to answering questions about the steps. Be sure to provide feedback about the accuracy of learners' responses when engaging with worked examples.

COMING NEXT

In this chapter we have seen the instructional potential of replacing some practice exercises with examples. However you will still need to include practice opportunities as a fundamental way to engage learners. In the next chapter we will draw on research that answers basic questions about practice, including what kind of practice is effective, where to place practice in the instructional environment, and how much practice to include.

FOR MORE INFORMATION

Clark, R.C., and R.E. Mayer. (2011). *E-Learning & the Science of Instruction*, 3rd edition. San Francisco: Pfeiffer. See Chapter 10.

This book provides a review of many of the same points discussed in this chapter, applied specifically to e-learning. Note that the more recent studies (after 2010) mentioned in this chapter will not be included.

Nievelstein, F., T. van Gog, G.V. Dijck, and H.P.A. Boshuizen. (2013). The Worked Example and Expertise Reversal Effect in Less Structured Tasks: Learning to Reason About Legal Cases. *Contemporary Educational Psychology* 38(2): 118-125.

This is an interesting study illustrating the benefits of worked examples to strategic tasks. Reasoning about legal cases is a task analogous to many critical thinking tasks in the workplace.

Renkl, A. (2014). The Worked Out Examples Principles in Multimedia Learning. In *The Cambridge Handbook of Multimedia Learning*, ed. R.E. Mayer. New York: Cambridge University Press.

There is more to say about worked examples than I could accommodate in this book. If you are interested in recent research details I recommend this resource. This handbook chapter is written by one of the leading researchers on worked examples.

Wittwer, J., A. Renkl. (2010). How Effective Are Instructional Explanations in Example-Based Learning? A Meta-Analytic Review. *Educational Psychology Review* 22: 393-409.

This meta-analysis includes a good literature review and concludes that instructional explanations should not be used when adjunct questions are added; however, it also points out some situations where explanations of worked examples are helpful.

DOES PRACTICE MAKE PERFECT?

CHAPTER 10

Does Practice Make Perfect?

"One way of looking at this might be that, for 42 years, I've been making small regular deposits in this bank of experience: education and training. And on January 15, the balance was sufficient so that I could make a very large withdrawal."

—Capt. Chesley "Sully" Sullenberger, Pilot of US Air 1549,
"The Miracle of the Hudson"

From music to chess to golf, evidence from world-class performers reinforces the saying that success is 99 percent perspiration and 1 percent inspiration.

One of my core evidence-based themes is that engagement does not happen automatically. It is up to the instructional professional—you—to build and facilitate learning environments that promote deliberate engagement. We've considered how to engage learners with graphics, with their peers in collaborative learning, and with examples. However, your main engagement tool is practice activities. In this chapter, we will look at evidence behind six core guidelines to help you maximize the benefits of practice during training. Specifically we will review: 1) what kind of practice works best, 2) how much practice to include in your lessons, 3) where to place practice, 4) how to group practice, 5) how to leverage comparison exercises, and 6) how to maximize the benefits of feedback.

THE POWER OF PRACTICE

From Captain Sullenberger to Yo-Yo Ma, world-class performers do not arrive haphazardly. Star performers start young. Yo-Yo Ma started to study the cello with his father at age four and Captain Sully had his first pilot license when he was 14. Second, they invest countless hours in regular, focused practice even after reaching high performance levels. In fact, the best musicians, athletes, and chess players require a minimum of 10 years of sustained and focused practice to reach their peak performance period.

Naturally aptitude and attributes play a role. I'm a basketball fan. But at 5'2" (not to mention my age!), I doubt that any amount of practice will transform me into a professional-level player. Captain Sully is a smart man, having qualified for Mensa when he was 12. However, for the most part we underestimate the role of focused practice in building competence; and in fact, most of us fail to reach the full potential of our natural gifts. It's true. Expertise is 99 percent perspiration and 1 percent inspiration!

What Do You Think?

Place a check next to each statement you believe is true about practice:

- ❑ A. The more practice, the better the learning.
- ❑ B. Six practice exercises placed at the end of the lesson will lead to better learning than the same six exercises distributed throughout the lesson.
- ❑ C. When teaching two topics, it's better to group practice questions according to topic than to mix questions for both topics in the same section.
- ❑ D. "List the five steps to construct a formula in Excel" is an effective practice exercise.
- ❑ E. Effective feedback is corrective—it tells learners whether their response is right or wrong.

WHAT IS PRACTICE?

Practice in learning environments is a deliberate assigned activity designed to promote a behavioral and psychological response that will build goal-relevant knowledge or skills. Responding to a well-designed, multiple-choice exercise, repeating 20 free throws in basketball, engaging in role play with a classmate, working collaboratively on a case study, or dragging and dropping screen objects in response to an online question are but a few examples of practice formats. Let's look at this definition in more detail.

While learners can and do undertake practice on their own, the quality of that practice may not lead to optimal results. The practice may not be aligned to desired outcomes and feedback may not be available. Instead, a deliberate assigned activity is one that takes into account the instructional goals and incorporates evidence-based guidance on productive engagement. To qualify as practice, the learner must make some kind of behavioral response. For the purposes of formal training, that response usually generates a visible product—one that can be evaluated by the instructional environment. Naturally, learners can also practice without behavioral responses, such as silently repeating a vocabulary word or self-explaining an example. However, to maximize the benefits from feedback, I recommend embedding opportunities for behavioral responses in your instructional environments.

As we discussed in chapter 4, the behavioral response must coincide with the appropriate psychological activity. Activity itself does not necessarily lead to learning and can even depress learning. Therefore, practice is a specific assignment intended to help learners bridge performance gaps. Here I distinguish between practice in general and deliberate practice that focuses on specific skill gaps. Take, for example, a recreational golfer. She accumulates a great deal of practice hours over time but never improves beyond a baseline, which typically falls far short of her capabilities. Deliberate practice requires an analysis of skill gaps and a focus on those gaps, usually with the help of a skilled coach or instructor (Ericcson, 2006).

What Is Effective Practice?

There are two types of practice common in training settings: 1) recall assignments that ask the learner to repeat or recognize the content of the lesson and 2) application assignments that ask the learner to apply knowledge or perform job tasks. For example, in Figure 10-1 you can compare three practice assignments from an Excel training session. Which exercises promote effective behavioral and psychological responses?

Figure 10-1. Excel Formula Practice Versions A, B, and C

Practice Version A

List the three features of an Excel formula.

Practice Version B

Select the correctly formatted Excel formula:

= 4C x 9F

= 4C/3D

2B + 3A =

Practice Version C

Enter the formula in the spreadsheet to calculate third-quarter profit.

Version A is a recall assignment—what I call a regurgitation exercise. It promotes rote learning. Recalling the features of an Excel formula does not mean that the learner can identify or construct a viable formula. Version B is a closer reflection of actual job performance because it asks the learner to identify a correctly formatted formula. This is a useful exercise for an important knowledge topic associated with using Excel. However, you would not want to stop with this practice because it fails to require learners to actually perform the task of constructing and entering a formula. Practice Version C is the closest to the requirements of the job. In short, this exercise promotes both behavioral and psychological responses aligned to the workplace.

Why not assign all three types of practice? After all doesn't one need to know (in other words, memorize) the formula features to construct a formula? With a few exceptions, I discourage regurgitation types of practice exercises such as Version A. First, rote learning does not lead to understanding and most workplace performance benefits from understanding. Second, basic facts and procedures can often be provided in some form of performance support aid to minimize reliance on recall. Third, any job task that is repeated many times will become automated naturally on the job. Last, most trainers have limited time allocated for training. It makes sense to leverage that time by assigning practice that will lead most directly to effective job performance.

PRACTICE AND THE BRAIN

Recall from chapter 3 the three forms of cognitive load: intrinsic, extraneous, and germane. Germane is useful cognitive load. It promotes learning by stimulating active processing in working memory leading to encoding in long-term memory. Germane load is generated by your practice exercises. But it's not enough to get new knowledge and skills encoded into long-term memory. Those knowledge and skills must be retrieved from long-term memory later when needed on the job. Therefore, as you plan practice you need to consider how to get knowledge and skills into long-term memory and back out again.

Your training goal is to avoid "apparent" learning. Apparent learning occurs when learners respond correctly to exercises or quizzes in class but fail to apply skills to the job. Instead, your goal is transfer of learning. New knowledge and skills processed at the time of learning must transfer later to job settings. Fortunately for the passengers of U.S. Air Flight 1549, Captain Sullenberger was able to make a rapid and effective transfer of his years of accumulated knowledge and skills. Unfortunately, the trainee pilot of Asiana Airlines Flight 214 had practiced landing with the aid of an Instrument Landing System—an airport navigation system for precision landing. Unfortunately, the system was temporarily off on the morning of the landing and the pilot had insufficient practice with visual approaches. In other words, his practice environment had not adequately mirrored all landing conditions.

Embed Retrieval Hooks During Learning

Suppose I asked you to state the months of the year. That would be no problem, right? However, what if I asked you to state them in alphabetical order? You could do it, but it would likely take you a bit longer because your learning cues were chronological—not alphabetic. Memory retrieval hooks must be implanted at the time of learning. It's too late to add them later.

For workforce learning, retrieval hooks are the sights, kinesthetics, and sounds of the workplace. In other words, it's all about context. To optimize transfer of learning, you need to embed the context of the job into your practice exercises. Rather than asking learners to recall the steps to perform a task or list the names of equipment parts, embed the job context into the exercise by asking learners to perform the task or circle the part of the equipment that performs a specific function. Based on the evidence and the psychology of learning, I offer my first recommendation.

Practice Guideline 1:

Incorporate the context of the job to build practice exercises that require application rather than recall of content.

One good way to implement this guideline is to develop job-realistic scenarios that embed the knowledge and skills of the job. Some scenarios can provide a basis for worked examples. Additional scenarios can become the context for various practice assignments. In some situations your entire lesson may be scenario-based. I will describe scenario-based lesson design in chapter 13.

HOW MUCH PRACTICE DO YOUR LEARNERS NEED?

Practice takes time and time is money, so deciding how much practice to include is an important issue. Top performers such as world-class musicians or athletes maintain a regular and rigorous practice regimen. Does this mean that the more we practice, the better we get? The answer is yes and no. In fact, you do continue to improve over time with practice—but at a diminishing rate. Instructional psychologists call this the power law of practice and skill. The power law means that skills build rapidly during the first few practice sessions; however, as practice continues, the rate of skill proficiency slows. The greatest improvements will accrue from the first practice sessions. Following the first few practice sessions, improvement continues but at a diminishing rate.

Evidence on Amount of Practice and Learning

Rohrer and Taylor (2006) measured learning of a mathematical procedure from two different practice regimens. All participants viewed a tutorial that demonstrated how to solve several example problems. Then, half the participants had a practice session consisting of three problems, while the other half completed nine practice problems. Some participants from each group were tested one week after practice and the others were tested four weeks later. Figure 10-2 shows the results.

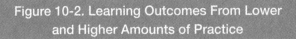

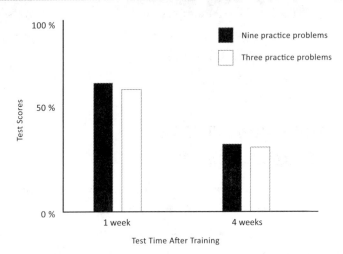

Source: Based on data from Rohrer and Taylor, 2006.

As you can see, everyone did better on the immediate test than on the delayed test. However, there were no real differences on either the immediate or the delayed test between the low and high practice groups. These results are an example of the power law of practice. The research team concluded that "the minimal effect of over learning on retention can be interpreted as an instance of diminishing returns. That is, with each additional amount of practice devoted to a single concept, there was an ever smaller increase in test performance" (1218).

Isaac Asimov wrote nearly 500 books during a 40-year period. Ohlsson (1992) calculated the average amount of time he took to write 100 books over an extended period of time. He measured in blocks of 100 to rule out individual variability around specific books. The first 100 books were completed in 237 months, the second 100 in 113 months, and the third in 69 months. His production speed increased steadily, with the greatest gains occurring in the first 20 years.

A Time for Over Learning

There are situations that benefit from extensive practice, which then leads to automaticity. Landing an aircraft is one example. Not only are the consequences of error very serious, but also multiple actions must be taken very quickly. In other words, the task imposes a high intrinsic load. There is no time to refer to a working aid to decide when to start the flare or to identify the correct power level for a given stage of descent. Over learning is expensive because it requires enough drill and practice to build automaticity. In many workplace settings, automaticity can evolve naturally through repetitive performance on the job—in other words through experience. However, in situations such as landing an aircraft, the first solo landing must be pretty good. Over learning is justified.

Over learning may also be needed when the final task is so complex that the underlying component skills must be automatic to free up working memory resources to devote to the entire task. I feel that the most important skill I learned in high school was typing. At least it is the one skill that I have continued to use more than 50 years later. With automated typing skills, I can devote most of my working memory capacity to expressing my ideas; however, my typing skill was an expensive investment requiring many hours of daily practice.

You will need to decide whether over learning through extensive and time-consuming practice is warranted for your learning goals. Performance criticality and the amount of intrinsic load in the final task are two determining factors.

So how much practice do you need? There is no universal rule. Based on the evidence and psychology of repetitive practice, consider the following recommendations.

Practice Guideline 2:

Adjust the amount of practice in your training based on:

- Consequences of error: If serious, you need more rather than less practice.
- Acceptability of a job aid: If yes, then fewer practice exercises might suffice.
- Complexity of the work: If high, drill and practice might be needed to automate requisite sub-skills.

HOW SHOULD PRACTICE BE SPACED?

Have you ever crammed for an exam? Most of us at one time or another waited until the last minute and then studied intensively. And in most cases cramming does work. On other occasions you may have been more organized and scheduled your study periods for several weeks prior to the exam. Cramming is called massed practice and can be contrasted with spaced practice. Which approach is better?

One of the first and most enduring principles of active learning is called the "spacing effect." First reported by Ebbinghaus in 1885, the spacing effect states that when practice opportunities are distributed over time, learning—especially delayed learning—is better. One often cited study evaluated different practice schedules for teaching postal workers to type (Baddeley and Longman, 1978). Learners practiced once or twice a day for either one or two hours at a time. The researchers found that those learners who reached criterion in the fewest total practice hours were assigned to the most distributed practice schedule, for example, once a day for an hour. Of course, those with more distributed practice required a longer calendar time to reach criterion levels. Often it may not be practical to extend overall learning time; in fact, a common goal in workforce learning is to accelerate job expertise.

As mentioned previously, we have all been successful at one time or another with cramming or massed practice. That is because the benefits of spaced practice are most pronounced on delayed learning. For example, Rohrer and Taylor (2006) compared learning of math skills from 10 practice problems. One group used a massed practice approach by working all 10 problems in a single session. The second group used spaced practice by working five problems in one week and the other five the following week. Learners were tested one week after the final practice session and again four weeks after the final practice session. Take a look at the data in Figure 10-3 and then select your interpretation(s):

Figure 10-3. Learning From Spaced and Massed Practice One Week and Four Weeks Later

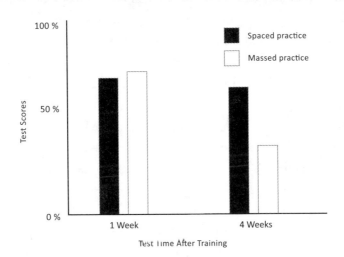

Source: Based on data from Rohrer and Taylor, 2006.

Your interpretation:

❏ A. Spaced practice works better for immediate learning.
❏ B. Spaced practice works better for long-term learning.
❏ C. Massed practice works better for immediate learning.
❏ D. Massed practice works better for long-term learning.

As you can see, both massed and spaced practice led to equivalent learning one week after study. However, the benefits of spaced practice are apparent after four weeks. Because many training organizations don't evaluate learning over time, the benefits of spaced practice are rarely seen. Based on a lot of accumulated evidence, however, spaced practice will give you a better long-term return.

Some Ways to Space Practice

There are several ways that you can space practice in an applied setting without disrupting the instructional schedule. One approach is to spread a given amount of practice over the duration of the training time. For example, imagine you have a course with six lessons and you plan on including six practice exercises with each lesson. At the end of the first lesson, assign two practice exercises. At the end of the second lesson, assign two exercises from lesson one and two from lesson two. You can see the pattern. Rather than placing all practice related to a specific lesson together, you distribute those exercises among your lessons. In that way, each lesson will have some review practice, as well as practice on new content.

A second approach is to use a blend of media to spread learning events over a longer timeframe. For example, you may initiate your training with some reading assignments, and a brief on-the-job assignment, followed by a virtual classroom session to discuss the outcomes of the job assignment. Following more workplace assignments, a face-to-face instructor-led session may leverage social presence via group problem solving or role plays. After the in-person session, asynchronous follow-up activities may include participation in discussion boards, submission of products to multimedia pages, and other assignments that require participants to continue to practice over time. Rather than an event, learning becomes a process. Rather than using instructional time to disseminate information, effective face-to-face learning leverages the opportunities inherent in high social presence with activities that involve engagement with others.

A third approach is to force frequent study by making shorter rather than longer assignment deadlines. Fulton et al. (2013) gave three different assignment deadlines in a 12-week online statistics course attended by healthcare executives. Participants were randomly assigned to deadlines that were either weekly, monthly, or end-of-course. Learners with weekly deadlines performed significantly better on exams than the monthly or end-of-course groups that were equivalent. The research team concluded that "provision of frequent, evenly spaced deadlines results in greater practice distribution which consequently predicts performance on tests of retention and transfer" (30).

In summary, even though the spacing effect has been reported and consistently demonstrated for well more than 100 years, this important principle is rarely applied. Perhaps because most learning from training classes is assessed soon after the instructional event (if at all), workforce learning professionals have not seen the benefits of spacing. The considerable evidence accumulated over a range of topics and time is the basis for this guideline.

Practice Guideline 3:

Distribute practice within your lessons and throughout your course rather than lumping them together. Convert learning events into learning processes.

HOW SHOULD PRACTICE BE SEQUENCED?

Imagine you have three or more categories of skills or problems to teach, such as how to calculate the area of a circle, a square, and a triangle. In traditional courses, a lesson on the area of circles would be followed by a lesson on squares and then triangles; each lesson including a presentation of the formula, some examples, and practice exercises. This type of organization is called blocked practice. An alternative sequence would combine all three types of calculations so that a practice on the area of a triangle would be followed by a practice on the area of a square and so on. This organizational scheme is called interleaved or mixed practice.

Rohrer and Taylor (2007) asked learners to calculate the number of faces, edges, corners, or angles in four unique geometric shapes. Following a tutorial that included examples, learners were assigned 32 practice problems—eight of each of the four types. The blocked group worked eight faces problems, eight edges problems, eight corners problems, and eight angles problems. The mixed practice group worked a practice problem from each of the four types eight times. For example, the learner would work a problem dealing with faces, followed by a problem focusing on edges, and so on. The research team reported practice scores achieved during the learning sessions as well as test scores achieved a day after practice.

The results of this experiment are shown in Figure 10-4. Learners in the mixed practice group scored lower on practice items but higher on the test. In other words, challenges faced during the lesson paid off in performance later.

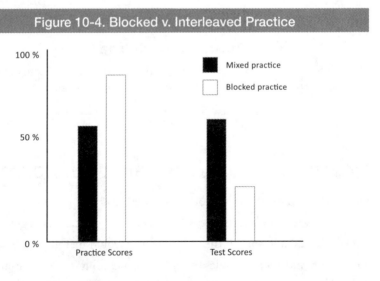

Figure 10-4. Blocked v. Interleaved Practice

Source: Based on data from Rohrer and Taylor, 2007.

A recent review on interleaving concluded that in a number of experiments that compared interleaving and blocking, interleaving resulted in better learning (Rohrer, 2012). For example, Kornell and Bjork (2008) taught college students to distinguish among different artists by viewing landscape paintings of each artist. Some lessons used a blocked approach in which students reviewed six paintings by one artist, followed by six of a second artist, and so on. The interleaved group reviewed one painting by Artist A, followed by one from Artist B, and so on. The final test asked learners to identify the artists of a series of paintings not seen during the lessons. Those in the interleaving group scored 59 percent compared with 36 percent in the blocked group. Similar results have been reported in experiments using mathematical content, such as algebraic rules and geometry.

Interleaving may help learners make discriminations among related categories and is therefore most beneficial with learning goals that require discrimination among classes of objects, concepts, or principles. For example, in an Excel class, an interleaved approach would combine calculations requiring addition, subtraction, division, and multiplication rather than grouping like calculations together. The evidence accumulated to date is the basis for the following guideline.

Practice Guideline 4:

When it's important to respond differently to different categories of problems, mix practice items rather than grouping similar practice types together.

As a trainer, this guideline may be a bit painful to implement. Because the learning experience will be more difficult, you will be tempted to make things easier for learners by organizing practice in blocks according to each topic. You will need to keep in mind the paradox that a more challenging practice organization (mixed practice) will yield better learning in the long term.

COMPARISON PRACTICE EXERCISES

We saw that mixing or interleaving assignments that involve related but distinct concepts or problems benefits learning perhaps by promoting comparisons among the different classes presented. Assignments in which learners are asked to make explicit comparisons between two sets of data, two mental models, or two scenarios have also proven effective.

Comparison as Prework

Several studies have shown that giving students a comparison assignment as prework before a lecture resulted in better learning from the lecture than students who read a summary of the comparison content. In a psychology class, Schwartz and Bransford (1998) asked college students to either compare data from two contrasting cases or to read summaries of the data. Following a lecture that focused on the theories that explained the data, learners who had analyzed contrasting cases as prework performed better on a transfer test than those who read summaries of the data. The research team suggested that the prework comparison activity prepared learners to learn more deeply from an explanation of the related concepts provided in the lecture.

Comparison as Lesson Practice

Gadgil et al. (2012) focused on teaching the correct double loop model of blood flow through the heart. First, they identified students with incorrect models, such as a single loop model. Their instructional goal was to correct misconceptions in these students. They tried two approaches. One group was shown a drawing of their flawed single loop model next to a drawing of a correct double loop model and was asked to compare the two drawings. A second group was shown only the correct double loop model and asked to explain it. On a post-test, those in the comparison group learned more.

The authors suggest that a comparison activity—especially one in which the learners compare their own flawed mental model with an expert model—helps learners correct misconceptions more than simply explaining a correct model.

Comparisons as Debriefs

A common technique in scenario-based learning is to track learner actions and then display those actions next to an expert trace. Figure 10-5 shows an example from a multimedia scenario-based learning course for automotive technicians. To promote reflection, the debriefing activity should ask learners to write a comparison of their approach to the expert approach.

Figure 10-5. Scenario Debrief Displays the Learner's Actions Next to Expert Actions and Asks Learners to Compare

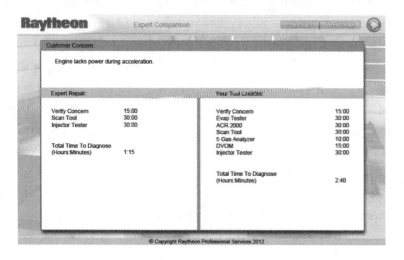

Source: Used with Permission from Raytheon Professional Services.

In summary, comparisons of data, examples, or models have proven effective as prework, training practice, and debrief. We need more evidence on these techniques, but the trend in the research available is the basis for this guideline.

Practice Guideline 5:

Assign comparison practice exercises to build relevant prior knowledge, to correct flawed or incomplete mental models, or to reflect on decisions made in a training scenario.

THE POWER OF FEEDBACK

Try a quick experiment. Close your eyes and on a piece of scratch paper, draw a line that is four inches long. Keep your eyes closed and practice by drawing five more lines that are four inches long. Do you think your line accuracy is better with your last attempt than at the start? Get a ruler and measure each line to see if you got more accurate with practice.

Now repeat the experiment. Close your eyes and draw a line four inches long. Then open your eyes and measure your line. Is it too long or short? Close your eyes and try again. After repeating this process several times, chances are your lines will get fairly close to the target of four inches. This experiment was first tried by Thorndike in the early part of the 20th century. Not surprisingly, Thorndike found that practice with no feedback did not improve performance.

Some tasks contain intrinsic feedback. By that I mean, you are able to immediately experience the results of your practice attempt. A good example is practice serving in tennis or entering a formula into a spreadsheet. As soon as you hit the ball you see where it goes. When you enter the formula correctly, you get no error message and you can see the results of your calculation. If the numbers are simple enough you can even confirm the accuracy of the calculation manually.

In contrast, other tasks may not provide immediate or obvious signs of successful outcomes. Consider learning how to input and refine search terms to locate relevant data in databases. You can input your search term and view the results. However, if you get only a few hits you won't know if it's because your term was not optimal, the databases you selected were not the best, or because there are not many items in the databases to satisfy your search. All practice exercises benefit from feedback. Even tasks with intrinsic feedback can benefit from feedback that helps the learners improve their response or correct errors.

What Is Feedback?

Feedback is information regarding the accuracy or technique of a practice response. It can be as simple as stating "right" or "incorrect" after a response. It can be as complex as a lengthy debrief of a simulated exercise in which instructors and participants review responses and discuss them in detail. Feedback can focus on the reason a response is correct or incorrect. It can also focus not only on the outcome but on the techniques used to achieve the outcome. For example, Figure 10-6 shows feedback from an online auto troubleshooting simulation that shows the learner's steps compared with an expert's steps.

Feedback can serve the following goals:

- to inform learners whether their responses are correct or incorrect

- to offer strategies, hints, examples—in other words, guidance to aid in arriving at a correct response

- to inform learners of the gaps between the instructional criteria and their own performance

- to inform learners of their own progress over time.

Perhaps it would be more accurate to use the term *feed forward* than feedback. In other words, by learning better strategies or considering ways to adjust techniques, feedback should have a future orientation looking toward the goal of improving skills on the next attempt and on the job.

Evidence on Feedback

Feedback is commonly recognized as an essential condition for efficient learning. In a comprehensive review of many meta-analyses, Hattie and Gan (2011) reported an average effect size of 0.79, which is high. However, not all feedback has proven effective. Kluger and DeNisi (1996) found that one-third of all feedback in the experiments they reviewed actually depressed learning! So the power of feedback comes down to factors, such as the type of feedback given, when feedback is given, as well as how the learner receives and processes the feedback.

Corrective v. Elaborative Feedback

The easiest kind of feedback is to simply tell learners that their responses are correct or incorrect. However, when Moreno (2004) compared this type of feedback to feedback that told learners whether they were right or wrong and gave them a brief explanation, the more detailed feedback led to better learning. In a learning game that focused on botany, she found that a comment such as, "Yes, in a low sunlight environment, a large leaf has more room to make food by photosynthesis," led to better learning than a response of "correct." Even when a response is correct, it may have been arrived at accidently at least in a multiple-choice or true-false type of question. Therefore, it's a good idea to elaborate on correct as well as incorrect responses.

The Focus of Feedback

Feedback should always focus the learner's attention to the task at hand and avoid directing attention to the ego. Even praise has come into disfavor because it tends to direct attention to the ego rather than on the task. Hattie and Yates (2014) contend: "We know of no research finding suggesting that receiving praise itself can assist a person to learn or to increase their knowledge and understanding" (p. 67). To ensure that feedback is reviewed and integrated, it should be given on work in progress with tips for improvement followed by another similar assignment. Furthermore, feedback that reflects progress over time leads to improved learning. My grandchildren's teacher posts writing samples for each child each month. Comparing the April writing of an individual child with the October writing gives dramatic evidence of growth over time—much better than comparing one child's writing with another.

Frequency of Feedback

Is it better to give feedback immediately after the learner responds or to delay feedback? Research is inconsistent on this question. The answer likely depends in part on the type of task involved in the training. For example, Corbalan et al. (2010) compared learning from feedback given at every step with that given at the solution stage in an algebra tutorial. You can see the learning and ratings results in Figure 10-6.

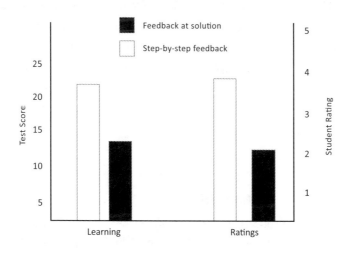

Figure 10-6. Effect of Frequency of Feedback in Mathematics on Learning and Student Ratings

Source: Based on data from Corbalan et al., 2010.

Keep in mind that in this math lesson, if a mistake were to be made at step 2 or 3, that mistake would cascade into an inaccurate final solution. Therefore, immediate feedback with each step was more effective. Perhaps in a more complex, problem-solving scenario designed for learners with some background experience, feedback would be more effective if delayed until the solution stage. For example, Kellogg and Whiteford (2009), in a review of best practices to build writing skills, suggest that specific suggestions for improvement on early drafts is most useful and that this type of feedback could be provided on an intermittent basis. In Figure 10-5, you see feedback presented at the solution stage. End-of-scenario feedback allows the learner to make mistakes along the way and then to learn from those mistakes at the conclusion of the exercise. We will need more research to be definitive about the best timing and placement of feedback for different instructional goals and learner backgrounds.

What About Peer Feedback?

In chapter 4 we reviewed a study that showed the learning benefits of peer review. The benefits were mostly reaped by the reviewers—those giving the reviews. Peer reviews can be used to supplement instructor feedback; however, the instructor will need to provide clear criteria and training before asking participants to engage in reviews. Further, the instructor should monitor all such reviews, adding any moderating comments needed.

The evidence we have on feedback is the basis for my next recommendation.

Practice Guideline 6:

Provide detailed task-specific feedback to practice exercises that explains why a response is correct or incorrect. Give feedback not only on outcomes but also on techniques and processes. For procedural tasks, provide step-by-step immediate feedback.

THE BOTTOM LINE

What Do You Think?

Now that you have reviewed the evidence, here are my responses to our initial questions.

A. The more practice, the better the learning.

It's *TRUE* that you get better learning with more practice. However, according to the power law of practice, the improvements will diminish over time. Although effective practice can lead to improved performance, the biggest skill gains accrue in the first few practice sessions. You will need to consider the criticality of the task and the need for automaticity as you weigh the return on investment of extensive practice.

B. Six practice exercises placed at the end of the lesson will lead to better learning than the same six exercises distributed throughout the lesson.

FALSE. Putting all of your practice in one spot in your lesson or course is not as effective as dispersing it throughout. We have ample evidence that practice spread out over a learning event leads to better long-term learning.

C. When teaching two topics, it's better to group practice questions according to topic than to mix questions for both topics in the same section.

FALSE. Although it will make the instructional event more challenging, you will get better learning from mixed practice. If your content includes concepts and strategic skills and it is important to determine when to use which, blend questions from the different topics to maximize learning.

D. "List the 5 steps to construct a formula in Excel" is an effective practice exercise.

FALSE. The Excel practice item is a regurgitate question. It asks for memorization and does not require any understanding. Because the job requires actual construction of formulas, a better use of instructional time is to ask learners to create formulas.

E. Effective feedback is corrective—it tells learners whether their response is right or wrong.

TRUE, but knowing whether your answer is correct or incorrect is necessary but not sufficient for full learning. The best type of feedback provides an explanation for why a response is correct or incorrect, which may include comments on techniques or problem-solving processes.

APPLYING PRACTICE TO YOUR TRAINING

How can you apply the research we've reviewed in this chapter to your own learning environment? First, remember that to learn a new skill does require practice; and depending on the criticality and complexity of the task, it may require a great deal of practice. However, practice is expensive and unless optimized, it may not give you a return on investment. As you plan your lessons and courses, apply the following guidelines:

- Resist the temptation to "cover" more material at the expense of practice opportunities.

- Create practice exercises that mirror the knowledge and skills of the work environment.

- Avoid "regurgitate" exercises that promote rote learning in favor of application exercises that incorporate the context of the job. Use realistic job scenarios as a springboard for practice questions.

- Adjust the amount of practice based on the criticality of the task performance and the need for automatic responses on the job.

- Distribute practice throughout your learning events. Take advantage of virtual learning environments to spread practice opportunities over time.

- Vary the context of practice when the goal is both how to perform a skill as well as knowing when to apply that skill. As you distribute your practice sessions among lessons mix the skills practiced and reap the benefits of spaced practice and varied context practice.

- Remember that practice in the absence of knowledge of outcomes fails to improve performance. Offer explanatory feedback to practice responses. For procedural tasks, step by step feedback is generally better than end-of-problem feedback.

- Focus feedback on the outcome of the practice as well as on the process or techniques used to reach the outcome.

- Move toward feed forward by using feedback to tell learners about their progress over time, to comment on work in progress, and to ask learners to revise based on feedback.

COMING NEXT

This chapter includes a summary of evidence on two of the most powerful tools to promote learning: examples and practice. In the next chapter we will review evidence on how to prepare and deliver effective explanations. From classroom instruction to multimedia lessons, explanations are a staple of just about all training. In chapter 11, we will review evidence-based guidelines regarding use of text, graphics, audio, examples, and engagement applied specifically to instructional explanations.

FOR MORE INFORMATION

Evans, C. (2013). Making Sense of Assessment Feedback in Higher Education. *Review of Educational Research* 83: 70-120.

A detailed technical review of 240 research articles focusing on feedback in higher education. Includes guidelines for effective feedback.

Hattie, J., and G. Yates. (2014). *Visible Learning and the Science of How We Learn.* New York: Routledge. (See chapter 8.)

A clearly written book that draws on the evidence regarding key instructional methods.

Kellogg, R.E., and A.P. Whiteford. (2009). Training Advanced Writing Skills: The Case for Deliberate Practice, *Educational Psychologist* 44: 250-266.

An interesting article on practice and feedback focused on an advanced skill.

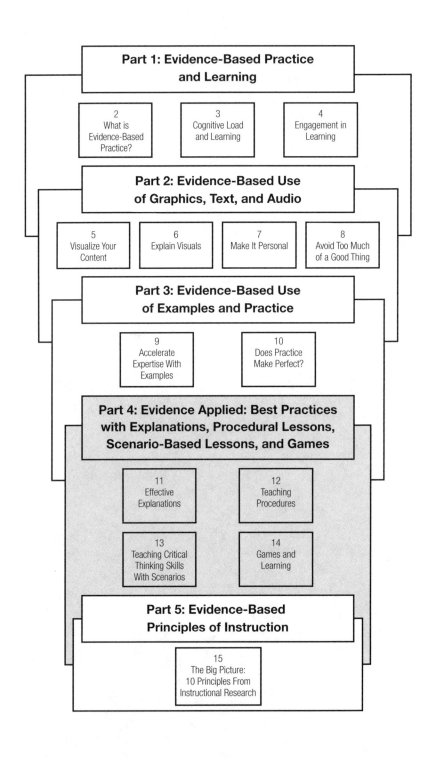

Part 1: Evidence-Based Practice and Learning

2
What is Evidence-Based Practice?

3
Cognitive Load and Learning

4
Engagement in Learning

Part 2: Evidence-Based Use of Graphics, Text, and Audio

5
Visualize Your Content

6
Explain Visuals

7
Make It Personal

8
Avoid Too Much of a Good Thing

Part 3: Evidence-Based Use of Examples and Practice

9
Accelerate Expertise With Examples

10
Does Practice Make Perfect?

Part 4: Evidence Applied: Best Practices with Explanations, Procedural Lessons, Scenario-Based Lessons, and Games

11
Effective Explanations

12
Teaching Procedures

13
Teaching Critical Thinking Skills With Scenarios

14
Games and Learning

Part 5: Evidence-Based Principles of Instruction

15
The Big Picture: 10 Principles From Instructional Research

PART 4

Evidence Applied: Best Practices With Explanations, Procedural Lessons, Scenario-Based Lessons, and Games

The previous chapters have summarized evidence on the basic communication modes of text, graphics, and audio, as well as the core instructional methods of examples and engagement. In this section we will apply many of the previous guidelines in the context of the kinds of instructional products you create. Just about all learning environments include explanations. Chapter 11 describes how to maximize the learning value of your explanations as well as ways to avoid common pitfalls. Chapter 12 is similar to chapter 11 with a specific focus on teaching procedural skills. Chapters 13 and 14 review high engagement instruction, including scenario-based e-learning and games. The goal of these chapters is to offer guidance on how to apply evidence-based strategies in the context of the instructional environments you design, develop, and deliver.

EFFECTIVE EXPLANATIONS

CHAPTER 11

Effective Explanations

If you have been in the training business for a while, no doubt you have heard the adage for instructors: "Move from sage on the stage to the guide on the side." This mantra and the expression, "death by PowerPoint," allude to the evolution from passive to active learning environments. The underlying premise is that learning environments that rely primarily or completely on instructional explanations are ineffective. However, we have evidence that when well designed, explanations are an effective instructional method. In addition, just about all forms of training rely to a greater or lesser extent on explanations.

In this chapter we will review research that focuses on explanations used for direct instruction. Some of the guidelines are based on evidence we have reviewed in previous chapters and some are new to this chapter. All of the techniques will focus on ways to get your learners engaged in your presentation. The most relevant explanation, if unattended, offers no benefit. Your goal is to prepare and deliver explanations that engage your learners. These guidelines apply to explanations delivered online in self-study lessons, in books, or classrooms—both virtual and in-person.

THE IMPORTANCE OF PRESENTATIONS

Presentations are ubiquitous—conferences, meetings, webinars, manuals, classroom and e-learning lessons. Worldwide, presentations are the most common method for training adults (Bligh, 2000). Some training events rely just about 100 percent on presentation alone. Other training events include presentations as one ingredient in the instructional mix. For example, a lecture with slides might be followed by a case study and discussion. Alternatively, an asynchronous online lesson might include brief narrated presentations followed by online activities.

I believe that explanations are one of the most used and abused instructional methods—often lacking techniques that promote learner engagement and subsequent learning. In spite of the hype on high engagement environments, such as games and scenario-based learning, I predict presentations will continue to dominate the instructional landscape either on their own or as part of a larger instructional event. They are fast. They are easy. They can be cheap to produce and efficient to distribute via the Internet. They allow the sponsoring organization to document that the content was "covered."

Because direct instruction based on explanations is a useful and ubiquitous instructional method, it's worthwhile to consider how to leverage it most effectively. There are plenty of books and resources full of tips and techniques for presentations. Unlike those resources, I will emphasize principled explanations that reflect research evidence in their planning, development, and delivery.

What Do You Think?

Place a check next to each statement you believe is true about explanations:

- ❏ A. Asking the audience to respond to questions with clickers during a lecture will improve learning.
- ❏ B. Explanations should rely heavily on visuals.
- ❏ C. You should add questions to instructional explanations.
- ❏ D. When it comes to explanations, less is often more.

WHAT IS A PRINCIPLED EXPLANATION?

A principled explanation is instructional content delivered via text, graphics, or audio that typically addresses the what, when, why, and how of a work domain. For example, in an Excel class, some topics might include: What is Excel? When might you use Excel? What are the basic components and functions of Excel? How do you use Excel to achieve the results you want? The explanation can be given in a face-to-face setting such as at a conference or in a classroom. The explanation might be delivered via text in a book or a combination of graphics and audio in a self-study computer lesson. Alternatively, explanation snippets may form the basis for embedded performance support. In order to keep experimental explanations consistent for comparison purposes, many of the research studies we will review used computer-delivered explanations. However, some studies are classroom based; and those that are not, generally report findings that can be applied to instructor-led training.

What are the key instructional features that distinguish a principled presentation from just a presentation? See Table 11-1 for a summary.

Table 11-1

FEATURE	DESCRIPTION
Engaging	Explanations intended for novice learners incorporate behavioral activites.
Visual	Explanations incorporate explanatory visuals and minimize decorative visuals.
Illustrated	Explanations include examples to demonstrate application of concepts, procedures, and principles.
Social	Explanations leverage social presence appropriate to the delivery medium.
Concise and Focused	The explanation is succinct and does not maunder.
Efficient	In a blended learning environment, explanations are delivered via computer or books, reserving classroom time for questions and activities that leverage social presence.
Individualized	Explanations are adjusted for learners with lower or higher levels of prior knowledge.

GUIDELINE 1: INCORPORATE QUESTIONS

Since the first edition of this book, several research studies have focused on how best to actively engage learners in your explanations. The main guideline to emerge from these studies is: Add questions! Let's take a look at some specific questioning methods.

Use Clickers in the Classroom

A clicker is a handheld device (perhaps soon to be replaced by smartphones) that allows the learners to select a number or letter in response to a question. Typically the instructor will project a multiple-choice question on a slide. After most students have made their selections, the instructor projects the aggregated responses in the form of a bar or pie chart and facilitates a discussion about the various options.

What evidence do we have that using clickers during presentations improves learning? Mayer, Stull et al. (2009) compared learning from three groups taking a college-level educational psychology class. One group responded to two to four questions per lecture with a clicker. After viewing the group responses, the instructor discussed the reasons for the correct answer. A second group (no clicker group) received the same questions but did not make any overt response. A control group attended the lectures with no questions. The clicker group gained approximately one-third of a grade point more than the other two groups, which did not differ from one another. In this experiment, a behavioral response led to better psychological activity than hearing questions with no response requirement. Perhaps in the no clicker group the questions were heard but not deeply processed because there was no active response requirement. The benefits of clickers have also been demonstrated by Shapiro and Gordon (2012) and Anderson et al. (2013). Active responses to relevant questions during a classroom presentation do improve learning.

Virtual classrooms offer multiple opportunities for responses during explanations. As you can see in Figure 11-1, the typical virtual classroom interface offers response tools including polling, chat, whiteboard markup, and audio. As with any technology, instructors can ignore these features and deliver a passive explanation. The effect can be soporific. In response, the audience can and will easily and unobtrusively minimize the virtual classroom window and focus on other activities.

Figure 11-1. The Virtual Classroom Offers Many Opportunities for Overt Engagement

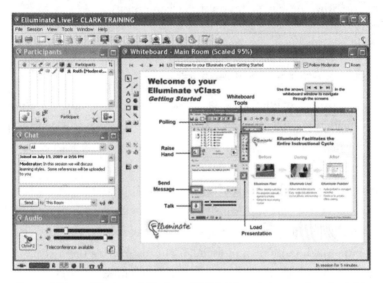

Source: From Clark and Kwinn, 2007 Material reproduced with permission John Wiley & Sons.

Follow Explanations With Questions

Imagine you have written an explanation for an asynchronous computer lesson or a book. Would learning from your explanation be improved if you added questions to it? Roelle, Berthold, and Renkl (2013) developed a computer lesson on the topic of management theory. Following an explanation of five to seven sentences, some learners answered questions in a box placed on the screen next to the explanation. For example, one question asked: "Why are whole tasks a good prerequisite for handling local problems in an organization?" Other learners received the same explanation minus the questions. Their screen also included a blank box; but rather than a question, they were instructed to write down their thoughts about the explanations.

The research team compared a 10-question post-test score, as well as the number of inferences each group made in the notes box during the lesson. Learners who answered inserted questions had written many more inferences in the note box and scored significantly better on the post-test, compared with those who did not receive questions.

Do All Learners Benefit From
Questions After an Explanation?

In the previous paragraphs we saw that adding meaningful questions to your explanations will improve learning. However, does this benefit apply to all learners? We have preliminary evidence that novice learners gain the most benefit. We saw a similar pattern in chapters 2 and 9 on graphics and worked examples. These powerful instructional methods are most beneficial as mental support mechanisms for those with minimal prior knowledge. For individuals with prior knowledge, additional support does not contribute much more than individuals already provide themselves; and in some cases, it interferes with what they already know.

To determine whether adding questions to explanations would have different effects on learners with high and low prior knowledge, two different studies created "experts" by giving half of the students additional instructional materials. For example, in one study the "basic" text of 684 words and three graphics was expanded to 1,139 words and eight illustrations. This enhanced lesson was used to build higher levels of expertise compared with the basic text. Next, "experts" who received the more detailed text and "novices" who received only the basic text were given explanations with or without questions.

One experiment focused on use of a statistical analysis program (Rey and Fischer, 2013) and the other (Roelle and Berthold, 2013) used the management content described in previous paragraphs. In both experiments, novices benefited by receiving questions but experts did not. Adding questions provides a source of external guidance that is helpful for novices but not for those with more expertise.

Psychological Activity During Presentations

There are some presentations devoid of behavioral interactivity that are nevertheless effective for learning. In these situations your presentation promotes psychological processing in the absence of behavioral responses. Presentations that are brief and targeted to an experienced audience motivated to learn the content can be effective without overt audience response. For example, medical residents rated a standard one-hour lecture higher than a more interactive session that included discussion (Haidet et al., 2004). Furthermore, learning was about the same from both versions. The medical residents had sufficient context and interest to process the content of the lecture in the absence of overt activity.

In summary, a well-organized, noninteractive presentation that uses engagement methods, such as visuals or rhetorical questions followed by Q and A, can be effective in brief timeframes when targeted for an experienced and focused audience.

GUIDELINE 2: INCORPORATE RELEVANT VISUALS

I reviewed solid evidence in chapters 2, 5, and 8 regarding the power of visuals to promote learning. A useful visual is one that shows the relationships among ideas in the presentation. For example, the graphic map of this book included with the part introductions offers a quick way to see the location and relationships among sections and chapters. For more details on effective visuals, please refer to the chapters indicated.

GUIDELINE 3: INCORPORATE EXAMPLES AND MODELS

We saw the power of examples to accelerate expertise in chapter 9. If your goal is to build problem-solving or other complex skills, you can dissect the appropriate behaviors by observing experts and defining specific problem-solving sub-skills. For example, Figure 11-2 includes a partial list of thinking skills defined for a history class. Rather than teach a series of history facts, the goal of the lessons was to teach how to review source documents to derive credible historical conclusions. The instructor used five teaching sessions to explain each strategy and to model each technique. Compared to classes that were not given explicit guidelines and examples, the experimental group wrote final test essays that were longer, more accurate, and more persuasive (De La Paz and Felton, 2010).

Figure 11-2. A Partial List of Analytic Strategies to Apply to Historical Source Documents

STRATEGY	QUESTIONS
Consider the author	1. What do you know about the author? 2. When was the document written? 3. How did the author know about the event?
Understand the source	1. What type of document is this? 2. Why was it written? 3. What assumptions underlie the argument?
Critique the source	For each source: 1. What evidence does the author give? 2. Are there errors? 3. Is anything missing from the arguments?

Source: Adapted from De La Paz and Felton, 2010.

Don't underestimate the power of skill modeling. But first be sure that you have identified appropriate skill models based on expert observations.

Then spend time providing explanations and models (demonstrations) of each sub-skill followed by ample practice. In other words, you can demonstrate problem-solving skills in much the same way that you would demonstrate a procedural skill. During problem-solving demonstrations, show the actions an expert would take, but also incorporate her thoughts—giving learners access to expert rationale. You could use a thought bubble in multimedia learning or print materials. This technique will implement a cognitive worked example as discussed in chapter 9.

GUIDELINE 4: MAKE YOUR EXAMPLES AND MODELS INTERACTIVE

For maximum benefit make your examples interactive. To follow is a brief review of techniques discussed in chapter 9.

1. Add Self-Explanation Questions

As you present an example, add questions linked to one or more steps in your illustration that require the learner to 1) attend to the example and 2) process it at a meaningful level.

2. Use Completion Examples

After showing perhaps one or two complete examples, you can provide additional examples that omit one or more of the final steps for the learner to finish.

3. Ask Learners to Compare Examples

This technique might be especially useful when your goal is to discriminate among two or more related approaches to a problem or instances of a concept. Display two examples and ask learners to identify the similarities and differences between them. For example, in a management class, you may show two videos—one illustrating a directive approach to management and the other a facilitative approach. After viewing each video, learners can construct a list of differences as well as discuss when one approach might be more effective than another.

4. Ask Learners to Compare Their Solution Approaches With an Expert Approach

Gadgil et al. (2012) identified students who held an inaccurate view of how the heart circulates blood. The research goal was to determine how best to correct these misconceptions. Half of these students were shown their own drawing illustrating an incorrect model next to a correct drawing and asked to write a comparison of the two. The other half reviewed and explained a correct model. The learners who compared their flawed model to a correct model learned more. Figure 10-5 (chapter 10) illustrates a multimedia case study in which the learner compared her solution steps against expert solution steps and wrote an explicit comparison of the two. This research suggests that learning is better when learners actively compare their own steps or products with expert steps or products.

5. Initiate an Explanation With a Discussion of an Example or Counter Example

Figure 11-3 shows a slide from a presentation I make on evidence-based e-learning. The screenshot links to a brief multimedia lesson on Excel, which violates most of the major guidelines of my explanation. I show the counter-example demonstration during my introduction and ask attendees to grade it and to discuss their grade in a small group. In a large face-to-face session, the discussion takes place in small buzz groups; and in a virtual session, participants talk in breakout rooms. Alternatively, you could make a similar assignment as a prework exercise. Ask individual learners to review examples and write up their own comparisons. Then in a synchronous setting, initiate a review and critique of the examples. Use this activity to launch an explanation of the critical features of the examples relevant to your instructional goals.

Figure 11-3. A Counter Example Serves as a Kickoff Activity

Grade this sample (A–F) and state your reasons.

Source: Example created by Frank Nguyen.

Show examples not only at the beginning but also throughout your presentation. Examples establish relevance, are concrete, and serve as a bridge from the content to the brain. Maximize the benefit of your examples by asking participants to respond to them. See chapter 9 for additional ideas to make your examples interactive.

GUIDELINE 5: LEVERAGE SOCIAL PRESENCE

Humans have an ancient imperative to learn from observation and talking with other humans. Our social nature is an evolutionary feature that can be profitably leveraged in instruction. Social presence in the classroom arises from communication between the audience and the instructor as well as among audience members. The instructor should leverage social presence by looking and sounding "approachable" rather than "on a pedestal." An available instructor is one of the features of any learning event shown to correlate with higher course ratings (Sitzmann et al., 2008) and with better learning (Mayer, 2009). A win-win! Specifically, the instructor should use a conversational tone and language, smile and maintain eye contact in a physical setting, speak to individual learners in smaller settings, reveal his own opinions or experiences relevant to the content, invite questions and comments, and encourage interactions among the attendees such as brief buzz groups. In short, audience ratings and learning will be higher when the instructor is a learning host. A good host makes the guests feel comfortable with him and with other guests.

Social Presence Online

You don't need to have an in-person class to leverage social presence. In chapter 7 we reviewed the personalization effect in detail and found you can improve learning by using first- and second-person language and online learning agents. The most recent evidence suggests that agents are most effective when they stimulate human social responses through realistic gesture and eye contact.

GUIDELINE 6: KEEP EXPLANATIONS CONCISE AND FOCUSED

I recall hearing a conference attendee in the elevator after my presentation on cognitive load theory. He was unaware that I was one of the many in the crowd on their way to the next session. "Gosh", he said, "I don't really know what she said but I know it's really important stuff!" When I reviewed my hour-long presentation I realized that my 120-slide lecture was way too ambitious for the timeframe and the attendees. Like a typical subject matter expert, I had tried to squeeze in just about everything I knew about cognitive load theory. Over time, I've gotten more disciplined in my presentations—and in my writing—by weeding out extra topics, tossing irrelevant examples and stories, and skipping or adapting activities that are too ambitious for the time allotted. Rather than "cheating" attendees, I do them a favor when I implement the "less is more" principle.

Most of us have an attention span of about 15 to 20 minutes before our minds start to wander (Hattie and Yates, 2014). This suggests that you make explanations concise. Try for explanations of 15 minutes or less, write short chapters, and design e-learning lessons of 10 minutes or less. Of course, most training classes are based on increments of hours and days. So the wise instructor or instructional designer mixes it up. For example, a pre-exercise is followed by an explanation of 10 minutes, interactive modeling examples, and then a practice activity. Breaks are inserted at regular intervals. Instructor-led sessions embed a chorography of activity ranging from listening, movement into small groups and then back into a larger group setting.

CREATING PRINCIPLED EXPLANATIONS

A "successful" principled explanation is the offspring of 60 percent planning and development prior to the event, 20 percent delivery proficiency, and 20 percent environmental and situation-specific factors, such as the physical setting, the audience, the technology, and so on.

I could write a whole book on the details associated with each of these phases. But others have written such books. Instead, I summarize common presentation problems in the four key phases of presentation development: 1) scoping the event, 2) planning the presentation, 3) developing the presentation materials, and 4) delivering the presentation.

WHAT CAN GO WRONG AT THE SCOPING PHASE

Scoping involves up-front research and reflection regarding the intended purpose of your explanation, features of your audience, time allotted, and presentation media and context. Some common problems that emerge from either failure to scope or getting incomplete, inaccurate scoping data are detailed in the following section.

Wrong Goals for a Presentation

Have you ever tried to achieve goals in a presentation that would have been better realized by other instructional methods? Your sponsor may impose unrealistic goals; for example, teach a group how to respond to a production plant emergency in a 30-minute lecture. When fielding inappropriate requests from clients, respond by offering more appropriate alternatives that may not even involve training. My colleague Chopeta Lyons has a great response to clients with ill-advised requests: "Yes, I can do that. But I would be remiss if I did not tell you . . ."(continue on to explain why the approach won't work).

Goals Don't Fit Audience Needs or Timeframe

Are your goals too ambitious (or too watered down) for the time allotted and the audience? I told you about my overly detailed presentation on cognitive load theory. It had way too many details and too many slides for a one-hour presentation. By the way, I've seen the opposite as well— under-developed presentations that had too little meat for the timeframe and audience. I have generally erred on the side of too much rather than too little. In so doing, I mentally flag some content as optional, which can be adapted to each situation. For example, if there is relevant participant discussion that eats into your presentation time, I will generally encourage that discussion and skip some of my slides.

Irrelevant Goals

Will your presentation goals be relevant to the audience's context or background? Irrelevant presentation goals got me fired! I was commissioned by an equipment manufacturer to teach a one-day session on the psychology of learning and evidence-based training methods. The audience was field staff—primarily sales people who also had collateral training duties. I had asked them to bring a sample lesson with them—thinking that reviewing their samples would make the session relevant. When I asked for a show of hands as to who had brought a lesson with them, guess what? Not one!

The presentation bombed completely. That particular audience had not the slightest interest in learning psychology or training techniques. Nor was there any accountability for their learning. I finally abandoned my script and asked the participants to meet in groups and list their main training challenges. My goal was to respond to their agenda rather than force mine. Unfortunately, this activity resulted in lists of complaints about how the central training staff (my sponsors) made their lives miserable. Things deteriorated from there.

WHAT CAN GO WRONG AT THE PLANNING PHASE

During planning you get specific about the overall organization of your presentation, the components of your introduction, and what kinds of activities you will include. Three common presentation frameworks are summarized in Figure 11-4. Of course, there are others, and also you can mix and match these. The point is to select an organizing framework that best matches what you discovered during your scoping research—especially the purpose of the explanation. Once you have a rough idea of your overall scheme, pay special attention to planning the introduction. Getting off to a good start is perhaps the single most important presentation event; it's hard to get an audience back once they are gone—either physically or mentally.

Figure 11-4. Three Common Organizational Schemes for Presentations

SCHEME	DIAGRAM	BENEFITS
Hierarchy	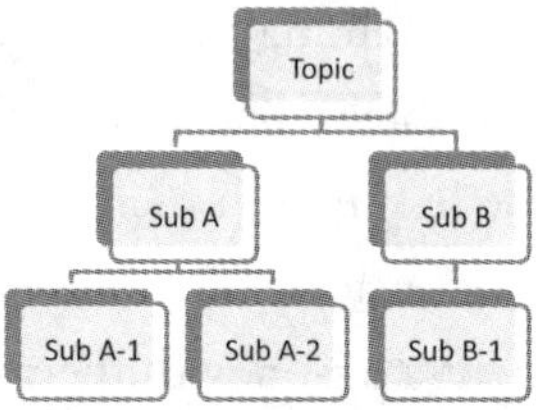	Logical Clarity of relationships Good for complex information Good for related content
Scenario-Based	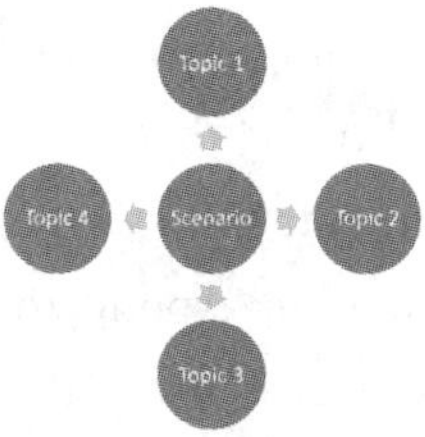	Can establish relevance Useful to set context Engaging to participants
Sequential		Nice for case study approach Adapts to a narrative approach Good for time-based or cause-effect content

Common problems with presentation introductions include the following.

Audience Confusion

Will your attendees immediately understand what the presentation is about, what it might accomplish, or how it will be organized? If not, they have no framework and no basis for deciding if it's relevant to their needs. Confusion may be the result of a divagating presentation with insufficient structure or failure to communicate the structure to the audience.

Death by Speaker Introduction

Well-intended event hosts can take up to 15 minutes of your allotted speaking time with various housekeeping, acknowledgment, and marketing duties, as well as with a lengthy speaker introduction often read word for word. In the interest of time, I usually ask my host to let me make my own introduction. Keep your personal introduction very succinct. At the start of a presentation, no one is that interested in your company, its products, your detailed educational history, your grandchildren, and so on. I recommend just a single slide that establishes your credibility and expertise on your topic. As the presentation evolves you can insert information about yourself and in that way build a more natural relationship.

No Visual Interest

The worst case is an explanation with no visuals. There are no slides, or the slides are walls of words. There are a few talented speakers who can command and sustain attention through their voice and narrative alone. But for the purpose of learning, even a talented speaker can get a better result by using effective visuals. Be visual from the start. I like a title slide like the one in Figure 11-5 that uses a visual to generate interest, spark curiosity, and convey the theme of the session.

Figure 11-5. A Visual Title Slide Engages From the Start

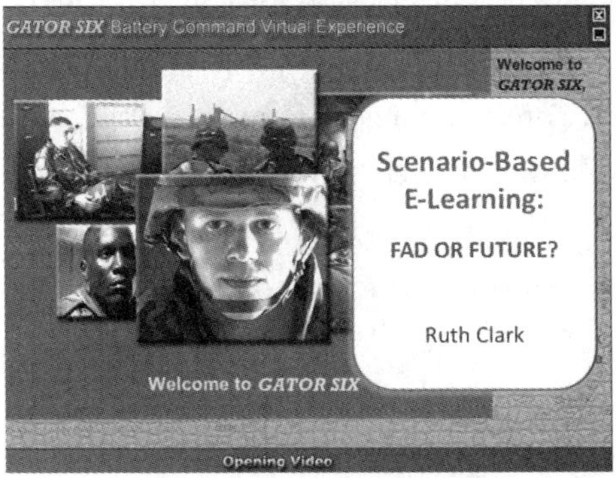

Source: Used with permission from Wills Interactive.

No Audience Engagement

Whether you are working with 20 or 120 people, insert some opportunities for overt engagement. You could use clickers, show of hands, buzz groups, and mini activities. Plan responses that require the attendees to connect your explanation to their own work domains. My presentations usually focus on evidence-based guidelines. I typically will show two or three lesson samples and ask participants to select the one they think is most effective. Next I show the research evidence. Most are interested to see if their initial selections were correct. Later I ask them to evaluate their own instructional environments for application of evidence-based principles.

WHAT CAN GO WRONG AT THE PREPARATON PHASE

Now your presentation plan comes to life. You are creating slides, writing handouts, jotting down talking points. Development is the incarnation of your scoping and planning phases. At this stage you will confront many questions. How many slides to produce? Should you have a handout? If yes, what type? What kinds of presenter notes to develop? Here are some common mis-steps during development.

Death by PowerPoint

How many slides should you develop for your presentation? Presentations such as classroom lectures or webinars are paced by the presenter—not the learners. Therefore, presentations run greater risk of causing mental overload than self-paced media, such as books or asynchronous e-learning. Too many complex slides can overload the learner. Alternatively, too few slides can fail to sustain attention due to lack of visual interest and stagnation.

I know of no evidence supporting any specific metric for numbers of slides. In my own presentations I average one slide per minute. So for an hour-long conference session, I'll typically develop 55 to 75 slides. This does not mean I necessarily show one slide every minute. During a short activity a single slide might remain in place for several minutes. During an explanation, I might have six slides for one topic and two for another. You will need to consider the complexity of the topic, the background of your audience, and what audience activities you plan as well as when and where you anticipate questions. I recommend you build in some extra slides which you can skip during the presentation if you run out of time.

Handouts

Handouts can be any kind of guide, physical or online, for the participants to use. There are many options for guides, and Table 11-2 summarizes the benefits and drawbacks of the most common alternatives. Often, guides consist of copies of the slides. That is certainly the easiest route for the presenter; however, slides are typically only part of the story and often omit major chunks of content. Consider alternatives even though they will take more time. For example, rather than (or in addition to) slides posted online, consider a text summary, annotated slides, references, or a job aid to help attendees apply the ideas of the presentation later.

Table 11-2		
FORMAT	**BENEFITS**	**DRAWBACKS**
Slides	Participants like them. Easy for speaker to prepare. Keep participants oriented.	Will require participant note taking. Can waste a lot of paper if hardcopy. Usually a poor reference resource.
Text Outlines	Easy for speaker to prepare. Provides an organizer. Consume less paper if hardcopy.	Generally less popular than slides. Will require participant note taking. Usually a poor reference resource.
Detailed Notes	Minimize note taking. Provide a useful reference.	More work for presenter. Can consume a lot of paper if hardcopy. Participants may get lost in presentation.
Mixed: Slides + Text	Popular Can be useful reference. Minimize note taking. Guide participants.	More work for presenter. Can consume a lot of paper if hardcopy.
Articles	Popular Can be useful for reference. Easy for speaker if already published.	Usually lack direct correspondence with presentation so audience gets lost. Can consume a lot of paper if hardcopy.

As you can see in Table 11-2, there is no single best handout. Your handout format will depend on the following:

- Do you want to provide a useful reference resource? Slides alone are incomplete and don't usually make good references.

- Do you want the attendees to devote full attention to your presentation? Slides alone will encourage note taking and in many situations lead to split attention.

- How much time and resource investment can be devoted to adjunct guides? Concise guides are more popular.

- Is your goal skill building? A job aid should be included.

- What is your context: conference, meeting, or class? Each benefits from a different type of guide.

Many conference organizers will dictate the type of handout to contribute (which will be slides in most cases). For classes or smaller presentations you will need to consider the factors in Table 11-2 to make a good decision. I typically prepare a handout for a class with tables summarizing the content and checklists to serve as job aids. I also include brief engagement activities.

WHAT CAN GO WRONG AT THE DELIVERY PHASE?

Imagine that you have invested sufficient time and effort planning and developing. You have a solid presentation. But at "show time" it's up to the speaker to breathe life into the event. What can go wrong the day and hour of the event?

Technical Glitches

You know the saying: What can go wrong, will. Technology can let you down. When presenting at a physical or virtual event, use your own computer and double check that it has the needed capacity and software for your presentation. Bring a second copy of the presentation on a memory stick in case you need to use a backup computer. Second, insist on a rehearsal prior to the event. Test everything. Third, don't include unreliable technology as part of your event. Depending on the setting, I may be reluctant to access the Internet as a critical part of my presentation. Even in our advanced Internet age, connectivity in the presentation room can be poor or the Internet may go down. At a minimum, have a backup of essential screen captures. Fourth, always have a plan B for critical elements of your presentation. If a multimedia presentation fails, revert to backup screen captures or substitute a different presentation. When giving virtual classroom sessions, I always send the event sponsor a copy of my slides and make a paper copy for myself. That way if I lose connectivity (it has happened to me more than once), the sponsor can load the slides allowing me to continue my presentation (on a telephone) referencing my printed copy.

Getting Derailed

Have you ever been thrown off your presentation plan? It's easy to get off track during the actual presentation. Meandering speakers and audience questions are two common culprits. Good planning and development should help with meandering. I usually print out thumbnails of my slides and write time guidelines in them. For example, I mark the slide where I should be at the halfway point. I prefer to invite audience questions during the presentation in most cases. It's part of being a good host. And it helps you see where you are or are not connecting. The trick is to use your responses to audience questions to forward your presentation agenda by adding an example, clarifying, or briefly discussing a different facet of your topic. Often you can use audience questions to lead to your next point.

The Inflexible Speaker

I told you about my presentation from hell. I should have abandoned my entire plan much earlier and asked the participants what they would like to know or do. Most situations are not that dire. A common problem is too little time for your agenda. It's always good to have some optional slides as part of a presentation. If questions are raised or an activity takes longer than anticipated, skip the extra slides. It is important to stick to 80 percent or more of the agenda, which has usually been published ahead and which is presented as part of the introduction. But good planning leaves your presentation scalable—you can skip some of the detail without short changing your agenda.

No Social Presence

If you can arrive early, take advantage of the wait time to meet and greet your attendees. Smile. It's simple but speakers are often nervous or concentrating on their performance and they forget to smile and look the audience in the eye. Use a conversational approach. Don't read a script. Build up passion for your topics—it will come through in your voice, words, and body language. Finally, never "take on" an audience member who voices a disagreement with your thesis. Always say thank you for the contribution and respond with either a clarification or a noncommittal statement such as: "Well, that's another way to look at it," or, "Hmm, it would be interesting to test out that idea."

SPIRAL V. LINEAR PRESENTATION DEVELOPMENT

I don't want to leave the impression that each phase summarized above proceeds in a linear manner. Good presentations, like all training events, typically evolve over time and over iterations. You pick up techniques by attending other presentations; you get ideas from ongoing research; you assess the strengths and weaknesses of your presentation from audience input. Don't wait until a week before a deadline to start working on your presentation. Plan and draft ahead giving yourself the opportunity to revisit and expand on your initial ideas.

THE BOTTOM LINE

What Do You Think?

Now that you have reviewed the evidence, check off each statement you believe is true:

❏ **A. Asking the audience to use clickers to respond to questions during a classroom lecture will improve learning.**
Using clickers is one technique proven to promote learning during a lecture. There are many others that you can consider, such as show of hands, buzz sessions, as well as polling and chat in virtual settings.

❏ **B. Explanations should rely heavily on visuals.**
We have seen the value of visuals to illustrate explanations in chapters 2 and 5. However, for maximum benefit the visuals should be relevant rather than decorative, simple rather than complex, and used more extensively in explanations for novice learners.

❏ **C. You should add questions to instructional explanations.**
Adding questions to explanations delivered via text or computer has been shown to benefit novices but to have minimal benefits for learners with prior knowledge.

❏ **D. When it comes to explanations, less is often more.**
Remember that human adult attention spans about 10 to 15 minutes. Therefore option D is especially true in settings in which explanations are presented outside the pacing control of the learner such as a classroom explanation.

APPLYING EVIDENCE-BASED TECHNIQUES TO YOUR EXPLANATIONS

Use this checklist as a guide when developing and delivering presentations. Add your own lessons learned to this list:

❏ The explanation is accompanied by questions that stimulate job-relevant processing of the content.

❏ The explanation is illustrated by relevant visuals.

❏ The explanation is supplemented by interactive examples and models.

❏ The explanation is concise and incorporates attention boosters, such as questions, short discussions, and breaks.

❏ The speaker invites social presence through a conversational approach, informal body language, and responses to questions.

❏ The goals of the presentation are realistic and achievable within the timeframe allowed.

❏ Handouts help the participants follow the presentation logic and provide follow-up reference.

COMING NEXT

Many training environments focus on teaching procedures, which are tasks that are performed more or less the same way each time, such as logging into a software application. Chapter 12 focuses specifically on the tools and techniques that best teach procedures, and includes a general template for procedural lessons that you can adapt to your own context.

FOR MORE INFORMATION

Clark, R.C., and A. Kwinn. (2007). *The New Virtual Classroom*. San Francisco: Pfeiffer.

We included a number of techniques to support high engagement in the virtual classroom in this book.

Eysink, et al. (2009). Learner Performance in Multimedia Learning Arrangements: An Analysis Across Instructional Approaches. *American Educational Research Journal* 46: 1107-1149.

Consider a deeper dive by reviewing this rather lengthy technical article. It compares learning from four different multimedia designs, including hyper-media learning, observational learning, self-explanation-based learning, and inquiry learning.

Hattie, J., and G. Yates. (2014). Acquiring Complex Skills Through Social Modeling and Explicit Teaching. *In Visible Learning and the Science of How We Learn*. Routledge: New York.

I recommend this book to all instructional professionals because it includes a synthesis of evidence that focus on a number of the topics I've outlined in this book.

Wittwer, J., and A. Renkl. (2008). Why Instructional Explanations Often Do Not Work: A Framework for Understanding the Effectiveness of Instructional Explanations. *Educational Psychologist* 43: 49-64.

I found this to be a very helpful review of evidence-based techniques that can make explanations effective.

TEACHING PROCEDURES

CHAPTER 12

Teaching Procedures

- Give the learner immediate feedback.
- Break down the task into small steps.
- Repeat the directions as many times as possible.
- Work from the most simple to the most complex tasks.
- Give positive reinforcement.

—Technology of Teaching (Skinner, 1968)

Sound familiar? These instructional prescriptions were written in the 1960s by Skinner, the father of behaviorist psychology. Behaviorism is the source for the core instructional methods for teaching procedures using a directive or part-task design.

In this chapter, we will draw on the proven guidelines reviewed in previous chapters to apply them to lessons that use a directive approach most appropriate for teaching procedures. Specifically we will review: 1) the components of and evidence for effective directive lessons and 2) what can go wrong in directive lessons. We will also look at recent research on design of performance support for procedural tasks.

WHAT ARE PROCEDURES?

Procedures are routine tasks that are performed more or less the same way each time. Some examples include many software tasks, taking routine customer orders, taking blood pressure, and equipment start-up tasks. In contrast to procedures are non-routine or strategic tasks that require problem solving and adjustment for effective results. Some examples of strategic tasks include troubleshooting unusual failures, many sales and customer service tasks, and diagnostic problem solving, to name a few.

Many jobs include a combination of procedural and strategic tasks. Routine operations may rely on procedures while unusual occurrences depend on strategic tasks. Sometimes similar tasks may be trained as procedures or as strategic tasks depending on the organizational context. For example, fast food restaurants generally have a high turnover of relatively low-skilled staff. Their goal is a fast, consistent, and safe product. They rely on a procedural approach to food preparation based on a combination of training and performance aids. In contrast, chef training takes a more strategic approach by teaching the economics, aesthetics, and safety of food preparation. The trained chef can create unique and cost effective menu options that maximize the flavor and appearance using ingredients available to him. In the next chapter, we will focus on techniques for teaching strategic tasks that involve judgment and problem solving.

The best approach to teaching procedural skills is a design called direct or part-task instruction. Direct instruction includes three core elements: explanations (as summarized in the previous chapter), demonstrations of skills, and student practice with feedback.

What Do You Think?

Place a check next to each statement you believe is true about directive lessons. Hint: If you have read previous chapters you should know many of these answers.

❑ A. Learning is better when topics are presented in small chunks.
❑ B. Learning is better when facts or concepts related to a procedure are sequenced prior to task steps.
❑ C. Performance support for procedures is most effective when steps are presented visually rather than in text.
❑ D. Learning is better when practice exercises are distributed throughout directive lessons.

THE ANATOMY OF A DIRECTIVE LESSON

A typical directive lesson includes a highly guided series of short topics with practice and feedback for each topic, concluding with the task steps. Directive lessons can be effectively designed for classroom or e-learning (synchronous and asynchronous). Because the "tell and show" parts of the lesson are usually delivered by a presentation either in the classroom or online, many of the techniques I described in the previous chapter on explanations apply to directive lessons.

I divide directive lessons into three main parts: introduction, supporting topics with practice and feedback, and lesson task with practice and feedback. Note that for some purposes, elements of a procedural lesson may be used as performance support linked to a software or hardware task. For the purpose of performance support, one or more of the three elements summarized here may be truncated or even omitted completely.

THE LESSON INTRODUCTION

The lesson introduction is critical to set the stage for learning and motivation. Don't shortchange it. You need to accomplish several goals, which I illustrate in my Excel sample classroom lesson handout in Figure 12-1. First, learners need to know the anticipated outcome and road map of the lesson. I use the learning objectives and lesson overview for this purpose. Second, learners need to see the relevance and work-related context for what they are about to learn. For an Excel lesson, I would use a simple demonstration illustrating how a formula automatically updates calculation results when spreadsheet data are changed. A good technique for the relevance and context portion of the introduction is to show the benefits of the lesson skills in a work setting. This can be through a "What went wrong?" or a "What went right?" demonstration, scenario, video, or data. Third, the introduction should activate relevant prior knowledge stored in long-term memory. This can be accomplished by starting the lesson with some review questions from prior lessons, presenting an analogy, or initiating a discussion about participant previous experiences related to the instructional goal. For example, in a management lesson on using Excel for budgeting, an introductory discussion could focus on previous budgeting challenges either at home or in a work context.

The introduction should be concise, informative, and promote active engagement of participants. As a result, learners should know the expected outcomes and road map of the lesson, appreciate the relevance of the skills to their work, and have conscious awareness of related prior knowledge or experience.

Figure 12-1. An Introduction Page in an Excel Training Manual

Lesson 2
Using Formulas in Excel

Introduction   In this lesson you will apply the power of Excel formulas allowing fast and accurate updates to your spreadsheets.

Importance   Have you ever added a long column of numbers only to have to change one number and then recalculate the whole column? Watch the demonstration to see how an Excel formula can save you time with updated calculations.

Lesson Overview   In this lesson we will learn to use formulas and graph the results of the calculations. Along the way you will learn to:

1. use cell references
2. format formulas to achieve calculation goals
3. input formulas into the spreadsheet
4. create bar and pie charts for your results.

Lesson Objective   You will input the correct formula to achieve calculation goals and graph the results.

Order of Topics   This lesson includes the following topics:

Topic	See Page
Cell references	4
Exercise 2-1: Name that cell	5
Formula formats	6
Exercise 2-2: Using formulas	7
How to enter a formula	8
Exercise 2-3: Enter formulas	9
How to create a charts and graphs	10
Exercise 2-4: Create charts for your data	

THE SUPPORTING TOPICS

One of the characteristic features of a directive design is the sequencing of the main supporting topics prior to the steps to perform a task. As you can see in the order of topics at the bottom of Figure 12-1, the Excel lesson sequenced two main topics: Cell references and formula formats prior to the steps of entering a formula and creating a chart. Most main supporting topics involve "What is it?" content along with any facts related to that topic. "What is it?" knowledge is best taught by tell (give an explanation usually in the form of a definition or description), show (give some examples), followed by practice (identify a valid example from samples or produce a valid example), and feedback.

In Figures 12-2 and 12-3 you can see the workbook pages for the "What is it?" lesson topic: formula formats. The explanation summarizes the key elements of a formula. The three examples incorporate all of the elements in various legal combinations. Remember from chapter 9, evidence recommends adding questions to examples to ensure their processing. I use that technique here in the section labeled "format questions." The goal of these questions is to encourage learners to review the examples carefully and induce some critical rules such as "all formulas begin with an equal sign." Following the tell and show sections, I added some important rules (facts) about order of operations along with a mnemonic to help recall the correct sequence.

Figure 12-2. Handout for Excel Supporting Topic

Formula Formats

Parts	Excel formulas can include the following elements: • equal sign (required) • cell references • operators (+, -, *, /) • numbers • parentheses
Examples	= C3 + D6 - (E 9 + 6) = E4*B3/12 = A3/B4*G5

Format Questions	Look at the samples above:
	1. How do all formulas start?
	2. There are four possible operators. What does each mean:
	   + means
	   - means
	   * means
	   / means
	3. What is the result of the second equation if E4 has a value of 4 and B3 has a value of 6?

Order of Operations	= A3*B4/D2+ 3 When A3 = 2 B4 = 3 D2 = 4 Does this mean 6 divided by 7 OR 2 multiplied by 3/7?
Clue	Use this clue to help you remember the order of operations: PDMAS: Prices Drop Most at Sales First calculation: Any elements in parentheses Second calculation: Division Third calculation: Multiplication Fourth calculation: Addition Fifth calculation: Subtraction

Figure 12-3. Practice for Excel Supporting Topic

Exercise 1-2: Using Formulas

Directions   Using the values in the spreadsheet below, answer the formula questions.

Questions   1. What is the numeric result of the following formulas:

A.   = D6 – C6

B.   = D5 * C14/C6

C.   = (C6 – C14)/C10

2. Write the correct formula to calculate:

A. Total sales for January

B. Net sales for toys for January

C. Percentage of total sales from feed

Exercise 1-2 shown in Figure 12-3 directs learners to use spreadsheet cell values to manually calculate formula outcomes, as well as to construct some formulas to achieve assigned calculation goals. This exercise requires learners to apply an understanding of how formulas work—not just parrot back the information given in the "tell and show" sections. In the classroom, the instructor allocates a few minutes to the exercise and when she sees that most are finished, asks pairs of participants to compare their answers and resolve any discrepancies. The instructor then shows all correct responses and answers any questions. While participants are working on the exercise, the instructor moves around the room checking for any misconceptions and helping individuals as needed.

In a virtual classroom shown in Figure 12-4, the instructor enhances engagement by summarizing the main components of a formula and asking learners to type into chat the common elements in the structure of all formulas based on the two examples displayed on the screen.

Figure 12-4. A Virtual Classroom Lesson on Excel Formulas

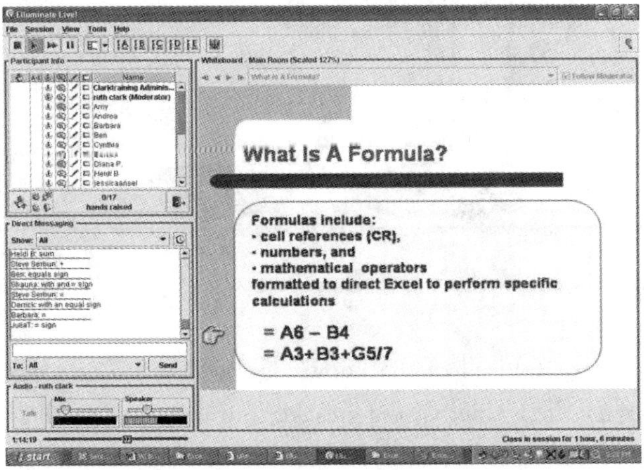

Source: Clark and Kwinn, 2007. Material reproduced with permission John Wiley & Sons.

Evidence for Sequencing Supporting Topics First

What evidence do we have for the learning benefits of sequencing the supporting knowledge prior to the major lesson task? Mayer, Mathias, and Wetzell (2002) created two lesson versions on how brakes work. One version gave a multimedia explanation of how brakes work. A second version included the same explanation but preceded it with a short description of each part, as illustrated in Figure 12-5. Learners who received the part explanations before the full description scored higher on a problem-solving test with a high effect size of 0.9.

Figure 12-5. A Topics-First Lesson Begins With an Explanation of Each Part

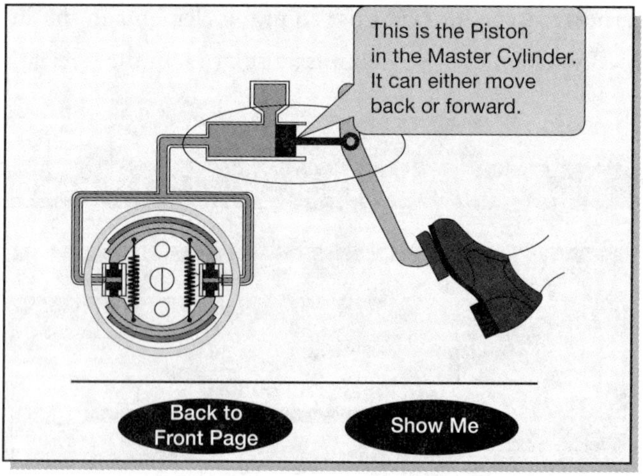

Source: Mayer, Mathias, and Wetzell, 2002.

Lessons that fold all of the knowledge topics into one meaty explanation barrage the learner with a great deal of information all at once. By teaching key concepts first, the amount of new information the learner must acquire all at once is greatly reduced. This sequencing helps mitigate mental overload.

Teach Supporting Topics in Context

To help learners connect the relationships between the parts and the whole, always teach supporting topics in the context of the whole task. For example, in Figure 12-5 each individual part is explained in a visual that shows the structure of the entire brake. Likewise, in Figure 12-3 the formula practice exercise makes use of a spreadsheet example. If you teach a series of supporting topics out of context, the result can be fragmented knowledge and confusion regarding the relations between task elements and the whole task.

THE TASK STEPS

So far we have seen how to develop the lesson introduction followed by the key supporting topics. The next part of the lesson uses tell, show, and practice with feedback to teach the steps of the procedure. As an example, Figure 12-6 shows part of an asynchronous demonstration of how to enter a formula in Excel. The main instructional method for teaching tasks is a "follow-along" demonstration given by the instructor in the classroom or shown on the screen in multimedia lessons.

Figure 12-6. An Animated Demonstration of Inputting a Cell Formula Described by Audio Narration

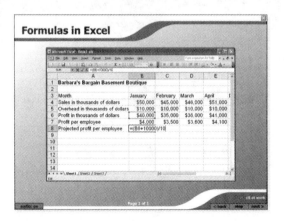

Evidence shows that brief animations described with audio are the best way to demonstrate procedures in multimedia environments. The animations could be rendered as computer-generated drawings, screen captures, or video. Simpler drawings impose less mental load and might be preferable for complex procedures and/or novice learners. Whatever form of animation you use in multimedia, include "pause" and "replay" buttons. Be sure to orient the animation from the visual perspective of the performer—that is, illustrate with an "over the shoulder" depiction as shown in Figure 12-7. In Figure 12-7 note the inclusion of a series of still shots under the running video. The still shots help the learner keep previous steps in mind as they view the demonstration.

Figure 12-7. An Animation of Origami Folding

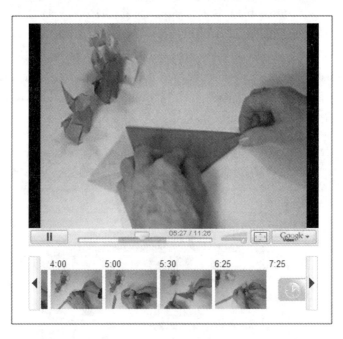

Source: Used with permission of Chopeta Lyons.

For reference purposes, the learner benefits from a documented summary of the steps. The best documentation during initial learning includes a visual of the work interface (screen or equipment) with text captions placed close to the relevant portion of the visual, as shown in Figure 12-8.

Figure 12-8. Handout for Excel Lesson Procedure

How to Enter a Formula

Introduction Follow the steps below on your spreadsheet to enter a formula.

Procedure To calculate total product costs for January:

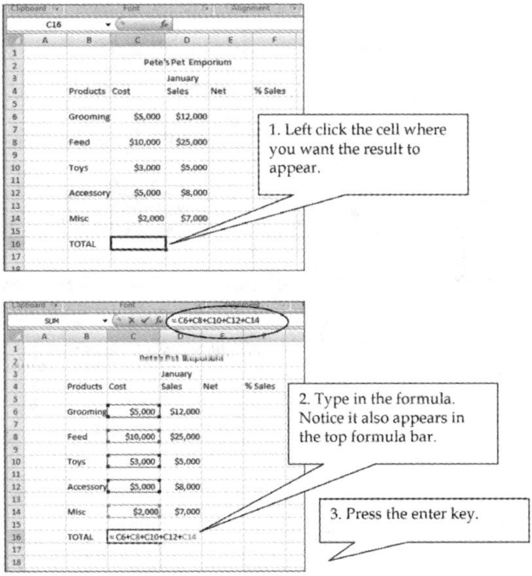

For tasks that will be repeated many times in training and on the job, a condensed working aid such as the example in Figure 12-9 may suffice.

Figure 12-9. A Working Aid for the Excel Lesson

FORMULAS
- Start with equal sign
- Operators: + - * /
- Order of operations: PDMAS

Examples:
= A3 + B4/C6
= A3 / (B4 - D8)

ENTERING FORMULAS

1. Enter data in cells
2. Right-click in cell where result should appear
3. Type in formula
4. Press Enter key

Practice in Directive Lessons

Following an interactive demonstration, practice exercises require learners to apply the same steps to some new scenarios or data sets. Figure 12-10 shows the practice for the Excel lesson in a virtual classroom. This practice illustrates a spiral technique in which the formulas constructed in the initial portion of the lesson are reused with a different data set. In part 2 of this practice, the benefit of formulas is reinforced by asking learners to change data values in the spreadsheet and document the results.

Figure 12-10. Practice Assignment in Virtual Classroom

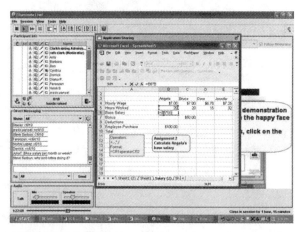

Source: Clark and Kwinn, 2007. Material reproduced with permission John Wiley & Sons.

In a classroom setting, the instructor moves around the room checking on progress and giving assistance as needed. At the end of the exercise, the instructor can give feedback by simply stating the answers or if she noted confusion during the exercise, demonstrating how to obtain the results.

When to Use Drill and Practice

In some situations, workers must be able to perform a procedure on the job quickly and accurately without benefit of a working aid. These procedures may involve high-risk tasks such as landing an airplane; or alternatively, require a rapid response, such as when learning a new language. In other situations, the overall task is quite complex and only by automating lower level procedures can the entire task be performed. For example, driving a car involves a number of sub-skills, many of which must be learned to automaticity to permit the focus of attention onto the traffic and driving conditions. Use drill and practice exercises in these situations.

Drill and practice requires learners to perform the procedure many times until it becomes automatic. Recall from chapter 3 that once automated, the procedure is stored in memory in a way that can be accessed and executed with minimal load on working memory. For example, automated typing allows me to think about the composition rather than the mechanics of typing. Computer simulations and games may be useful for drill and practice exercises as the computer program can measure both accuracy and speed of response, and assign points accordingly. In an adaptive exercise or game, accuracy and response time can be measured and practice continued until automaticity is reached.

Because drill and practice can become rather boring, some types of repetitive exercises can be embedded in a game format. We will discuss games in more detail in chapter 14.

Feedback in Directive Tasks

Is your feedback effective? You may recall from chapter 10, reviews of feedback research have reported that often feedback actually impedes learning. To maximize the value of feedback in directive lessons apply the following guidelines:

- Focus on progress of the individual over repetitions; avoid comparisons with other performers.

- Give immediate feedback when the consequence of an error on one step will affect the performance of future steps and the ultimate result.

- Provide explanatory feedback that tells why a given answer is correct or incorrect.

- Focus on specific techniques to improve performance—not just the final result or answer.

Review chapter 10 for a summary of evidence on feedback.

PERFORMANCE SUPPORT FOR PROCEDURES

Some tasks may not require training. Many procedural tasks are simplifying due to technological advances in software. For example, e-learning authoring systems used to require considerable knowledge of coding. Many contemporary authoring systems use icons or actions based on familiar software such as PowerPoint. In other situations, a particular task is performed only once or infrequently. Training to perform such tasks may be replaced by some form of performance support or job aid.

Performance support is a set of directions or demonstrations that guide the worker through a procedure with no intention that the steps will be learned. Furniture assembly directions are good examples. Once assembled, the task will hopefully not be repeated. Training would be a wasted effort. What is the best way to provide performance support for a procedural assembly task?

In chapter 8, I reviewed research by Watson et al. (2010) that compared time to assemble an artificial device over five trials using three forms of performance support: text directions, a series of still photos with no words, and an animation with no words. You can review the results summarized in Figure 8-5.

On the first build the animated displays (with no words) led to 56 percent faster build times than text directions. By the second build, the animated and still photographs supported the same build times—both faster than text. By the third build, all three formats resulted in equivalent build times. It is possible that by the third build the procedure was learned and there was minimal reliance on the directions. We need more studies to confirm these results; but based on this data, visual representations were the most efficient format for performance support of a manual assembly task.

REFERENCE SUPPORT FOR PROCEDURAL TASKS

Evidence is mixed about the learning value of taking notes during a lesson. No doubt potential benefits depend on the rate of content delivery, note-taking skills, as well as learner familiarity with the content. Marsh and Sink (2010) found that students preferred receiving handouts and learning was better when handouts were provided. Rather than allocating attention to taking notes, learners can devote their mental capacity to the explanations and invest mental resources in practice exercises. Because training time in adult learning settings is generally limited, I recommend providing relatively detailed handouts—at least when the content is stable and the quality and consistency of the training is important.

Memory support aids can be reproduced in paper or in software for display either in mobile devices or embedded in the software. Many software producers incorporate step-by-step help screens available adjacent to the application as performance support. Increasingly, documentation and training staff work together to ensure consistency and integration of documentation into hardware, software, and training.

WHAT CAN GO WRONG WITH PROCEDURAL TRAINING?

As with any training approach, things can go wrong that degrade the learning potential of the event or product. Remember that the most expensive element in any training program is the time participants are away from the job. Shortchanging the instructional environment may save some money in the short run but can be exponentially expensive across the delivery landscape. Here is a summary of common short falls in procedural lessons.

Content Sequenced Outside of Job Context

The basic goal of directive lessons is to teach procedural tasks along with the associated knowledge needed to perform those tasks. Most of the lessons should be rooted in a task such as how to update a budget in Excel, how to assemble the Erylitizer, how to troubleshoot the Cam Loader, or how to verify the customer's credit. To ensure job context, conduct a job analysis to identify and segment the core tasks associated with a work role. Without a pervasive and authentic job context, the lessons will seem (and may be) irrelevant to your learners.

I saw an example of decontextualized training in a course on electrical troubleshooting. It began with a lesson on Ohm's law to include definitions of voltage, amperage, and resistance. The next lesson introduced the components of a circuit followed by a lesson on different types of circuits. Later in the course testing equipment was explained in conjunction with procedures to measure voltage, resistance, and amperage. The initial lessons conveyed the important concepts of electrical theory and were attempting to teach supporting knowledge first. However, lacking context, the learner has to more or less memorize the definitions and relationships. How would you reorganize this content?

I would start the course by introducing a simple circuit to include the different elements and how they affect the flow of electricity and the operations of the equipment they support. Then, bring in the testing equipment, allowing the learner to measure the different values involved; and from there lead into Ohm's law. In short, begin your lessons with a very simple but real job task that involves only a few elements and integrate the needed concepts and theories into those tasks.

Similar out-of-context instances are seen in software training that explains all the tool bars and icons outside of how they may be used to perform a specific task. Instead, a task-focused approach shows only the icons or tool bars relevant to that task.

A common dilemma involves building procedural lessons, such as software training, intended for a broad audience with diverse work roles. In this situation, define the most common tasks to be performed by users and create scenarios to illustrate and practice those tasks. To customize the training, require participants to complete a project in which they apply the skills to their own work-related data. In the Excel course I created a demonstration and practice spreadsheet based on Pete's Pet Emporium. I could ensure learning transfer by asking participants to apply their Excel skills to a work-related project such as preparing a budget.

Suboptimal Sequencing and Segmenting

Sometimes procedural lessons get out of control by mushrooming beyond the learner's attention span and working memory capacity. At the other end of the spectrum, you can overdo segmenting by creating lessons that are too small to be meaningful and rapidly become tedious. There are always exceptions, but for e-learning, aim for lessons not to exceed five to 10 minutes in length; and classroom lessons that include practice opportunities should not exceed an hour. My own experience teaching in virtual classes is a limit of about 1.5 hours (assuming engagement during that time) without a break. When I have longer sessions, I break after each hour.

A common sequencing mistake is to place most of the main knowledge topics into one of the first lessons in a course in the form of a "technical terminology" lesson. This approach is usually quite boring and fails to teach the terminology in job context. Most of the knowledge topics should be placed in the same lesson that teaches a specific task—usually sequenced just prior to the actual task. In the Excel formula lesson, the knowledge topics "what is a valid formula" and "cell references" are sequenced prior to the procedure of "how to enter a formula."

As you plan your instructional sequence, consider not only the content placement but also the diversity of learning events. For example, follow a brief presentation with a practice or case study. When it's time for debriefs, select one or two student products to review rather than five or more at once. Interweave individual assignments with pair collaboration, as well as small group work. In classroom settings, encourage participants to move around for various learning events by joining different teams, working on wall charts, and so on.

Ineffective Practice

Frequent practice with feedback is one of the core features of the directive lesson design. Practice failures range from little or no practice (with the excuse, "we just don't have time—we have to 'cover' the material") to regurgitate practice that asks learners to parrot back what they have been told or read. Instead create application exercises that mirror the work role as closely as possible. Remember from chapter 10 that it's better to distribute practice exercises within a lesson and among lessons than to lump them all in one place. Also, practice without feedback is of little value. Feedback should go beyond "right or wrong" to provide an explanation or focus on techniques that will improve performance.

Ineffective Pacing

Years of classroom instruction have shown me that it is just about impossible to maintain an optimal pace for all. One of the drawbacks of the classroom as a delivery medium is instructor-pacing rather than learner-pacing. No matter what, you will be too slow for some and too fast for others. I tend to pace my presentations fairly quickly because I provide a complete reference handout and because I want to invest most of the time in practice opportunities, which is when the real learning happens.

Some techniques to optimize pacing include: 1) assign prework to convert a diverse background audience to a more homogeneous group, 2) have participants work or debrief together, 3) include extra "bonus" assignments for fast finishers, 4) have an ongoing project that fast finishers can work on while others complete assignments, 5) get pacing feedback from your learners early in the event, and 6) be flexible. Flexibility means setting your instructional priorities ahead of time and skipping lower priority content or activities.

A recent virtual classroom session I led had a large class size and we soon fell behind the planned schedule. I adjusted the design by collapsing two breakout room exercises into one and skipping a section of content in lieu of more case study work on a skill set I considered more important for the particular group. In a different class, I discovered that many of the trainers attending did not know the difference between a recall practice and an application practice. I abandoned my agenda completely instead asking each individual to post an application practice on a wall chart. A gallery tour identified any remaining recall exercises and the class worked collabo ratively to revise them to an application level.

Failure to Connect

Student ratings and learning are enhanced by a social connection between the instructor and the learners. In addition to the opening introductions and greetings, one of the best times to connect is during practice exercises and case work. Often, instructors are reluctant to move into the learner's space while they are working, when in fact, these times offer a great opportunity to verify that participants are "getting it," catch misconceptions, reinforce effective approaches, and establish relationships with individual participants.

THE BOTTOM LINE

What Do You Think?

Now that you have reviewed the evidence, check off each statement you believe is true:

- ❑ A. Learning is better when topics are presented in small chunks.
- ❑ B. Learning is better when related knowledge content is sequenced prior to task steps.
- ❑ C. Performance support for procedures is most effective when steps are presented visually rather than in text.
- ❑ D. Learning is better when practice exercises are distributed throughout directive lessons.

All of the statements are true. By chunking the content and sequencing key knowledge topics first, you minimize mental overload. It's important, however, that each topic reflect the work context so the learner can see its relationship to the lesson task.

We need more research on formats for performance support. But we do have one study showing that diagrams—animated or still—led to a more efficient first build compared to text descriptions. However, after three or more builds, the advantage of visuals disappeared as the procedure became familiar through repetition.

The spacing effect is a classic principle of instructional psychology. Find ways to distribute practice opportunities among and within learning events. Remember that the benefits of spacing apply primarily to delayed learning and may not be seen during the instruction.

APPLYING METHODS FOR TEACHING PROCEDURES

Consider the following guidelines when faced with helping learners acquire procedural skills.

- Use a directive approach for procedural tasks and/or novice learners.

- Focus each lesson on a job task plus associated knowledge topics.

- Segment content into brief topics followed by practice with feedback.

- Sequence knowledge topics prior to task steps.

- Make the work context of the lesson salient in the introduction and throughout the lesson.

- Use a "tell, show, practice, feedback" pattern in each lesson.

- Use visuals described by audio in explanations.

- Provide varied and interactive examples (including demonstrations).

- Plan application level practice exercises distributed throughout the lessons.

- Provide explanatory feedback for practice exercises.

- Include working aids to guide performance after training.

- Build and sustain learning relationships with the participants during instructor-led events.

COMING NEXT

Now that we've looked at ways to teach procedural skills, we will turn to instructional methods best suited for strategic skills that involve problem solving and/or critical thinking. The next chapter will focus on scenario-based learning designs.

FOR MORE INFORMATION

Clark, R.C. (2008). *Developing Technical Training.* San Francisco: Pfeiffer.

This is the first book I wrote based on some of the early work of David Merrill and Robert Horn. In this book you can read basic instructional methods for teaching facts, concepts, processes, procedures and principles.

TEACHING CRITICAL THINKING SKILLS WITH SCENARIOS

CHAPTER 13

Teaching Critical Thinking Skills With Scenarios

"We learn geology the morning after the earthquake."

—Ralph Waldo Emerson

Confronting a realistic but unfamiliar problem or situation creates a moment of need for learning. Faced with a task or challenge we must resolve, we are most open to acquiring the knowledge and skills required to respond. And when that task or problem is clearly work related, we are engaged by the relevance of the exercise. This is the motivational power of scenario-based learning environments in which an authentic work problem initiates and drives learning.

In this chapter, we apply proven guidelines to lessons that use job scenarios as the engine for learning. Specifically we will review: 1) the components of scenario-based lessons, 2) the evidence for a scenario-based approach and, 3) the use of media in scenario-based lessons.

WHAT IS SCENARIO-BASED LEARNING?

Scenario-based learning, also called whole task, problem-based, or immersive learning, is a preplanned guided inductive learning environment designed to accelerate expertise. The learner assumes the role of a staff member responding to a realistic work assignment or challenge, which in turn responds to reflect the learner's choices. Scenario-based lesson designs can be delivered in instructor-led in-person or virtual classrooms, as well as via asynchronous multimedia. Let's consider this definition in more detail using the multimedia scenario-based lesson illustrated in Figure 13-1.

Figure 13-1. A Virtual Repair Shop Includes Normal Testing Tools

Source: Used with Permission of Raytheon Professional Services.

The Learner Responds to a Job-Realistic Situation

In the automotive troubleshooting lesson designed for apprentice technicians, the learner is assigned a work order and has access to testing devices in a virtual shop to respond. As in real life, he uses the diagnostic tools to gather data, define the failure, and repair the car. In a classroom setting, a laboratory would include the tools needed to identify and repair automotive failures.

The Scenarios Are Preplanned

As with all forms of effective instruction, each scenario is defined by learning objectives that summarize desired knowledge and skill outcomes derived from a job analysis. In the automotive troubleshooting lesson there are two objectives. Obviously one goal is to accurately define the failure.

In addition, there is a process objective focusing on the efficiency of the diagnostic process. Each diagnostic test device is tagged with a realistic use time and some tests are irrelevant to the symptoms described on the work order. The program tracks which testing tools the learner uses and in what sequence. Therefore, learners get feedback not only on the accuracy of their diagnosis but also on the process they used to define the failure.

An Inductive Rather Than an Instructive Approach

In chapters 11 and 12 we focused on instructional environments that were relatively instructive. By that I mean the instruction provides explanations typically accompanied by examples and demonstrations, as well as practice with corrective feedback. Mistakes are generally flagged sooner rather than later and corrected promptly. In contrast, scenario-based designs rely on problem-solving experience as the main source of learning. Mistakes may or may not be corrected immediately and often the learner experiences the consequences of his mistakes rather than being told. For example, in the automotive lesson, if the learner selects an incorrect failure, he sees that the symptom persists and the customer is unhappy. From this result he infers that his solution was not correct and he must revise his analysis.

The Instruction Is Guided

We have a great deal of evidence showing that pure discovery learning is both inefficient and ineffective. A meta-analysis synthesizing more than 500 studies that compared a discovery approach with either a directive or guided discovery approach reported significantly better learning among the more guided versions (Alfieri et al., 2011). In one experiment Lazonder et al. (2010) developed a computer simulation in which learners were to discover which combination of several factors led to best sales in a shoe store. Factors included type of background music, location of the stockroom, and the type of floor cover, among others. In the simulation, participants varied values within these factors, which then altered the sales figures. Three groups worked with the simulation and received a performance score based on the proximity of their models to the simulation's underlying model. The control group worked with the simulation but received no guidance. Subjects in a second group received an information guide prior to starting the simulation. The guide summarized the different factors and their values but did not explain how they affected sales. A third group received the same guide prior to starting the simulation and also had access to it during their work in the simulation. Figure 13-2 summarizes the performance scores. The research team concluded that providing domain-specific information to learners with low prior knowledge both before and during the simulation led to the best performance.

Figure 13-2. Effects of Guidance on Learning From a Simulation

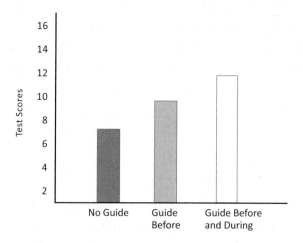

Source: Based on data from Lazonder et al., 2010.

In the sales simulation experiment, guidance took the form of traditional domain-specific content available prior to and during the simulation. Guidance can take other forms as well. In the automotive troubleshooting lesson, when the learner clicks on a test instrument that is not relevant to the problem, a notice appears on the screen stating that the test is not appropriate.

The Goal Is to Accelerate Expertise

How is expertise built? Research on a variety of high-level performers in sports, games (such as chess), and music have pointed to the role of extensive and focused practice over an eight- to 10-year period (Ericsson, 2006). In other words, expertise grows from focused experience, often with the support of a coach. Many work domains require considerable time to build experience because some tasks occur rarely or are too risky to learn on the job. For example, in troubleshooting, some failures may be relatively infrequent. Having the opportunity to resolve these in a compressed time period accelerates expertise. Compressed experience is especially feasible in a multimedia delivery environment where a test can be performed or a decision made with the click of a mouse.

WHEN TO CONSIDER SCENARIO-BASED LEARNING

Scenario-based lessons are motivating to many learners. By starting a lesson with a real-world task assignment, the relevance of the training is immediately salient. Scenarios with an optimal level of challenge and guidance have the potential to increase learner engagement leading to deeper processing and better learning of new skills.

A second benefit is transfer of learning. Because in scenario-based designs most learning occurs in the context of real-world tasks and problems, the cues accumulated in memory will lead to better retrieval later. When facing a new problem on the job, most experts search their memory banks for a similar situation they faced in the past. Problem-based lessons give learners an opportunity to build those memory repositories for later use.

Scenario-based learning is generally most appropriate when teaching learners with some relevant prior knowledge or experience how to perform tasks that rely on critical and creative problem solving. They are especially useful to teach skills that are difficult to acquire on the job because of safety concerns or scarcity of real-world opportunities. Teaching new military officers to make good combat decisions is one example. Decisions can have life or death consequences, and a scenario-based approach to learning offers at least a partial substitute for real-world experience.

What Do You Think?

Place a check next to each statement you believe is true:

- ❏ A. Multimedia scenario-based lessons require computer simulations.
- ❏ B. Scenario-based lessons are more expensive to develop than traditional directive lessons.
- ❏ C. Scenario-based lessons should include feedback.
- ❏ D. Learning from scenario-based lessons is better when realistic multimedia such as video is used to portray the scenarios.

THE ANATOMY OF A SCENARIO-BASED LESSON

There are four essential elements of an effective scenario-based lesson: 1) an authentic scenario or task assignment that serves as a context for learning, 2) learner guidance while responding to and resolving the problem, 3) feedback on problem solutions or problem-solving processes, and 4) explicit opportunities to reflect on problem solutions.

I'll describe each of these in a bit more detail and illustrate with the Excel content used in chapter 12, as well as with the automotive troubleshooting lesson introduced in Figure 13-1.

THE SCENARIO

Case study scenarios commonly appear in procedural (part task) lessons and sometimes even in explanations. In procedural lessons a problem or case study usually serves as an end-of-lesson (or unit) practice opportunity. But in the scenario-based approach the lesson starts (rather than ends) with a problem or scenario that serves as a context for learning. I introduced one example in Figure 13-1. Figure 13-3 shows a case that initiates an Excel classroom lesson with some business analysis goals for Pete's Pet Emporium.

Figure 13-3. An Excel Assignment Initiates and Drives a Scenario-based Lesson

Excel Case 1: Pete's Pet Emporium

Pete has always done his bookkeeping manually and is looking to you for help as he converts to an online spreadsheet. Your first task is to show Pete the value of using formulas in his spreadsheet. For Pete's first lesson, you plan to show him how to use a formula to calculate total costs, sales, and net gain for January.

	A	B	C	D	E	F
				C16		
1						
2			Pete's Pet Emporium			
3				January		
4		Products	Cost	Sales	Net	% Sales
5						
6		Grooming	$5,000	$12,000		
7						
8		Feed	$10,000	$25,000		
9						
10		Toys	$3,000	$5,000		
11						
12		Accessory	$5,000	$8,000		
13						
14		Misc	$2,000	$7,000		
15						
16		TOTAL				
17						
18						

Designing an effective problem or scenario is one of your biggest challenges. First, your scenario must require the participant to learn and apply the key skills needed to resolve it. In the Excel class, the business analyst will require the use of formulas to perform calculations and charts to display data. In the troubleshooting lesson, the technician must learn the mechanical and electrical components of the automotive systems involved, which diagnostic tests might be most appropriate at a given time, and how to interpret diagnostic data to identify a likely cause of failure.

As you plan your scenario, define the desired outcome and the criteria for success. These elements correspond to the action and criterion of a traditional lesson objective. Your outcome may involve a decision, actions, rationale for actions, a problem-solving path, or a product. Your criteria may be a correct answer, an answer that matches rationale, a decision path that is efficient and effective, solution time, or specified features of a product deliverable. For example, the Excel scenario will initially require the construction and input of accurate formulas to achieve the assigned goals. The outcome will be a correct answer because the spreadsheet incorporates specific data values. In contrast, the automotive troubleshooting class will require selection of a correct diagnosis, as well as an efficient, logical, problem-solving process in which irrelevant tests are bypassed.

Many scenarios will require the learner to access related problem data. In Figure 13-1 the simulated automotive shop offers the technician access to a variety of common diagnostic tools and tests. This part of your design will correspond to the "givens" in your learning objective. When you do your job analysis, note the common sources of data that experts use to solve problems and plan ways to incorporate these into your lesson. Typical examples include documents, technical diagrams, computer programs, client interviews, and test equipment—any resource that would be normally used on the job to define and analyze the problem.

THE GUIDANCE

One of the potential mine fields in scenario-based lessons is mental overload and learner confusion leading to frustration and drop out. Devote careful thought to the placement and type of guidance in the lessons. Instructional psychologists call this type of guidance scaffolding. For the initial problems in your course, provide heavy doses of guidance and gradually remove support as learning progresses. The most common types of guidance reviewed here involve: problem sequencing, learner control, examples, and knowledge resources such as experts, tutorials, and references.

Sequence Problems From Simple to Complex

The initial problem or task assignment should be the simplest instance you can build of an authentic job problem appropriate for your target audience. Easy problems will have fewer variables, relaxed constraints, straightforward solutions, and limited data to consider. The first Excel problem might require a column addition or row subtraction. A later problem might require several operations such as subtraction and division. For automotive troubleshooting, initial cases could involve a single system with a straightforward failure that can be defined with a few tests.

Constrain Learner Control

Learner options are limited in a more structured scenario design called a branched scenario. Figure 13-4 shows a screenshot from a customer service branched scenario lesson. The learner hears the customer's comments and has a choice of three response options. Upon clicking any of the options, the learner sees and hears the customer response and receives commentary from the virtual coach in the lower left corner. Branched scenarios are especially effective for problems in which one choice leads to another and then another in a linear sequence. Note that compared to the design of the automotive troubleshooting scenario, in the branched scenario, the learner makes only one decision per screen and gets immediate feedback on her response.

Figure 13-4. A Branched Scenario Immersive Lesson on Customer Service

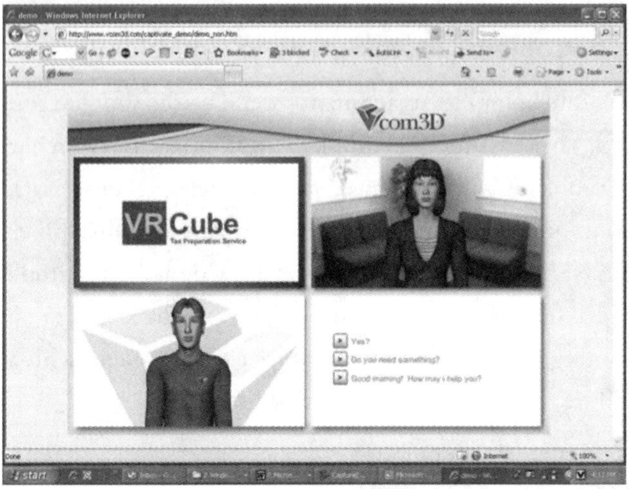

Source: Used with permission from VCOM 3D.

Alternate Problem Demonstrations With Assignments

Start with a demonstration (also called a worked example) of how to solve a problem or at least include a link to such a demonstration. For example, the instructor might demonstrate how to add a column of numbers in the spreadsheet. Next, learners are asked to perform a similar task using different data. For example, the learners would add or subtract a different column or row. An alternative technique is to start with a partial demonstration in which the instruction demonstrates the first solution steps and the learner finishes it. Follow with another scenario in which the learner does more or all of the work.

Offer Knowledge Resources

Some scenarios can benefit from a variety of perspectives. For example, a medical ethics scenario provides links that access virtual experts including lawyer, ethicist, clergy, psychologist, and colleague. A course for new supervisors offers links to manager, experienced supervisor, legal staff, and human resources, to name a few. The automotive troubleshooting course includes a hotline telephone that offers advice about which tests to try. In addition, learners can work on problems collaboratively. Discussion of alternatives in a group setting encourages deeper processing of information.

Nievelstein et al. (2013) compared learning outcomes among novice law students who worked with either a full civil code or a reduced code that included only material relevant to the case provided. Individual learners researched and wrote argumentation for a civil law case using either the complete civil code or a condensed version. Test case performance was better among those who used the condensed reference. The research team recommends: "Rather than losing precious cognitive resources on searching through large amounts of information, students' attention can be entirely devoted to making sense of the relevant information in the code in relation to the case" (412). Over a sequence of diverse cases, learners would become familiar with much of the full code.

THE FEEDBACK

All learning benefits from feedback. In scenario-based learning environments you can use two types of feedback: intrinsic and instructive. Instructive feedback, described in chapter 10, informs the learners that their responses are correct or incorrect and provides an explanation. The virtual coach in the lower left of Figure 13-4 offers this type of feedback. Intrinsic feedback shows the outcomes of the learners' actions or decisions as they resolve the problem. In other words, the learner acts and sees how the situation plays out for better or for worse. For example, when the learner selects a rude comment in the customer service branched scenario shown in Figure 13-4, the customer responds with negative body language and reply. Therefore, the scenario lesson in Figure 13-4 includes both instructive and intrinsic feedback. In the automotive repair scenario, selecting an incorrect diagnosis leads to a screen showing the failure symptoms continue to display. A debrief at the end of the lesson provides instructive feedback.

Intrinsic feedback can also reveal environmental responses that may be normally hidden. For example, a food handlers' lesson scenario incorporated a germ meter that reached the danger zone when food was improperly handled. A supervisory lesson on giving performance feedback included a "motivation" dial to reveal the feelings of the employee receiving feedback.

THE REFLECTION

One of the big differences between scenario-based and directive lessons is the instructional response to learner errors. Based on behaviorist roots, directive lessons attempt to minimize learner errors. When a mistake is made, the learner usually gets immediate corrective feedback. In contrast, scenario-based course designs view mistakes as an opportunity for learning. Feedback may not come until several actions have been taken or even until the end of the scenario. To learn from mistakes, it is important to prompt learner reflection on what they did and what they might do differently.

One powerful form of feedback that encourages reflection is an expert comparison. Figure 13-5 shows a screen from the automotive troubleshooting lesson that compares the diagnostic actions taken and time consumed by the learner with those of an expert. Gadgil et al. (2012) found better learning when students were able to do a side-by-side comparison of their incorrect explanations with expert solutions rather than to view an expert solution alone. Another approach to reflection is to let the learner experience intrinsic feedback followed by an opportunity to reconsider his responses and replay his choices.

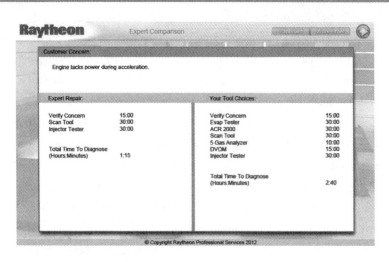

Figure 13-5. Comparison of Learner's Solution Process With an Expert's

Source: Used with Permission from Raytheon Professional Services.

CLICKER CASES IN THE CLASSROOM

Scenario-based learning designs can be implemented in instructor-led training, as well as in asynchronous multimedia lessons. One approach in large instructor-led classes is clicker cases. In an in-person setting, learners use handheld devices that allow them to select letters or numbers corresponding to instructor-projected questions. A similar technique in the virtual classroom could use polling. How effective are clicker cases in classroom settings?

In a multi-university test, faculty developed cases relevant to various topics in an introductory biology course (Lundeberg et al., 2011). For each topic, students received either a standard PowerPoint lecture or a clicker case. The cases unfolded over a series of class sessions. Six cases were developed corresponding to topics such as cell division and Mendelian genetics. Learning from the cases was compared with learning from standard lectures. For some topics the lectures led to better learning while for others the clicker cases were more effective. Outcomes varied based on the quality of the cases and the presentations.

In a comparison of highest and lowest faculty-rated cases, the more effective cases had an intriguing storyline, promoted emotional engagement, were well organized, generated interaction, and contained strong visual material. For example, a highly rated clicker case focused on the story of Santhi Soundararajan, a female athlete from India who was stripped of her Olympic medal after failing to pass a sex test. The case was introduced through an Internet video followed by PowerPoint slides that included information on gender testing in athletes, genetic criteria to determine sexuality, and an assignment in which students served as members of an Olympic committee to determine whether Santhi was female and make a decision based on her genetic makeup. The Santhi case was effective because it was based on a true story, used multimedia and controversy to stimulate emotional engagement, and gave learners an active assignment to make a decision.

MEDIA IN SCENARIO-BASED LEARNING ENVIRONMENTS

Is it better to present a problem scenario in text or with more visual forms of media such as video or computer animation? We have some preliminary data suggesting that often learners will become more engaged when the scenario is presented at least in part with visuals rather than text. My colleagues at Microsoft taught an instructor-led security networking course for years using a case study presented primarily in text. The case was based on a fictitious pharmaceutical company. The instructors converted the text case into a multimedia format by creating a mock website for the case company and adding video interviews and online networking diagrams.

The instructors reported that the learners were much more engaged with the multimedia version and treated the scenario more like an actual client engagement.

There is some research evidence that supports this anecdotal observation. For example, Kamin and her colleagues (2003) compared collaborative discussions among medical students who reviewed a case in text with discussions among medical students who reviewed the same case in video. The discussions were much richer in groups using the video case. Of course in medicine, the sights and sounds of the patient can be presented in a more authentic manner with video than with text. Moreno and Ortegano-Layne (2008) compared learner ratings and learning among student teachers who reviewed case examples presented either in text, computer animation, or video. Both ratings and learning were better from the computer animated and video examples than from the text examples. The computer animated and video cases resulted in equivalent learning outcomes.

The question of which media will best present your scenarios will be resolved in part by your development resources and delivery technologies. Based on the limited data we have, I recommend adding visual elements to a problem scenario whether it will be conducted in a classroom or computer setting. Realistic media is likely to be especially helpful to portray case elements that involve sights and sounds that cannot be authentically represented in text. Visual media can create a more compelling environment that engages learners on an emotional level, which in turn leads to deeper learning.

WHAT CAN GO WRONG WITH SCENARIO-BASED LESSONS

There are a number of potential traps to avoid in scenario-based lessons.

Learner Overload

Perhaps the most common problem encountered in scenario-based lessons is mental overload. Asking learners to solve a problem unfamiliar to them and to learn the knowledge and skills they need to resolve that problem at the same time can be overwhelming. One solution is to design scenario-based lessons for learners with some prior experience. Another solution is to incorporate guidance. Learners new to the domain need higher levels of guidance such as branched scenarios or pre-scenario tutorials.

Unbalanced Skill Set

So far I've focused primarily on the elements of a single scenario-based lesson. Imagine a medical education in which all of your case problems focus on a broken leg. Clearly the range of knowledge and skills acquired would be very limited. To achieve balance, you need to identify "problem classes" based on the diversity of work role functions you identify during your job analysis. For example, you might have problem classes that focus on cardiac issues, oncology, orthopedic problems, and so on. Within each problem class, you will need to identify a series of cases that incorporate the required knowledge and skills of that class and that progress from easy to complex.

Inefficiency of Learning

Inefficiency is an offspring of high "flounder factor" lessons. When learners start to take random actions to progress through a problem, the result can be both ineffective and inefficient learning. Learner control is one of the major tools you can use to minimize inefficiency. As mentioned above, present more constrained interfaces (branched scenarios, limited active objects) to guide learners during early problem-solving stages. Also be more aggressive with imposing guidance and directions when learners get off track.

Instructor Roles

In the classroom it is up to the instructor to administer and facilitate the case problems. Specifically, the instructor can present the problem, provide relevant clarifications, facilitate group discussions, help locate relevant resources, and facilitate problem debriefs. Note that this is quite different from a more traditional role. Instructors must be agile and flexible—able to provide just-in-time explanations but also willing to let learners make some errors and learn from them. The degree of ambiguity in the process and in the final results may be difficult for some instructors to accept—especially if they are used to working in highly directive learning environments.

THE BOTTOM LINE

Now that you have reviewed the evidence, here are my comments on the questions at the start of this chapter.

A. Multimedia scenario-based lessons require computer simulations.
FALSE. Scenario-based lessons do not require computer simulations. Some can be produced with simple branching. More complex forms, such as the automotive troubleshooting example, do involve some level of simulation.

B. Scenario-based lessons are more expensive to develop than explanatory lessons.
TRUE. Many factors affect development costs, including the media used, the incorporation of simulations, and the complexity of the case problems,

among others. Presentations—even when augmented with examples and questions—are generally much faster and easier to design and develop, hence their popularity. In contrast, scenario-based designs are very interactive and in general will require more time and cost. However, after developing one or two whole-task lessons, a template can be adapted to accommodate new case variables and data. Also some authoring systems include a programming interface for branched scenario designs. Two popular systems as of this writing are Articulate Storyline and Adobe Captivate.

C. Scenario-based lessons should include feedback.

TRUE. Actually this is a true statement for any lesson that involves learner practice. However, in scenario-based lessons you can decide whether to provide instructive or intrinsic feedback or both. You can also decide whether to provide immediate or delayed feedback or a combination.

D. Learning in scenario-based environments is better when realistic multimedia such as video is included.

We don't really have sufficient evidence to make blanket generalizations on this issue. It is likely that more visual media such as still photos or video will be more engaging and also may be essential when the sights and sounds of the workplace are critical data to consider. When comparing video to computer-generated animation, keep in mind that video may be more difficult to update than an animated interface.

APPLYING SCENARIO-BASED LEARNING TO YOUR TRAINING

Use the following checklist to guide your design and development of scenario-based learning environments.

❑ Consider a scenario-based approach for tasks that involve decision making and critical thinking or for tasks that are challenging to learn in the work environment.

❑ Provide a more constrained design and higher levels of guidance for novice learners.

❑ Initiate the lesson with a work-authentic assignment or scenario.

❑ Design an interface which is clean and in which learner response options are clear.

❑ Incorporate fewer variables and less data in initial scenarios.

❑ Offer less learner control in initial scenarios.

❑ Provide guidance to minimize learner frustration and ensure learning.

❑ Fade guidance as learners gain more experience.

❑ Provide both intrinsic and instructional feedback.

❑ Use feedback to illustrate both visible and "invisible" consequences of actions.

❑ Allow learners the opportunity to make mistakes, experience the results, and reflect in order to learn from their mistakes.

❑ Present scenarios with visuals rather than text alone.

❑ As an instructor, assume a facilitative role rather than a knowledge source.

❑ Consider clicker cases to apply scenario-based learning principles to larger classroom settings.

❑ Ensure the full range of knowledge and skills through the scenarios selected to fulfill the goals of the instructional program.

COMING NEXT

An exciting new instructional approach has emerged in the form of games or gamification. Although much has been written about serious games, only in the last few years has sufficient research accumulated to warrant a chapter in this book. In chapter 14, you will be updated on three tracks of research on the effects of games on learning.

FOR MORE INFORMATION:

Clark, R.C. (2013). *Scenario-Based E-Learning*. Pfeiffer: San Francisco.

See my book for detailed information on the design and development of multimedia scenario-based lessons.

GAMES AND LEARNING

Games and Learning

"The design of games for learning should be based on rigorous scientific evidence rather than on strong opinions."

—Mayer (2014b, 254)

On a typical day in 2009, 60 percent of eight- to 18-year-olds were playing video games compared with 52 percent in 2004. No doubt by the time you are reading this, the proportion is closer to 70 or even 75 percent! In 2012 more than $20 billion were spent on games and associated hardware (ESA). The escalating popularity of digital games among young and old alike suggests a seductive path to the marriage of motivation and learning. A growing number of books and articles tout the benefits of gamification as a preferred approach to learning environments that are both fun and effective. In spite of the hype, a 2013 survey indicates that only 20 percent of workforce learning organizations are using serious games (ASTD, 2014).

What evidence do we have about the effectiveness of games? Are games better for learning than more traditional instructional approaches such as computer tutorials or lectures? What kinds of games are most effective? Are some game features more important than others when it comes to learning? The popularity of games in general and the ongoing interest in games for learning has stimulated quite a few research studies and several recent reviews, including a 2014 book by Richard Mayer, *Computer Games for Learning*. In this chapter we will survey the current landscape of game research to answer these questions.

WHAT IS A GAME?

Just about every research report and review includes a definition of games. I reviewed a number of these and abstracted the most common features as the foundation for the following definition: "Games designed for learning purposes (also called serious games) provide an environment that is both entertaining and educational characterized by high interactivity and responsiveness, specific challenging goals, and rules and constraints that guide how the player engages with the game."

These basic features are sufficiently broad to incorporate a range of games including more traditional board and puzzle games, as well as graphic intensive video-based adventure or role-playing games. Let's look at each feature individually.

Interactive and Responsive

Learners are highly engaged in a game environment when they're making frequent physical responses that often reflect psychological engagement. When the learner interacts with the game interface, there is an immediate response in the form of points, scores, or in a change in the environment itself. For example, in arcade games, rewards in the form of points, tokens, or prizes are given for player actions that align to the game goals. In strategy games such as Lemonade Tycoon 2, players attempt to maximize profit by applying lean manufacturing principles, making decisions about a lemonade recipe, purchasing supplies, setting prices, hiring employees, and making other decisions about location and expansions. The physical and mental exchange between player and game is one of the core features that initiates and sustains continued playing.

Specific Challenging Goals

The point of a game is to achieve a goal. The goal may be to win points, to beat a competitor, or to create an environment with specific properties. Games that are too easy fail to hold interest. Games that are too challenging lead to discouragement and drop out.

Many games use levels as a mechanism to gradually increase game challenge. As players move through levels, more difficult goals require improvements in player speed, accuracy, agility of response, or strategic decisions. Games maintain challenge by adapting to the player; that is, they adjust difficulty based on player's success at lower levels. A study by Sampayo-Vargas et al. (2013) evaluated an adaptive bubble game in the domain of foreign language vocabulary, which adjusted the difficulty level based on player performance. They compared motivation and learning from an adaptive version that increased difficulty based on player performance, a nonadaptive version that increased difficulty automatically in one-minute play time increments, and a paper worksheet (not a game) that asked students to perform similar vocabulary matches as the game. They found no differences in motivation among the three versions. However, the pretest and post-test gains shown in Figure 14-1 reflect significant learning benefits of the adaptive game version.

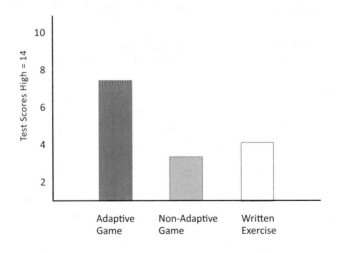

Figure 14-1. Pretest and Post-Test Gains in Two Game Versions and a Paper-Based Worksheet

Source: Based on data from Sampayo-Vargas et al., 2013.

Rules and Constraints

The game goal cannot be achieved arbitrarily. The player moves and game responses are guided by rules and constraints. Sometimes these must be discovered inductively by game play; other times the rules are made explicit from the start. Game goals, rules, and constraints should align with the learning objective. If misaligned, learning will be depressed. For example, a game designed to teach physics principles rewarded learners for speed of response, which precluded reflection and depressed learning compared to non-gaming approaches.

TYPES OF GAMES

Games that meet the three criteria described above encompass a diverse landscape of game types. Qualifying games range from Angry Birds to SimCity to Scrabble. Unfortunately, there is no single agreed upon categorization system. Many game scholars refer to the entertainment game categories summarized in Table 14-1. While these categories may not be especially helpful for instructional purposes, their general familiarity at least communicates the genre of game being evaluated.

Table 14-1

GENRE	DESCRIPTION	EXAMPLES
Casual, Arcade, Puzzle	Simple rules and strategies. The goal is to entertain with relatively low psychological commitment from the player.	Angry Birds Pac Man Tetris
Action	Requires quick reflexes, accuracy, and timing to overcome obstacles. Often has an emphasis on combat. This genre includes shooter games.	Pong Ultra Street Fighter IV Call of Duty Medal of Honor Midnight Racer Unreal Tournament
Action-Adventure	Has a focus on exploration and usually involves gathering items, solving puzzles, and combat.	Myst Resident Evil 6
Role Play	Players assume the role of one or more avatars that specialize in specific skill sets while progressing through a predetermined storyline.	Final Fantasy Dungeons & Dragons World of Warcraft

GENRE	DESCRIPTION	EXAMPLES
Simulation	Designed to emulate aspects of a real or fictional reality, including construction, vehicle operations, biology, and so on.	SimCity Flight Simulator The Sims
Strategy	Focus is on game play that requires careful and skillful thinking and planning to achieve victory.	Civilization Age of Empires Dune
Sports	Emulates playing of traditional sports.	FIFA Soccer Madden NFL

There is some confusion on the terms *games* and *simulations*. A simulation is a simplified model of an actual event, process, set of principles, or system. Simulations may be operational, such as a simulation of a software system or a flight controller; or they may be conceptual, such as a simulation of pendulum movement or economic principles like those in the business simulation Lemonade Tycoon. Operational simulations are generally intended to build procedural skills while conceptual simulations focus on strategic tasks.

Like games, simulations are generally interactive and responsive according to the rules and constraints of the systems they model. Some simulations incorporate game features such as rewards or points for achieving goals. Some researchers have adopted the terminology *simulation-games* (Sitzmann, 2011; Mayer, 2014b). Others treat them as two quite separate methods. Perhaps the distinction is not worth the quibble; it is the design for learning of either a game or simulation-game that is most important.

GAME DESIGN FOR LEARNING

Games have been shown to be especially effective for second-language learning (Young et al., 2012; Mayer, 2014b). Language learning relies on automaticity to formulate sentences and therefore benefits from drill and practice made more palatable by a gaming veneer. For example, imagine a computerized concentration type game to learn language vocabulary. The player faces a matrix of face-down cards that have either a picture or a written vocabulary word on the back. The player can turn over two cards at a time to match picture and word. If there is no match, the cards revert to face down. You win by matching all of the cards in the least amount of time. Do you think this a well-designed game for the goal of learning vocabulary?

My answer is no. Success in the concentration game relies on recalling the spatial position of each card, as well as the translation of the word in order to make successful matches. The need for spatial recall imposes extraneous cognitive load that detracts from learning of vocabulary. How could this game be designed more effectively? One approach is to convert it to a drag-and-drop matching game in which all cards are face up and the player drags matching cards together. The score can be based on the speed at which cards are correctly paired. The game could be adapted to learning progress by replacing pairs once they have been correctly identified three or more times. An alternative is to play a vocabulary word (or sentence) in audio and ask the player to click on the correct picture. As learning progresses, the sentence structures can become more complex and eventually include multiple sentences.

To successfully design a serious game, the learning objectives must be drivers for the engagement and response, the challenge of the goals, and the rules and constraints. At the same time, all of these core features should avoid extraneous load that would detract from learning.

What Do You Think?

Based on your own experience with games, indicate which of the following statements are true:

- ❑ A. Overall there is substantial evidence for the effectiveness of serious games.

- ❑ B. Narratives in games make them more effective for learning.

- ❑ C. Entertainment games can affect basic cognitive skills and behaviors.

- ❑ D. Learning from games can be improved by aids that explain the principles underlying the game rules and responses.

Mayer (2011; 2014b) organizes game research into three main questions:

- Do games change cognitive skills such as spatial aptitudes or behaviors such as aggression or helpfulness?

- Do people learn better with games compared to alternative instructional methods such as lectures or computer tutorials?

- What features of games promote learning?

Let's look at the evidence accumulated to date on each of these questions.

DO GAMES AFFECT COGNITIVE SKILLS OR BEHAVIORS?

There have been a number of claims about the secondary effects of entertainment games. For example, do violent video games lead to aggressive behaviors? Or, can game playing improve basic cognitive skills such as spatial aptitude? While very interesting, most of this research is a bit tangential to the main theme of this chapter, so I will provide only a couple of representative research reports to illustrate the focus of this research stream.

On the Down Side

Fischer et al. (2007) conducted three experiments to determine whether playing racing games such as Need for Speed, Burnout, or Midnight Racer is associated with or can lead to an increase in high-risk driving behaviors. A correlational study evaluated the association between self-reported frequency of playing these racing games and risky driving behaviors. Significant correlations of 0.5 for men and 0.33 for women were reported. A second study used an experimental approach. Men and women were randomly assigned to play either a racing game or a neutral game. They then completed a risk-taking scenario test in which responses to risky road situations portrayed on video were recorded. They found that men who played the racing games took more risks on the test than those who played neutral games. Women were not affected. The research team concluded that playing of racing games can lead to greater willingness to take driving risks—more so in men than women.

Do Games Improve Spatial Ability?

If you ever saw the film *The Last Star Fighter*, you are familiar with this premise. In the film, an alien defense force has installed first-person shooter game consoles throughout the earth and selected the best players to serve as fighters in an interstellar war. Naturally, the video game was a mirror image of the space fighting environment. After all of the game playing, the hero was able to successfully respond to the challenge. Sorry for the spoiler for those of you who have not seen the film.

In his review of the cognitive consequences of games, Mayer (2014b) finds that action games, especially first-person shooter games "resulted in greater improvements in perceptual attention skills than engaging in a control activity, with a median effect size in the large range" (p. 191). In contrast, brain-training, spatial action, and real-time strategy games did not yield these benefits. Playing Tetris over time led to an improvement in 2-D mental rotation with Tetris and non-Tetris shapes but not with other forms of mental rotation. Mayer concludes that playing a particular game can improve cognitive skills that are tapped and reinforced by that game.

Connolly et al. (2012) conducted a review of research to identify positive outcomes of games. They looked at evidence reported on both entertainment and educational games published from 2004 to 2009. They concluded that digital entertainment games can lead to attentional and visual perceptual advantages as summarized in the previous paragraph. However, when it comes to educational games, evidence showing the benefits of games on learning is not strong.

Can Games Promote Positive Health?

Primack et al. (2012) reviewed 38 studies comparing the benefits of video games on behaviors or attitudes linked to health benefits. Some of the outcomes reported include physical therapy, psychological therapy, health education, and disease self-management. The research team noted some limits in the research. Two-thirds of the studies had follow-up periods of less than 12 weeks and only 11 percent used evaluators blind to treatments. They conclude that there is potential for video games to improve health outcomes, particularly in the domains of psychological and physical therapy. Specifically they report that only 50 percent of the studies focusing on disease self-management had positive outcomes, compared with 67 to 100 percent of the studies focusing on physical and psychological therapy.

The Bottom Line

The cognitive and behavioral consequences of games are a sufficient topic for a book in itself. Based on my limited review, it appears that there is potential for both negative and positive effects depending no doubt on features unique to the game itself, to the game player, and to the context—such as the number of times a game is played or the sex of the player. We will look to future research to specify guidelines regarding positive and negative effects of specific games on specific behaviors in particular contexts. For more detail I recommend chapter 6 in Mayer (2014b).

DO GAMES PROMOTE BETTER LEARNING THAN ALTERNATIVE INSTRUCTIONAL METHODS?

Quite a few studies have compared learning outcomes among individuals playing a game with individuals assigned to a more traditional instructional method such as lectures or computer tutorials. In these studies the same content is presented in a game version and in a traditional version and learning is measured with a test. Three recent reviews have summarized these kinds of studies: Sitzmann, 2011; Wouters et al., 2013; and Mayer, 2014b.

Sitzmann (2011) reported that overall, simulation games resulted in learning gains 9 to 14 percent higher than comparison groups. However, I find the details of her analysis offer a different perspective. She categorized both the simulation-games and the comparison methods as involving active engagement or as being passive (such as reading or listening to a lecture). The comparison groups learned more than the game groups when taught with active instructional methods, whereas the game groups learned more than the comparison groups when the comparison group was taught with passive instructional methods. Interestingly, she reports that computerized tutorials were much more effective than simulation games and that hands-on practice was slightly more effective than games.

My conclusion from her review is that active engagement leads to learning and any method that incorporates relevant active engagement (with feedback) will lead to better learning than a method that relies primarily on passive learning environments such as lectures or reading. In previous chapters we have discussed the benefits of behavioral responses that receive feedback and are aligned to desirable psychological engagement.

Wouters et al. (2013) conducted a similar review on the learning and motivational benefits of games. Their review included game experiments published from 1990–2012. Overall they reported a positive effect of serious games with a small effect size of 0.29. Among the studies they reviewed, only two involved adults and these showed no significant differences compared to the alternative method. More importantly, research studies that used random assignment of students showed a very small effect size advantage for games—too small to be of much practical value. As discussed in chapter 2, a critical feature in experimental research is random assignment of subjects to treatments. Research studies without random assignment of participants are open to the potential flaw of systematic differences among participants in the subject pools. For example if subjects self-select to play a game rather than study via a more traditional method, the game players may have individual differences such as experience with games that give them a learning advantage.

The Wouters (2013) meta-analysis reported that games were most effective when they: 1) were supplemented with other instructional methods rather than used as the sole instructional approach, 2) are played in teams—usually pairs, 3) focus on language learning, and 4) are played over multiple sessions rather than just once. They also reported that game outcomes were not enhanced by high-end graphics or by narratives.

In his book on game research, Mayer reviews research on the effectiveness of games compared with alternative methods. He identifies two promising academic domains in which games appear to be most effective: science and second-language learning. Like the previous reviews he did find positive effects for games over conventional instruction, especially when compared to classroom or paper-based alternatives.

Overall, all three reviews gave a positive nod to the benefits of games on learning. However, digging a bit deeper, I see a number of qualifying statements. In fact, the learning benefit of any instructional method will likely depend on the instructional techniques used that support the key psychological learning events discussed in chapter 3. This leads to our last and perhaps most productive research question.

WHAT MAKES GAMES EFFECTIVE?

This type of research involves measuring learning from different versions of the same game that systematically vary game features. This research stream does not argue whether games are more effective than other methods; instead it looks for those features of games that lead to better learning. If you want the short story, I have summarized what we have learned from this research in Table 14-2. In the next few paragraphs I will describe guidelines derived from research that asks: What works in game design?

Table 14-2	

FEATURE	DESCRIPTION
Active Engagement and Feedback	Behavioral responses coupled with feedback lead to learning in games.
Engagement and Progress Aligned to Learning Objective	The actions taken and consequences of those actions must be aligned to the learning objectives. Most learning will be linked to those game activities that lead to progress or rewards.
Minimize Irrelevant Cognitive Load	Games such as the vocabulary concentration game described in this chapter demand mental activity that is irrelevant and would deplete the learning resources of working memory.
Add Self-Explanation Questions	When learners must take action or make a decision in a game, adding a question that requires the learner to reflect and select reasons for that action can improve learning.
Add Instructional Feedback	Game responses are often intrinsic, meaning the game world makes some change or awards points. However, traditional instructional feedback that explains why a response is correct or incorrect can increase learning.
Add Attention-Focusing Worksheets	Adding a worksheet or adjunct activity that directs learners to the most relevant aspects of a game environment can improve learning.
Add Working Aids or Pre-Training Sessions That Explain Guidelines	Adding a brief summary of the main principles or guidelines that are the foundation for game progress can promote learning. These can be presented as a mini lesson prior to game play or as a working aid that lists the principles.
Adapt Game Challenge Based on Learning	Optimal game challenge levels can be maintained by adapting the difficulty or content of the game based on the player's learning progress.
Supplement Games With Other Instructional Methods	To aid in reflection and articulation of lessons learned, incorporate games into a set of instructional methods, including explanations, discussions, and so on.
Assign Pairs to Play Games	For more challenging games, playing with a partner can promote discussion and articulation of game principles.
Integrate Personalization Principles Into the Game	In chapter 7, I summarized a number of methods that improve learning through personalization. For example, include an agent in your game who can give feedback or hints.
Offer Multiple Opportunities to Play a Game	Research has shown that playing a game one time has little positive benefit. To maximize learning, arrange for multiple plays. This would be especially relevant for goals that benefit from drill and practice.

1. Promote Active Engagement and Feedback on Instructional Content

In the Sitzmann (2011) review summarized previously, we saw that the learning environment (either a simulation game or a traditional lesson) that engaged learners with content in a relevant manner was most effective. In fact, some studies found computer tutorials characterized by frequent learner responses and feedback more effective than simulation games. We can conclude that active engagement coupled with feedback is an essential ingredient of any learning environment including games.

2. Align Engagement With the Learning Objective

Active engagement is not enough. It must align with the learning objective. For example, an effective second-language game shown in Figure 14-3 uses a grid with first-, second-, or third-person (singular and plural) indicators down the vertical axis and a visual of an action across the horizontal axis. When the player clicks on a square in the grid, she is required to speak a sentence using the correct verb conjugation. For example, if the vertical grid says "we" and the horizontal grid shows a visual of playing a game, the correct response is: "We are playing soccer" (translated into the appropriate language). If the learner does not make an appropriate response, the correct sentence is shown for the learner to read aloud. The activity in this game design requires the player to apply real-world language skills. Progress scores could be based on the number of correct sentences, as well as the time needed to complete all the squares.

Figure 14-3. An Effective Second-Language Game

In contrast, an early version of Oregon Trail, an adventure game designed to teach children the problems faced by American pioneers, incorporated guns for killing game for food. The children, however, misused this feature—converting the game into a first-person shooter genre. In this situation, features placed in the game resulted in unintended player goals and engagement that distracted from the learning objectives.

3. Add Self-Explanation Questions

Another effective approach is to promote reflection on the game by adding self-explanation questions. In several chapters throughout the book, we have reviewed the learning benefits of adding explanation questions to examples, to scenario-lessons, and to graphics. It would not be surprising to find similar benefits with games. Basically an effective self-explanation question will encourage the learner to carefully review the game actions and results and focus on the underlying concepts or principles. In other words, the questions convert an instructional method such as an example or graphic from a potentially passive learning method to an engaging event.

Mayer and Johnson (2010) evaluated the effects of game features using The Circuit Game shown in Figure 14-4.

Figure 14-4. The Circuit Game

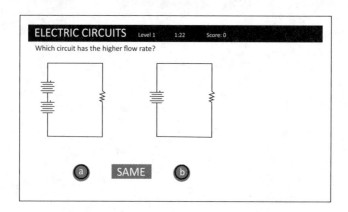

Source: Fiorella and Mayer, 2012; Mayer and Johnson, 2010.

The goal of the game is to teach basic principles of electronics based on resistors and batteries in circuits. For example, at Level 1 in Figure 14-4, players are shown two circuits that differ in one circuit element and are asked to choose the circuit with a higher rate of current. The research team compared learning from the following four versions: 1) basic as shown in Figure 14-4; 2) self-explanation in which after responding, the player is asked to select the reason for their answer from eight alternatives; 3) feedback in which after responding the correct answer is marked and accompanied by an explanation; and 4) both questions and feedback. Take a look at the data in Figure 14-5. Mark the versions that resulted in best learning.

- ❏ Basic version
- ❏ Self-explanation version
- ❏ Feedback version
- ❏ Versions with self-explanations and feedback

Figure 14-5. Learning From Four Versions of the Circuit Game

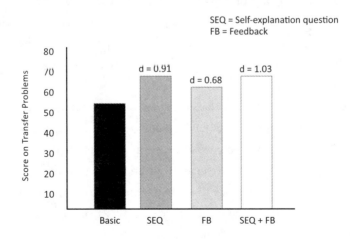

Source: Based on data from Mayer and Johnson, 2010.

The game versions that encouraged reflection through self-explanation questions or gave feedback on correct answers or included both questions and feedback all led to better learning than the basic version. From this research we learn two important instructional methods you can use to improve learning from games: self-explanation questions that require players to articulate their rationale for moves and feedback that provides an explanation for the correct answer.

4. Minimize Features That Impose Extraneous Cognitive Load

Previously in this chapter I discussed the concentration vocabulary game. Having to recall the spatial location of the cards imposes irrelevant mental load that interferes with the desired learning outcome. Narratives are a second feature that appears to interfere with learning from games. A narrative is a story line such as found in an adventure-type game. Adams et al. (2012) measured learning of electro-mechanical concepts from a narrative game shown in Figure 14-6 compared with the same content presented in a noninteractive slide show. In the game, the player assumes the role of an individual searching a World War II bunker for lost art. To move through the bunker and open doors, the player must apply electromechanical concepts and principles such as wet cell batteries presented on the mobile device shown. The slide show simply showed the content presented on the mobile device in the game.

Learning was better from the slide show than the game—even though the slide show did not require behavioral engagement. Perhaps the activities required by the narrative become a distraction and interfered with learning by imposing irrelevant cognitive load. In addition, the time required to play the game was more than twice that to view the slide presentation. At the very least, the narrative approach in this game was a very inefficient learning vehicle. In their review, Wouters et al. (2013) support this conclusion stating that, "including a narrative is counterproductive . . . because players will use too much of their cognitive capacity for processing the narrative information that is not directly related to the learning content" (260).

Figure 14-6. A Screenshot From the Cache 17 Game

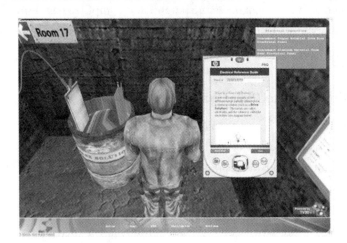

Source: Adams et al., 2012.

Another potential source of extraneous load is a game interface that is overly complex. We saw in chapter 8 that when it comes to graphics, simpler versions are generally more effective. The Wouters (2013) review concurs reporting that games using schematic visuals or text are more effective than those using cartoonlike or photo-realistic images.

5. Supplement Games With Other Instructional Methods

Games may be designed to be played as stand-alone activities or as an adjunct to other instructional events. Three reviews of research on games concur that games exert their best effects when used in conjunction with other instructional methods (Hays, 2005; Sitzmann, 2011; Wouters, 2013). There are no doubt a number of ways that games can be integrated with other instructional events. For example, games such as the language drill and practice games I described previously in this chapter could augment traditional tutorials on grammatical language rules. Alternatively, a strategy game could be followed by a group debrief in which different actions and responses are discussed and principles made explicit. Sitzmann (2011) recommends that "to maximize the potential of computer-based simulation games, they should be used as a supplement to lecture, discussion, tutorials, or other instructional methods" (517).

6. Assign Pairs to Play Challenging Games

Consider collaborative play to promote learning from a game. In their meta-analysis Wouters et al. (2013) reported that games that involved playing with another person resulted in a higher positive effect size of 0.66 compared to games played solo that yielded a lower effect size of 0.22. Along similar lines, Sears and Reagin (2013) reported that advanced learners achieved more when solving math problems on their own, whereas more novice learners benefited from solving problems in pairs. Collaboration when playing a challenging game may benefit players who are more likely to articulate game goals and underlying principles to one another than a solo player.

7. Make Games Available for Multiple Plays

Many research studies evaluated the learning benefits of games played only one time. Two research reviews (Wouters et al., 2013; Young et al., 2012) compared the benefits of games played only once to games played multiple times and found significant benefit from games when played multiple times.

8. Provide Instructional Support

Some games use a discovery approach that requires learners to induce underlying principles or relationships—in other words, by trying actions and seeing how the game responds. Alternatively, games can take a more directive approach by adding instructional support. Fiorella and Mayer (2012) added working aids to the basic circuit game shown in Figure 14-4. They included two aids. One was a pregame worksheet that required learners to identify the components of the circuit such as batteries and resistors. In this way, the elements of the circuit schematics would be familiar prior to game play. Second, they provided a game aid that listed principles such as, "If you add a battery in serial, the flow rate increases." The transfer test scores were better among players who used the worksheets with a high effect size of 0.77. In addition, player satisfaction was higher in the version with the worksheets.

9. Apply Personalization Principles

In chapter 7 we reviewed the benefits of informal language on learning. Mayer has found similar benefits of informal language in games. Subjects were assigned to either a formal or informal version of a botany game called Design-A-Plant. In the game the player is told the conditions of a fictitious planet and must create a plant with appropriate roots, stems, and leaves to survive in those conditions. An on-screen agent called Herman the Bug explained the conditions of the planet and gave feedback to player responses. In a formal version Herman might say: "In very rainy environments, plant leaves have to be flexible so they are not damaged by the rainfall. What really matters for the rain is the choice between thick and thin leaves." In contrast, the informal narration stated: "This is a very rainy environment and the leaves of your plant have to be flexible so they're not damaged by the rainfall. What really matters for the rain is your choice between thick and thin leaves." In five separate experiments, Moreno and Mayer (2000, 2004) found better learning from the more informal versions with a median effect size of 1.58, which is very high.

10. Reconsider Competitive Elements in Games

A competitive element is game feedback in the form of scores or points. The competition may be individualized in the form of scores posted over play rounds or among different players. DeLeeuw and Mayer (2011) added competitive elements to the circuit game shown in Figure 14-4. In the competitive version the players saw a graphic of their scores on each level. Based on these scores they could earn tickets that were entered into a raffle for a prize. Adding competitive elements did improve retention of information but not transfer learning. In other words, competition improved memory outcomes but not deeper learning. The research team noted differences in outcomes among men and women. Men did worse in the competitive version than in the base version, whereas women did better.

The value of a competitive element may depend on the basis for the score and on the instructional goal. For example, in language learning, a cumulative graph showing speed or accuracy of response over multiple game plays may be valuable feedback for players as progress indicators. However, for some learning goals, a score—especially one displayed frequently—may become a distraction. We will need more research on what kinds of competitive elements are most beneficial for different game types, learning goals, and learners.

In conclusion, you may have noted that many beneficial instructional methods that we have reviewed throughout this book also apply to serious games. Relevant engagement with feedback, personalization in language, self-explanation questions, and explanations of principles are four examples. As a general observation, in designing a game, applying instructional techniques shown to benefit traditional learning environments may often result in a more effective game.

THE BOTTOM LINE

Now that we have reviewed the evidence accumulated to date on the effects of games, let's revisit your original ideas about them.

What Do You Think?

Based on my interpretation of the evidence in this chapter, I summarize my answers below:

A. Overall there is substantial evidence for the effectiveness of serious games.

FALSE. First, it is really difficult to make too many generalizations about a method as broad as games. As you know, there are many types of games and their benefits will depend on their design, features of the players, and the instructional goals. Further, even the more positive reviews of game research had qualifications that suggest a conservative interpretation. In the end, no doubt some games are useful for some individuals to achieve some learning goals. We will need more research to narrow down these generalizations.

B. Narratives in games make them more effective for learning.

FALSE. Based on evidence to date, narratives do not appear to make games more effective; in fact they often serve as a distraction from the instructional content. If this generalization holds up, it suggests that adventure games may not offer the best design approach.

C. Entertainment games can affect basic cognitive skills and behaviors.

TRUE. It appears that entertainment games can have both positive and negative cognitive and behavioral consequences. For example, games may promote aggressive or risk-taking behaviors or positive health practices. The effects will depend on the nature of the game, the player, and the context.

D. Learning from games can be improved by aids that explain the principles underlying the game rules and responses.

TRUE. We have ample evidence that unguided discovery learning is both inefficient and ineffective. By providing guidance in the form of learning aids, serious games can be more effective and more efficient. As this research stream expands, we will learn more about what types of guidance are most effective. For now, I recommend guidance regarding how to interact with a game, the basic instructional principles of a game, and explanatory feedback to accompany game responses.

APPLYING GAMES TO YOUR TRAINING PROGRAMS

While there may be solid potential in harnessing the motivational potential of games in the service of learning, as of yet, we do not have good guidelines for the types of games most useful for given learning objectives and players. The most useful stream of research delineates the features we can embed in games that boost learning. Evidence to date suggests the following guidelines:

- Design game engagement, rules, and progress to align with the learning objectives.

- Provide explanatory feedback.

- Ask learners to select reasons for their game moves (self-explanations).

- Avoid extraneous narrative treatments and overly complex interfaces.

- Combine games with other instructional methods such as tutorials.

- Provide for multiple game plays.

- Provide instructional support such as explanations of game interface elements or principles.

- Personalize games with first- and second-person informal language.

- Assign more complex games to pairs.

- Consider games for skills that benefit from drill and practice such as second-language learning.

COMING NEXT

In the final chapter I will summarize some of the themes that emerge from a consideration of the evidence across multiple chapters.

FOR MORE INFORMATION

Mayer, R.E. (2014). *Computer Games for Learning*. MIT Press Cambridge, MA.

This book presents a readable unbiased review of the evidence on games. It provides more detail on the themes I introduced in this chapter. I recommend it for every instructional professional interested in games for learning.

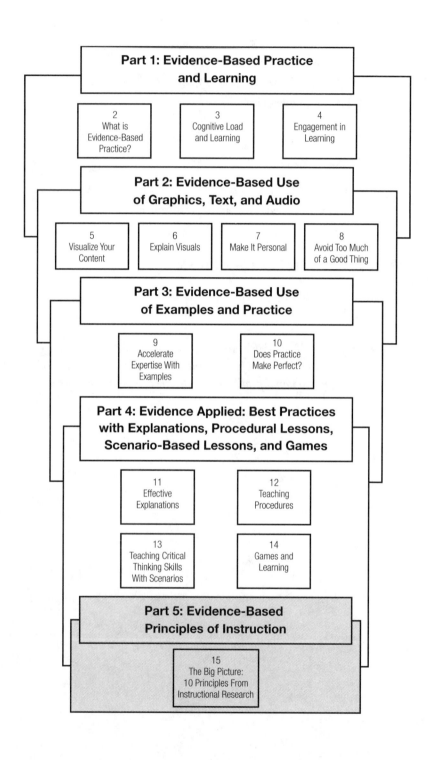

PART 5

Evidence-Based Principles of Instruction

From graphics to games, we have surveyed much of the current research landscape that offers specific guidelines for practitioners. However you'll notice that several themes emerge that go beyond the evidence presented in any one chapter. In this final chapter I briefly summarize 10 themes that were salient for me. Keep these themes in mind as you make decisions that go beyond any one instructional method in this book.

THE BIG PICTURE: 10 PRINCIPLES FROM INSTRUCTIONAL RESEARCH

Evidence Can Inform Practice

A Few Instructional "Laws"

No Yellow Brick Road

Prior Knowledge Is the Important Individual Difference

The Power of Self-Explanations

Exploit Examples

Psychological Engagement Is Essential to Learning

Cognitive Load Management

Workplace Context

Define Your Instructional Methods

CHAPTER 15

The Big Picture: 10 Principles From Instructional Research

In chapter 1, I mentioned the four humors of blood, phlegm, and black and yellow bile. Many medical treatments, such as bloodletting, were linked to flawed models and led to death. Today we have a more accurate understanding of disease with research accumulating yearly. Some of the myths that characterize workforce learning practices may not lead to death. But they do impede learning or at least divert resources from methods that have greater potential to give a return on investment.

From graphics to examples and from explanations to games, throughout this book I have offered guidelines based on the most recent research specific to the chapter theme. However, now that it's all said, I find there are some general themes that span a number of chapters that are worth underscoring. In this final chapter I will summarize a few "mega themes" not salient in any one chapter but that emerge across multiple chapters.

1. EVIDENCE CAN INFORM PRACTICE

My research for this book found quite a few experiments relevant to practitioners. Even better, there are a number of research reviews in the form of meta-analyses and books. The body of practical evidence that practitioners can use grows yearly and much of it focuses on questions and methods we consider daily—issues such as games, explanations, and graphics. The references cited throughout this book are at least double those in the first edition. In part, I decided to cite more of the sources than I did in the first edition to give credit to the scientists whose work I described. But also there is a growing body of evidence available. I suspect that most practitioners lack the time to search, read, and summarize this evidence and I hope this book fills that void. In any event, there is sufficient research on issues that practitioners face daily to guide our design, development, and delivery decisions.

2. A FEW INSTRUCTIONAL "LAWS"

Although many of the guidelines throughout the book are subject to qualifications (see next paragraph), we do have several universal guidelines that apply to most instructional contexts. I believe that some of these guidelines are as close as we will come to laws in our field. To qualify as a law, an instructional practice should be applicable to diverse content, learners, and instructional goals. A good example is the spacing effect discussed in chapter 10. Demonstrated with many types of content and learners, the spacing effect shows better long-term learning when practice opportunities are distributed within and across lessons. The spacing effect supports making learning a process, not just a single event. With current technology, we can develop learning events using a combination of synchronous and asynchronous media.

Another "law" relates to the benefits of explanatory feedback that informs learners not only whether their answer was correct but also states the reason. Effective feedback is acknowledged as one of the most important instructional methods in our tool kit.

3. NO YELLOW BRICK ROAD

As research on any given issue evolves, the new findings often specify the conditions under which that method is most successful. Consider graphics. There are a number of conditions under which a graphic will promote learning. And a few in which graphics impede learning. To be effective, the graphic must be relevant to the instructional goal. Explanatory graphics in particular can be helpful to show relationships in your content. Second, graphics are generally most effective for learners who are new to the content, rather than those with more experience. This is because often a more experienced learner can form a visual image by reading the text. Third, for many situations a simpler graphic such as a line drawing or a series of line drawings is more effective than a more complex rendering such as a photograph or an animation. Finally, graphics have more impact when learners are explicitly engaged with them. You may have noticed a number of questions I include in this book asking you to review a graphic and then select an interpretation of it. My goal is to draw your attention to the graphic and offer you the opportunity to engage with it.

I've used graphics as an example but in fact the "no yellow brick road" theme applies to a variety of instructional methods reviewed in the book, including the modality effect, worked examples, and games. No yellow brick road suggests that we will usually need to factor in the instructional goal and the learners' prior knowledge when applying many of the guidelines offered here.

4. PRIOR KNOWLEDGE IS THE IMPORTANT INDIVIDUAL DIFFERENCE

While individual differences such as learning styles and emotional intelligence are charismatic, for learning outcomes, the single most widely demonstrated difference is prior knowledge. A novice learner is more subject to cognitive overload and therefore benefits from different instructional methods than learners with experience in the domain. We saw this relationship with graphics, examples, questions, and use of audio to explain visuals. As I mentioned in chapter 1, if this book does no more than encourage instructional professionals to scrap resources invested in learning styles, the book will be a success.

5. THE POWER OF SELF-EXPLANATIONS

Learners with highly developed learning skills will spontaneously study instructional content such as worked examples and derive their underlying principles. But many will gloss over examples or give them only cursory attention. Several experiments have focused on the value of promoting self explanations by attaching a question to a given instructional element. In this book I have reviewed studies showing the benefits of self-explanations when learning from worked examples, graphics, and games. No doubt self-explanations benefit many instructional environments. Rather than give a detailed instructional explanation, provide a graphic or an example and ask learners to derive their own explanations. Follow up with an activity and feedback to ensure accuracy of those self-explanations.

6. EXPLOIT EXAMPLES

We have a rich body of evidence for the learning value of worked examples that illustrate high structure tasks, interpersonal skills, and problem-solving tasks. To maximize the value of your examples, make them engaging using the techniques summarized in chapter 9. These include adding self-explanation questions, creating faded worked examples and promoting comparison among examples. Be sure to apply the basic principles regarding text, audio, and graphics to the design of your worked examples. Research found that when an example violated contiguity by separating graphic from text, the instructional value of that example was negated.

7. PSYCHOLOGICAL ENGAGEMENT IS ESSENTIAL TO LEARNING

The "active learning" focus in our field is on the right track—but, the activity that is important is the mental activity. In some cases physical activity actually defeats the appropriate mental activity. For example, in some games, the physical actions or narratives absorb mental resources that detract from the instructional goal. I described a couple of games in chapter 14 that reflect this design flaw. Keep in mind the engagement matrix introduced in chapter 4. Learner overt responses (active learning) are useful when those responses align with the required psychological engagement of the job. Overt responses allow for feedback. At the same time, learning can occur in the absence of physical engagement. Brief explanations supported with visuals, personal wording, and examples are shown to activate psychological processes that promote learning.

8. COGNITIVE LOAD MANAGEMENT

Cognitive load is a helpful theory to guide our design, development, and delivery of instructional events. A focus on minimizing extraneous cognitive load by shortening, eliminating, or simplifying elements of the learning environment; by explaining complex graphics with audio; and by using worked examples is especially critical for novice learners. Less extraneous load frees working memory for germane load through activities such as practice exercises, self-explanations, and other forms of engagement that lead to learning.

9. WORKPLACE CONTEXT

The idea of context cropped up in a few of the chapters. It is mentioned in the chapter on examples, practice, and scenario-based e-learning. However, incorporating the context of the workplace is a fundamental principle of effective job training. Designing graphics, examples, practice exercises, games, and scenario-based learning lessons that reflect the sights, sounds, and psychological environment of the workplace will project greater relevance and will build skills that will transfer to the workplace. At the same time, instructional elements that do not embody job context such as irrelevant stories or narrative themes in games risk corroding learning outcomes.

10. DEFINE YOUR INSTRUCTIONAL METHODS

We have a tendency to use terms loosely. Take games for example. The term *game* includes a plethora of different approaches and features. Before we make generalizations about methods such as games we need to specify what we mean by that method. What type of game? What are the main features of a game? Next time you read or hear claims for any method such as games, review or discuss the features of that method. In our field we often use the same term to mean different things. At the same time we use different terms to mean the same thing. For example, what I call scenario-based learning, may be referred to as immersive learning, case-based learning, problem-based learning, or whole-task learning, to name just a few. Before you adopt a position on approaches such as these, take the time to get clarity on the approach in question.

WHAT'S NEXT

This chapter brings us to the end of this story. But the lessons from research will continue. I am certain there will be new guidelines available by the time this book is published. Keep in touch with the ATD Community of the Science of Learning for research updates. Another useful way to keep current is to purchase handbooks or review books and take classes that incorporate evidence for their guidelines. The second edition *Cambridge Handbook of Multimedia Learning* (Mayer, 2014a) and *Computer Games for Learning* (Mayer, 2014b) are two examples.

In the academic research, I predict greater emphasis on measures and methods aligned to motivation. In addition, we will see more value added research in which a given approach such as a game is tested with different features added. This type of research will yield a series of design guidelines that we can apply to our instructional methods. For example, in chapter 14 we saw that the addition of self-explanation questions or job aids improved learning from a basic game.

So, what's next for you? In the appendix, I include a synopsis of many of the instructional methods I have reviewed in this book. It's a job aid in which you can find an overview of many of the guidelines and link back to them in the book. My hope is you will be able to apply many of these guidelines to your decisions regarding the design, development, and delivery of instructional environments. I also realize that constraints such as time, budget, technology, policies, and other factors will preclude application of all guidelines all of the time. But it's a step forward to know the evidence and to be aware of the trade-off when your decisions supersede evidence-based guidelines.

Your comments are welcome. Contact me: Ruth@Clarktraining.com

A SYNOPSIS OF INSTRUCTIONAL METHODS

Evidence-Based Principles on Communication Modes
    (Text, Graphics, Audio)
Evidence-Based Principles for Examples
Evidence-Based Principles of Engagement
Evidence-Based Guidelines for Explanations
Evidence-Based Guidelines for Teaching Procedures
Evidence-Based Guidelines for Scenario-Based Learning
Evidence-Based Guidelines for Games

Appendix: A Synopsis of Instructional Methods

We've looked at quite a bit of instructional research in the past 15 chapters. In this appendix I will summarize most of the important guidelines. If you are interested in a specific issue, you can review the headings below to get a summary and then refer to the specific chapters to get the details. Remember that the effectiveness of many instructional methods will have qualifiers such as background knowledge of the learners or the instructional goal. There are few universal guidelines. As you review the guidelines below, I recommend you refer back to the chapter to read some of the details and the supporting evidence. That way, you can determine whether and when a guideline applies to your situation.

EVIDENCE-BASED PRINCIPLES ON COMMUNICATION MODES (TEXT, AUDIO, GRAPHICS)

All instructional environments from books to simulations rely on some combination of text, audio, and graphics to communicate content and instructional methods. We have quite a bit of research to guide best use of these modes.

MODE	GUIDELINES	CHAPTERS
Graphics	Relevant graphics will improve learning of novices compared to text alone. Avoid seductive or unnecessarily complex visuals that distract learners from the instructional content. Learners prefer materials with graphics of any kind. Photographs and animations are more effective than text for performance support of spatial tasks. More research is needed on motivational effects of decorative graphics.	2, 5, 8

Stills Versus Animations	Still visuals generally impose less mental load than animated visuals. Still visuals have been shown more effective to teach mechanical and scientific processes; animations have been shown more effective to teach procedures.	8
Computer Animation Versus Video	Video may offer a more emotive message and convey important details when high fidelity sights and sounds are needed. Computer-generated animations are easier to update and can impose less mental load than video. More research needed on when to use video versus animation.	8
Animated Visuals	Apply methods to manage cognitive load, including cues to direct attention, segmentation, controls to stop and replay, and explanations given in audio narration.	8
Text	Place text near a visual when the visual requires an explanation; otherwise omit words in any form. Write lean sentences. Chunk text into small segments allowing learners to access each chunk at their own pace in asynchronous e-learning. Use first and second person in your explanations.	6, 8
Audio	Explain complex graphics with audio rather than text to avoid split attention. Keep audio narration brief. See chapter 6 for exceptions.	6
Audio and Text	Avoid identical narration of written text. Narration that expands on short bulleted text is OK.	6

EVIDENCE-BASED PRINCIPLES FOR EXAMPLES

Humans are uniquely wired to learn by observation. You can save instructional time by providing examples of task completion. Referred to as worked examples, evidence has shown the benefits of demonstrations for learning structured tasks such as solving algebraic problems, interpersonal skills such as customer service, and critical thinking skills used in problem solving. Leverage your worked examples by applying the following guidelines:

GUIDELINE	DESCRIPTION	CHAPTER
Use high fidelity examples to illustrate routine tasks.	Worked examples for procedural tasks should mirror the sights and sounds of the workplace.	9
Use varied context examples for strategic tasks.	Provide two or more worked examples of tasks that involve problem solving or critical thinking that vary the cover story while illustrating the core guidelines.	9
Provide examples for novice learners.	Some worked examples have been shown to depress learning of individuals with background experience in the domain. More research needed on this relationship.	9

Engage learners in your examples.	Promote processing of your examples by: • Including a series of faded examples • Adding self-explanation questions to your examples • Assigning example comparisons.	9
Apply principles on text, audio, and graphics to examples.	When designing worked examples, use relevant visuals and keep text closely assigned to the visuals.	9

EVIDENCE-BASED PRINCIPLES OF ENGAGEMENT

Contrary to popular belief, not all engagement leads to learning. At the same time, engagement is essential to learning. Make a distinction between behavioral engagement and psychological engagement. In some cases, behavioral engagement leads to mental overload and depresses learning. In other cases, behavioral engagement does not align with the learning goal and thus does not promote the intended learning. However, effective behavioral engagement can maximize learning through feedback.

GUIDELINE	DESCRIPTION	CHAPTER
Some behavioral engagement depresses learning.	When behavioral engagement is unrelated to the learning objective, imposes extraneous mental load, or promotes incorrect or incomplete responses, learning is depressed. For example, filling in blank organizers led to less learning than reviewing a completed organizer.	4
Psychological engagement is essential with or without behavioral engagement.	Learning occurs when learners process and practice content and skills relevant to the learning objective. Relevant psychological processing can occur in the absence or presence of behavioral engagement.	4
Add techniques shown to promote psychological engagement.	Learning from explanations is best when you include: • relevant visuals • worked examples or demonstrations • personalization techniques.	2, 5, 7, 9
Best learning comes from relevant behavioral engagement with feedback.	Learning is optimized when the learner's response to a relevant behavioral engagement is followed by explanatory feedback. Some proven behavioral engagement techniques include adding questions to explanations and examples, using clickers during lectures, and assigning relevant collaborative exercises.	4, 10, 11, 12, 13

Optimize behavioral engagement in the form of practice exercises.	• Be sure the practice aligns to the learning objective. • Assign sufficient practice based on criticality of the task. • Space practice over and among learning events.	10, 12

EVIDENCE-BASED GUIDELINES FOR EXPLANATIONS

Almost all learning environments include explanations. They may be in the form of an instructor lecture or guidance, online tutorials, or hints provided during a game or simulation.

GUIDELINE	DESCRIPTION	CHAPTER
Add behavioral engagement to explanations.	Build in frequent activities during explanations, including questions (consider clicker questions), questions linked to examples (self-explanation questions), collaborative exercises, and drawing assignments.	11
Promote psychological engagement during explanations.	Incorporate relevant graphics and examples, keep explanations succinct, leverage social presence.	7, 8, 9

EVIDENCE BASED GUIDELINES FOR TEACHING PROCEDURES

A procedure is a task that is performed more or less the same way each time. Some examples of routine tasks include logging onto a computer, responding to routine customer transactions, or operating equipment in a consistent manner. Infrequent procedures can be guided by performance support to economize time spent training. Procedures are best trained with a part task approach.

GUIDELINE	DESCRIPTION	CHAPTER
Consider performance support to replace or supplement training.	For assembly tasks, visual performance aids (still graphics or animations) were more efficient for initial performance than text. After several task iterations, text, and graphics were equally effective.	8, 12
Break large tasks into sub-tasks, but teach in context of the whole.	To manage cognitive load, teach procedures in small chunks of 7-12 steps each. Be sure to illustrate subtasks in context of whole task.	12
Teach important concepts prior to the procedure.	Prior to demonstrating or practicing steps, teach critical concepts needed for understanding. Show concepts in context of the task.	12
Provide guided practice.	Depending on the complexity of the procedure, impose guidance in the form of demonstrations, guided practice, and feedback.	10, 12

EVIDENCE-BASED GUIDELINES FOR SCENARIO-BASED LEARNING

For tasks that involve critical thinking skills, or that are challenging to build expertise on the job due to safety or other constraints, consider scenario-based learning. Scenario-based learning, also called whole task, problem-based, or immersive learning, is a preplanned guided inductive learning environment designed to accelerate expertise. The learner assumes the role of a worker responding to an authentic job assignment or challenge, which in turn responds to reflect the learners' choices.

GUIDELINE	DESCRIPTION	CHAPTER
Use experts to identify realistic scenarios and the thinking processes to resolve them.	Build real-world scenarios that will be the driver of the learning. Ensure authentic scenarios by deriving them from experts.	13
Identify sufficient scenarios to reach competency.	Interview field supervisors to identify the number of problems or situations a worker should resolve to reach an acceptable level of competency.	13

Ensure sufficient guidance.	Some guidance techniques include: • transition from simple to complex scenarios • constrain learner control through scenario design with greater structure in initial scenarios • provide instructional support such as worked examples, and knowledge resources • provide consequential (intrinsic), as well as instructional feedback during and/or at the end of a scenario.	13
Provide opportunity for explicit reflection.	To maximize lessons learned, include techniques that encourage learners to review their decisions and actions and identify lessons learned. Some techniques include: • collaborative debrief • comparison of learner solution with expert solution • replay of the scenario • a learner statement of lessons learned.	13

EVIDENCE-BASED GUIDELINES FOR GAMES

There is currently a good deal about games and gamification. What evidence do we have for the benefits of serious games—that is games designed for both fun and learning? What techniques can be added to make games more effective as learning devices?

GUIDELINE	DESCRIPTION	CHAPTER
Align game progress to desired learning outcomes.	Design a game so that game actions and progress link to the learning goal.	14
Minimize complexity.	Avoid extraneous cognitive load in games by: • using a simple interface • avoiding narrative themes unrelated to learning • providing pretraining on principles underlying the game • avoiding mental work not directly related to the learning objective.	14

Promote reflection on lessons learned.	Learning from a game may result in tacit knowledge not readily articulated. Encourage conscious awareness of lessons learned through: • collaborative play • comparison of responses or results with expert responses or results • a learner statement of lessons learned.	14
Add known instructional methods to promote learning from games.	Some techniques shown to improve learning from a game include: • adding job aids such as an explanation of game principles • including a pregame exercise to familiarize players with game concepts and interface • giving explanatory feedback • adding self-explanation questions.	14

Glossary

A

Academic Evidence: Evidence derived primarily from research scientists in research facilities using scientific methods. For example, experiments and correlational studies.

Active Learning: The premise that learners must be actively engaged for learning to occur.

Application Practice: Assignments that ask learners to respond in ways they would respond on the job. Contrast with recall practice.

Asynchronous E-Learning: Computer learning environments in which individual learners study independently at their own pace usually in a self-study mode.

Automaticity: Any task that is hard wired into long-term memory can be performed without using working memory resources. Automaticity is built through repetition.

Avatar: An onscreen character. Also called pedagogical agent.

B

Behavioral Engagement: Active learning that involves an overt physical response.

Behaviorism: A psychological theory based on stimulus-response with reinforcement that is the basis for directive instuctional designs.

Blocked Practice: An organizational scheme in which practice exercises addressing a specific skill are grouped together. Contrast with mixed practice.

C

Clicker: A hand-held response technology that records and summarizes learner answers to projected questions.

Cognitive Overload: A condition stemming from exceeding the limited capacity of working memory. When overloaded, working memory processing becomes inefficient.

Collaborative Learning: Learning environments in which group participation is encouraged. Groups vary from two to six learners. Collaboration may be synchronous or asynchronous.

Comparison Experiments: Experiments in which two or more methods are compared for learning effectiveness and or efficiency. Characterized by random assignment of subjects and variation only of the method of interest. For example, learning is measured from two identical lessons: one with graphics and the other without graphics.

Correlational Studies: Research focusing on the relationship between two sets of data. For example, do individuals who smoke more have a higher probability of lung cancer?

D

Decorative Visual: A graphic added for visual appeal. Decorative visuals do not promote the learning objective.

Deliberate Practice: Engagement assignments that focus on individual gaps in performance often mediated by a coach.

Directive Instruction: Training design that is heavily guided and typically includes explanations, examples, practice, and feedback.

Dual Channel: Feature of working memory referring to components devoted to visual information and to auditory information.

E

Effect Size: The difference in outcomes between a test group and a control group expressed as multiplier of the standard deviation. Effect sizes of 0.3 and less are considered low; 0.3–0.7 medium and 0.8 and above high.

Evidence-Based Practice: The use of scientific evidence when making decisions regarding learning environments.

Examples: An instance provided in a learning environment to illustrate a task or a content topic. Includes demonstrations. Also called worked examples.

Expertise Reversal: A condition in which an instructional method that helps novice learners either does not help or even hurts more experienced learners. For example, visuals improve learning of novices but not more experienced learners.

Explanations: Words in audio or text intended to provide content.

Explanatory Visuals: A visual that depicts relationships among the content. *See also* organizational, relational, transformational, and interpretive.

Extraneous Cognitive Load: Irrelevant mental work imposed on working memory due to poor instructional design decisions.

Eye Tracking: A research technique in which the focus of attention on a display is measured through a trace of eye movements of the viewer.

F

Factorial Experiments: Experimental research in which two or more factors are varied across treatments. For example, the effects of a lesson with and without graphics are tested on novice and experienced learners.

Faded Worked Examples: A series of examples that starts with a full worked example and gradually imposes more work on the learner ending with a full problem assignment.

Feedback: Knowledge of results provided by the instruction typically in response to a practice exercise.

G

Game: An interactive environment characterized by a challenge, high levels of engagement, and responses in terms of changes in score or the game context. Serious games are designed to promote learning goals.

Germane Cognitive Load: Mental work imposed on working memory during learning in the service of learning. Relevant practice is one good example.

Graphics: A visual representation of content. Includes still visuals such as line drawings and moving visuals such as animations.

I

Instructional Media: The vehicle for delivering instructional events, including instructors, computers, workbooks, and video.

Instructional Method: A technique proven to make learning more effective or more efficient. Examples and practice are two important instructional methods addressed in this book.

Instructional Mode: Three basic communication mechanisms: graphics, text, and audio.

Interleaved Practice: An organizational scheme in which practice items from different problem categories are assigned together. Also called mixed practice. Contrast with blocked practice.

Interpretive Graphic: An explanatory visual that makes invisible phenomena visible. For example, a graphic of molecules.

Intrinsic Cognitive Load: Mental work imposed on working memory during learning due to the complexity of the instructional goals and content.

Intrinsic Feedback: Knowledge of results gleaned by seeing how a given action affects the environment. For example, after serving a tennis ball you can immediately see whether it landed where you intended. Often associated with scenario-based learning environments.

L

Learner-Centric View: A focus on the strengths and limits of human memory in the design, development, and delivery of instructional programs. Contrast with Techno-centric view.

Learning Style: Individual differences regarding how each learner would benefit from specific learning environments. Some of the more common learning styles include visual, auditory, and kinesthetic learners, the Myers-Briggs Inventory, and Kolb learning styles.

Level 1 Evaluation: An assessment of the quality of a learning event based on participant ratings.

Long-Term Memory: Permanent memory. The repository of our knowledge and skills. Contains organized knowledge and skills in structures called schemas.

M

Massed Practice: Organization of practice exercises in which most of the practice is assigned in one or two chunks. Contrast with spaced practice.

Media: *See* instructional media.

Mental Model: A representation of how something works stored in long-term memory.

Meta-analysis: A statistical technique in which multiple separate research studies can be synthesized to allow more robust generalizations about specific instructional tactics.

Method: *See* instructional methods.

Mixed Practice: An organization in which practice items that address several different topics are assigned together. Contrast with blocked practice.

Mode: *See* instructional mode.

O

Organizational Graphic: An explanatory visual that shows qualitative relationships among content topics. A tree diagram and a concept map are two examples.

Over Learning: Automaticity in task performance stemming from extensive practice.

P

Part-Task: An instructional design characterized by chunking content, which typically includes explanations, examples, and practice with immediate feedback. Contrast with whole-task.

Personalization Principle: Guidelines for making instruction more personal such as writing in first and second person. Evidence shows better learning in a personal environment.

Planning Phase: A stage in the creation of a presentation in which the sequence of topics, the introduction, and activities are specified. Usually takes the form of an outline.

Power Law of Practice: The relationship between the amount of practice and skill proficiency stating that proficiency continues to improve with continued practice but at diminishing rates.

Practice: Overt opportunities for learners to respond during a lesson in ways that support the objectives of the lesson. Diverse formats include multiple choice, drag and drop, projects, drill and practice, and so on.

Practitioner Evidence: Evidence derived by workforce learning practitioners to guide the selection, design, and development of instructional environments. For example, needs assessment and evaluation.

Principled Presentation: An audio explanation by a speaker or narrator that incorporates proven instructional modes and methods to promote learning.

Problem-Based Learning: A form of scenario-based learning design commonly used in medical education.

Procedural Skills: Tasks that are performed more or less the same way each time they are done. Step by step routine tasks. Examples include logging onto your computer and following a recipe.

Protocol Analysis: The coding of statements made during learning or during problem solving to derive the basis of decisions made or learning outcomes.

Psychological Engagement: Active learning that results in achievement of the instructional goal. May or may not be accompanied by behavioral activity.

Pumpkin Slides: Decorative visuals that do not promote the learning objective.

R

Recall Practice: Assignments that ask learners to repeat back content provided in the lesson. Also called regurgitate practice. Contrast with application practice.

Relational Graphic: An explanatory visual that summarizes quantitative data. Bar charts and pie graphs are common examples.

S

Scaffolding: Guidance included in lessons to reduce learner confusion and make learning more efficient. Scaffolding is especially needed in scenario-based learning designs.

Scenario-Based Learning: An instructional design in which the lesson starts with a problem or assignment that serves as the engine for learning. Also called whole-task learning.

Scoping Phase: A stage in the creation of presentations in which the purpose of the presentation, features of the audience and presentation setting are defined.

Self-Explanation: A form of active learning in which learners deeply process an instructional element, such as an example or graphic. Effective self-explanations connect the learning material with underlying principles or with prior knowledge.

Simulation: A model of a real-world or scientific phenomenon. Simulations may be operational or conceptual.

Social Media: Computer applications that connect individuals in a personal way. Examples include Twitter and Facebook.

Social Presence: The inclusion of interpersonal cues in a learning environment. Face-to-face environments typically have greatest potential for social presence while asynchronous e-learning has less.

Spaced Practice: Organization of practice assignments in which practice sessions are distributed throughout a lesson and among lessons. Contrast with massed practice.

Strategic Skills: Tasks that are performed uniquely each time. These tasks require adaptation and problem solving to accommodate changes in the performance environment. Examples include making a sale and conducting a performance appraisal.

Synchronous E-Learning: Computer-delivered instruction in which participants are geographically separate but online at the same time. Also called virtual classrooms. Contrast with asynchronous e-learning.

T

Techno-Centric View: A focus on the use of technology for learning often without regard for how technology features best support human learning processes.

Transfer: When new knowledge and skills acquired in a learning setting are retrieved and applied on the job, we say that transfer has occurred.

Transformational Graphic: An explanatory visual that shows changes in time or space. A cycle chart and animation of screen changes are two examples.

V

Varied Context Examples: A series of examples to illustrate a core principle in which the surface features of the examples change.

W

Whole-Task: An instructional design that uses an authentic task as the driver for learning. Also called scenario-based learning. Contrast with part-task.

Worked Examples: *See* examples.

Working Memory: Part of human memory that is responsible for conscious awareness, thinking, and learning. Working memory has a limited capacity of around four to six chunks of information.

References

Abercrombie, S. (2013). Transfer Effects of Adding Seductive Details to Case-Based Instruction. *Contemporary Educational Psychology* 38:149-157.

Adams, D.M., R.E. Mayer, A. MacNamara, A. Koenig, and R. Wainess. (2012). Narrative Games for Learning: Testing the Discovery and Narrative Hypotheses. *Journal of Educational Psychology* 104:235-249.

Adesope, O.O., and J.C. Nesbit. (2012). Verbal Redundancy in Multimedia Learning Environments: A Meta-Analysis. *Journal of Educational Psychology* 104:250-263.

Ainsworth, S., and S. Burcham. (2007). The Impact of Text Coherence on Learning by Self-Explanation. *Learning and Instruction* 17:286-303.

Ainsworth, S., and A. Loizou. (2003). The Effect of Self-Explaining When Learning With Text or Diagrams. *Cognitive Science* 27:669-681.

Alfieri, L., P.J. Brooks, N.J. Aldrich, and H.R. Tenenbaum. (2011). Does Discovery-Based Instruction Enhance Learning? *Journal of Educational Psychology* 103:1-18.

American Society for Training & Development (ASTD). (2013). *State of the Industry Report 2013*. Alexandria, VA: ASTD Press.

———. (2014). *Playing to Win: Gamification and Serious Games in Organizational Learning*. Alexandria, VA: ASTD Press.

Anderson, L.S., A.F. Healy, J.A. Kole, and L.E. Bourne. (2013). The Clicker Technique: Cultivating Efficient Teaching and Successful Learning. *Applied Cognitive Psychology* 27:222-234.

Atkinson, R.K., A. Renkl, and M.M. Merrill. (2003). Transitioning From Studying Examples to Solving Problems: Effects of Self-Explanation Prompts and Fading Worked Out Steps. *Journal of Educational Psychology* 95(4): 774-783.

Aydin, S. (2012). A Review of Research on Facebook as an Educational Environment. *Education Technology Research & Development* 60(6): 1093-1106.

Ayres, P., N. Marcus, C. Chan, and N. Qian. (2009). Learning Hand Manipulative Tasks: When Instructional Animations Are Superior to Equivalent Static Representations. *Computers in Human Behavior* 25:348-353.

Baddeley, A.D., and D.J.A. Longman. (1978). The Influence of Length and Frequency of Training Session on the Rate of Learning to Type. *Ergonomics* 21:627-635.

Bernard, R.M., P.C. Abrami, Y. Lou, E. Borokhovski, A. Wade, L. Wozney, P.A. Wallet, M. Fisher, and B. Huang. (2004). How Does Distance Education Compare With Classroom Instruction? A Meta-Analysis of the Empirical Literature. *Review of Educational Research* 74:379-439.

Bligh, D.A. (2000). *What's the Use of Lectures?* San Francisco: Jossey-Bass.

Boucheix, J.M., R.K. Lowe, D.K. Putri, and J. Groff. (2013). Cueing Animations: Dynamic Signaling Aids Information Extraction and Comprehension. *Learning and Instruction* 25:71-84.

Brewer, N., S. Harey, and C. Semmler. (2004). Improving Comprehension of Jury Instructions With Audio-Visual Presentation. *Applied Cognitive Psychology* 18:765-776.

Burkhardt, H., and A.H. Schoenfeld. (2003). Improving Educational Research: Toward a More Useful, More Influential, and Better-Funded Enterprise. *Educational Researcher* 32:3-14.

Butcher, K.R. (2006). Learning From Text With Diagrams. Promoting Mental Model Development and Inference Generation. *Journal of Educational Psychology* 98: 182-197.

Chi, M.T.H. (2000). Self-Explaining Expository Texts: The dual Processes of Generating Inferences and Repairing Mental Models. In *Advances in Instructional Psychology: Educational Design and Cognitive Science*, ed. R. Glaser. Mahwah, NJ: Lawrence Erlbaum Associates.

Chi, M.T.H., M. Bassok, M.W. Lewis, P. Reimann, and R. Glaser. (1989). Self-Explanation: How Students Study and Use Examples in Learning to Solve Problems. *Cognitive Science* 5:145-182.

Cho, K., and C. MacArthur. (2011). Learning by Reviewing. *Journal of Educational Psychology* 103:73-84.

Clark, R.C. (2008). *Developing Technical Training*. San Francisco: Pfeiffer.

———. (2013). *Scenario-Based E-Learning*. San Francisco: Pfeiffer.

Clark, R.C., and A. Kwinn. (2007). *The New Virtual Classroom*. San Francisco: Pfeiffer.

Clark, R.C., and C. Lyons. (2011). *Graphics for Learning*, 2nd ed. San Francisco: Pfeiffer.

Clark, R.C., F. Nguyen, and J. Sweller. (2006). *Efficiency in Learning*. San Francisco: Pfeiffer.

Clark, R.C., and R.E. Mayer. (2008). Learning by Viewing Versus Learning by Doing: Evidence-Based Guidelines for Principled Learning Environments. *Performance Improvement* 47:5-13.

———. (2011). *E-Learning and the Science of Instruction*, 3rd ed. San Francisco: Pfeiffer.

Clark, R.E., and D.F. Feldon. (2014). Six Common but Mistaken Principles of Multimedia Learning. In *Cambridge Handbook of Multimedia Learning*, 2nd ed., ed. R.E. Mayer. Boston, MA: Cambridge Press.

Connolly, T.M., E.A. Boyle, E. MacArthur, T. Hainey, and J.M. Boyle. (2012). A Systematic Literature Review of Empirical Evidence on Computer Games and Serious Games. *Computers & Education* 59:661-686.

Cook, D.A., W.G. Thompson, K.G. Thomas, and M.R. Thomas. (2009). Lack of Interaction Between Sensing-Intuitive Learning Styles and Problem-First Versus Information-First Instruction: A Randomized Crossover Trial. *Advances in Health Science Education* 14: 70-90.

Corbalan, G., F. Paas, and H. Cuypers. (2010). Computer-Based Feedback in Linear Algebra: Effects on Transfer Performance and Motivation. *Computers & Education* 95:692-703.

Cromley, J.G., B.W. Bergey, S. Fitzhugh, N. Newcombe, T.W. Wills, T.F. Shipley, and J.C. Tanaka. (2013). Effects of Three Diagram Instruction Methods on Transfer of Diagram Comprehension Skills: The Critical Role of Inference While Learning. *Learning & Instruction* 26:45-58.

De Koning, B.B., H.K. Tabbers, R.M.J.P. Rikers, and F. Paas. (2007). Attention Cueing as a Means to Enhance Learning From an Animation. *Applied Cognitive Psychology* 21:731-746.

———. (2011). Improved Effectiveness of Cueing by Self-Explanations When Learning From a Complex Animation. *Applied Cognitive Psychology* 25:183-194.

De La Paz, S., and M.K. Felton. (2010). Reading and Writing From Multiple Source Documents in History: Effects of Strategy Instruction With Low to Average High School Writers. *Contemporary Educational Psychology* 35:174-192.

DeLeeuw, K.E., and R.E. Mayer. (2011). Cognitive Consequences of Making Computer-Based Learning Activities More Game-Like. *Computers in Human Behavior* 27:2011-2016.

Dunlosky, J., and K.A. Rawson. (2012). Overconfidence Produces Underachievement: Inaccurate Self-Evaluations Undermine Students' Learning and Retention. *Learning and Instruction* 22:271-280.

Dunlosky, J., K.A. Rawson, E.J. Marsh, M.J. Nathan, and D.T. Willingham. (2013). Improving Students' Learning With Effective Learning Techniques: Promising Directions From Cognitive and Educational Psychology. *Psychological Science in the Public Interest* 14:4-58.

Ericcson, K.A. (2006). The Influence of Experience and Deliberate Practice on the Development of Superior Expert Performance. In *The Cambridge Handbook of Expertise and Expert Performance*, eds. K.A. Ericsson, N. Charness, P.J. Feltovich, and R.R. Hoffman. New York: Cambridge University Press.

Evans, C. (2013). Making Sense of Assessment Feedback in Higher Education. *Review of Educational Research* 83:70-120.

Eysink, T.H.S., T. de Jong, K. Berthold, B. Kolloffel, M. Opfermann, and P. Wouters. (2009). Learner Performance in Multimedia Learning Arrangements: An Analysis Across Instructional Approaches. *American Educational Research Journal* 46:1107-1149.

Fiorella, L., and R.E. Mayer. (2012). Paper-Based Aids for Learning With a Computer Game. *Journal of Educational Psychology* 104:1074-1082.

Fischer, M.H. (2000). Do Irrelevant Depth Cues Affect the Comprehension of Bar Graphs? *Applied Cognitive Psychology* 14(22): 151-162.

Fischer, P., J. Kubitzki, S. Guter, and D. Frey. (2007). Virtual Driving and Risk Taking: Do Racing Games Increase Risk-Taking Cognitions, Affect, and Behaviors? *Journal of Experimental Psychology, Applied* 13:22-31.

Fulton, L.V., L.V. Ivanitskaya, N.D. Bastian, D.A. Erofeev, and F.A. Mendez. (2013). Frequent Deadlines: Evaluating the Effect of Learner Control on Healthcare Executives' Performance in Online Learning. *Learning and Instruction* 23:24-32.

Gadgil, S., T.J. Nokes-Malach, and M.T.H. Chi. (2012). Effectiveness of Holistic Mental Model Confrontation in Driving Conceptual Change. *Learning and Instruction* 22:47-61.

Gentner, D., J. Loewenstein, and L. Thompson. (2003). Learning and Transfer: A General Role for Analogical Encoding. *Journal of Educational Psychology* 95:393-408.

Ginns, P. (2005). Meta-Analysis of the Modality Effect. *Learning and Instruction* 15:313-331.

———. (2006). Integrating Information: A Meta-Analysis of Spatial Contiguity and Temporal Contiguity Effects. *Learning and Instruction* 16:511-525.

Ginns, P., A.J. Martin, and H.W. Marsh. (2013). Designing Instructional Text in a Conversational Style: A Meta-Analysis. *Educational Psychology Review* 25:445-472.

Haidet, P., R.O. Morgan, K. O'Malley, B.J. Moran, and B.F. Richards. (2004). A Controlled Trial of Active Learning Strategies in a Large Group Setting. *Advances in Health Sciences Education* 9:15-27.

Hatala, R.M., L.R. Brooks, and G.R. Norman. (2003). Practice Makes Perfect: The Critical Role of Mixed Practice in the Acquisition of ECG Interpretation Skills. *Advances in Health Sciences Education* 8:17-26.

Hattie, J.A.C. (2009). *Visible Learning: A Synthesis of Over 800 Meta-Analyses Relating to Achievement.* London: Routledge.

Hattie, J., and M. Gan. (2011). Instruction Based on Feedback. In *Handbook of Research on Learning and Instruction,* eds. R.E. Mayer and P.A. Alexander. New York: Routledge.

Hattie, J., and G. Yates (2014). *Visible Learning and the Science of How We Learn.* London: Routledge.

Hays, R.T. (2005). *The Effectiveness of Instructional Games: A Literature Review and Discussion. Technical Report 2005-004.* Naval Air Warfare Center Training Systems Division, Orlando, FL.

Hegarty, M., H.S. Smallman, and A.T. Stull. (2012). Choosing and Using Geospatial Displays. Effects of Design on Performance and Metacognition. *Journal of Experimental Psychology: Applied* 18:1-17.

Heidig, S., and G. Clarebout. (2011). Do Pedagogical Agents Make a Difference to Student Motivation and Learning? *Educational Research Review* 6:27-54.

Hew, K.F., and W.S. Cheung. (2013). Use of Web 2.0 Technologies in K-12 and Higher Education: The Search for Evidence-Based Practice. *Educational Research Review* 9:47-64.

Johnson, C.I., and R.E. Mayer. (2012). An Eye Movement Analysis of the Spatial Contiguity Effect in Multimedia Learning. *Journal of Experimental Psychology: Applied* 18:178-191.

Jones, R., M. Panda, and N. Desbiens. (2008). Internal Medicine Residents Do Not Accurately Assess Their Medical Knowledge. *Advances in Health Science Education* 13:463-468.

Kalyuga, S. (2012). Instructional Benefits of Spoken Words: A Review of Cognitive Load Factors. *Educational Research Review* 7:145-159.

Kalyuga, S., P. Chandler, J. Tuovinen, and J. Sweller. (2001). When Problem Solving Is Superior to Studying Worked Examples. *Journal of Educational Psychology* 93:579-588.

Kamin, C.S., P.S. O'Sullivan, R. Deterding, and M. Younger. (2003). A Comparison of Critical Thinking in Groups of Third-Year Medical Students in Text, Video, and Virtual PBL Case Modalities. *Academic Medicine* 78(2): 204-211.

Kauffman, D.F., R. Zhao, and Y. Yang. (2011). Effects of Online Note Taking Formats and Self-Monitoring Prompts on Learning From Online Text: Using Technology to Enhance Self-Regulated Learning. *Contemporary Educational Psychology* 36:313-322.

Kellogg, R.E., and A.P. Whiteford. (2009). Training Advanced Writing Skills: The Case for Deliberate Practice. *Educational Psychologist* 44:250-266.

Kirschner, F., F. Paas, P.A. Kirschner, and J. Janssen. (2011a). Differential Effects of Problem-Solving Demands on Individual and Collaborative Learning Outcomes. *Learning and Instruction* 21:587-599.

Kirschner, F., F. Paas, and P.A. Kirschner. (2011b). Task Complexity as a Driver for Collaborative Learning Efficiency: The Collective Working Memory Effect. *Applied Cognitive Psychology* 25:615-624.

Kluger, A.N., and A. DeNisi. (1996). The Effects of Feedback Interventions on Performance: A Historical Review, a Meta-Analysis, and a Preliminary Feedback Intervention Theory. *Psychological Bulletin* 119:254-254.

Kornell, N., and R.A. Bjork. (2008). Learning Concepts and Categories: Is Spacing the "Enemy of Induction"? *Psychological Science* 19:585-592.

Kratzig, G.P., and K.D. Arbuthnott. (2006). Perceptual Learning Style and Learning Proficiency: A Test of the Hypothesis. *Journal of Educational Psychology* 98:238-246.

Krause, U., R. Stark, and H. Mandl. (2009). The Effects of Cooperative Learning and Feedback on E-Learning in Statistics. *Learning and Instruction* 19:158-170.

Lazonder, A.W., M.G. Hagemans, and T. de Jong. (2010). Offering and Discovering Domain Information in Simulation-Based Inquiry Learning. *Learning and Instruction* 20:511-520.

Lehman, S., G. Schraw, M.T. McCruddent, and K. Kartler. (2007). Processing and Recall of Seductive Details in Scientific Text. *Contemporary Educational Psychology* 32:569-587.

Leopold, C., E. Sumfleth, and D. Leutner. (2013). Learning With Summaries: Effects of Representation Mode and Type of Learning Activity on Comprehension and Transfer. *Learning and Instruction* 27:40-49.

Linek, S.B., P. Gerjets, and K. Scheiter. (2010). The Speaker/Gender Effect: Does the Speaker's Gender Matter When Presenting Auditory Text in Multimedia Messages? *Instructional Science* 38:503-521.

Liu, H., M. Lai, and H. Chuang. (2011). Using Eye-Tracking Technology to Investigate the Redundant Effect of Multimedia Web Pages on Viewers' Cognitive Processes. *Computers in Human Behavior* 27:241.

Lowe, R., W. Schnotz, and T. Rasch. (2011). Aligning Affordances of Graphics with Learning Task Requirements. *Applied Cognitive Psychology* 25:452-459.

Lundeberg, M.A., H. Kang, B. Wolter, R. delMas, N. Armstrong, B. Borsari, N. Boury, P. Brickman, K. Hannam, C. Heinz, T. Horvath, M. Knabb, T. Platt, N. Rice, B. Rogers, J. Sharp, E. Ribbens, K.S. Maier, M. Dechryver, R. Hagley, T. Goulet, and C.F. Herreid. (2011). Context Matters: Increasing Understanding With Interactive Clicker Case Studies. *Education Technology Research and Development* 59:645-671.

Marsh, E.J., and H.E. Sink. (2010). Access to Handouts of Presentation Slides During Lecture: Consequences for Learning. *Applied Cognitive Psychology* 24:691-706.

Mason, L., R. Lowe, and M.C. Tornatora. (2013). Self-Generated Drawings for Supporting Comprehension of a Complex Animation. *Contemporary Educational Psychology* 38:211-224.

Mayer, R.E. (2001). *Multimedia Learning.* New York: Cambridge University Press.

———. (2009). *Multimedia Learning.* 2nd ed. New York: Cambridge University Press.

———. (2011). Multimedia Learning and Games. In *Can Computer Games be Used for Instruction?*, ed. S. Tobias and D. Fletcher. Greenwich, CT: Information Age Publisher.

———. (2014a). Cognitive Theory of Multimedia Learning. In *The Cambridge Handbook of Multimedia Learning*, 2nd ed., ed. R. Mayer. New York: Cambridge University Press.

———. (2014b). *Computer Games for Learning.* Cambridge, MA: MIT Press.

———. (2014c). Incorporating Motivation into Multimedia Learning. *Learning & Instruction* 29:171-173.

————. (2014d). Principles Based on Social Cues in Multimedia Learning: Personalization, Voice, Embodiment, and Image Principles. In *The Cambridge Handbook of Multimedia Learning*, 2nd ed., ed. R.E. Mayer. New York: Cambridge University Press.

Mayer, R.E., A. Bove, A. Bryman, R. Mars, and L. Tapangco. (1996). When Less Is More: Meaningful Learning From Visual and Verbal Summaries of Science Textbook Lessons. *Journal of Educational Psychology* 88:64-73.

Mayer, R.E., and P. Chandler. (2001). When Learning Is Just a Click Away: Does Simple User Interaction Foster Deeper Understanding of Multimedia Messages? *Journal of Educational Psychology* 93:390-397.

Mayer, R.E., and C.S. DaPra. (2012). An Embodiment Effect in Computer-Based Learning With Animated Pedagogical Agents. *Journal of Experimental Psychology: Applied* 18:239-252.

Mayer, R.E., and L. Fiorella. (2014). Principles for Reducing Extraneous Processing in Multimedia Learning: Coherence, Signaling, Redundancy, Spatial Contiguity, and Temporal Contiguity Principles. In *The Cambridge Handbook of Multimedia Learning*, 2nd ed., ed. R.E. Mayer. New York: Cambridge University Press.

Mayer, R.E., and J.K. Gallini. (1990). When Is an Illustration Worth Ten Thousand Words? *Journal of Educational Psychology* 88:715-724.

Mayer, R.E., M. Hegarty, S. Mayer, and J. Campbell. (2005). When Static Media Promote Active Learning: Annotated Illustrations Versus Narrated Animations in Multimedia Learning. *Journal of Experimental Psychology: Applied* 11:256-265.

Mayer, R.E., J. Heiser, and S. Lonn. (2001). Cognitive Constraints on Multimedia Learning: When Presenting More Material Results in Less Understanding. *Journal of Educational Psychology* 93:187-198.

Mayer, R.E., and J. Jackson. (2005). The Case for Coherence in Scientific Explanations: Quantitative Details Can Hurt Qualitative Understanding. *Journal of Experimental Psychology: Applied* 11:13-18.

Mayer, R.E., and C.I. Johnson. (2008). Revising the Redundancy Principle in Multimedia Learning. *Journal of Educational Psychology* 100:380-386.

————. (2010). Adding Instructional Features That Promote Learning in a Game-Like Environment. *Journal of Educational Computing Research* 42:241-265.

Mayer, R.E., A. Mathias, and K. Wetzell. (2002). Fostering Understanding of Multimedia Messages Through Pretraining: Evidence for a Two-Stage Theory of Mental Model Construction. *Journal of Experimental Psychology: Applied* 8:147-154.

Mayer, R.E., and R. Moreno. (1998). A Split-Attention Effect in Multimedia Learning: Evidence for Dual Processing Systems in Working Memory. *Journal of Educational Psychology* 90:312-320.

Mayer, R.E., V. Sims, and H. Tajika. (1995). A Comparison of How Textbooks Teach Mathematical Problem Solving in Japan and the United States. *American Educational Research Journal* 32:443-460.

Mayer, R.E., A. Stull, K. DeLeeuw, K. Almeroth, B. Bimber, D. Chun, M. Bulger, J. Campbell, A. Knight, H. Zhang. (2009). Clickers in College Classrooms: Fostering Learning With Questioning Methods in Large Lecture Classes. *Contemporary Educational Psychology* 34:51-57.

McCrudden, M.T., G. Schraw, S. Lehran, and A. Poliquin. (2007). The Effect of Causal Diagrams on Text Learning. *Contemporary Educational Psychology* 32:367-388.

McDaniel, M.A., K.M. Wildman, and J.L. Anderson. (2012). Using Quizzes to Enhance Summative Assessment Performance in a Web-Based Class: An Experimental Study. *Journal of Applied Research in Memory and Cognition* 1:18-26.

Moreno, R. (2004). Decreasing Cognitive Load for Novice Students: Effects of Explanatory Versus Corrective Feedback in Discovery-Based Multimedia. *Instructional Science* 32:99-113.

———. (2006). Does the Modality Principle Hold For Different Media? A Test of the Methods-Affects-Learning Hypothesis. *Journal of Computer Assisted Learning* 33:149-158.

———. (2007). Optimizing Learning From Animations by Minimizing Cognitive Load: Cognitive and Affective Consequences of Signaling and Segmentation Methods. *Applied Cognitive Psychology* 21:765-781.

Moreno, R., and R.E. Mayer. (2000a). Engaging Students in Active Learning: The Case for Personalized Multimedia Messages. *Journal of Educational Psychology* 93:724-733.

———. (2000b). A Coherence Effect in Multimedia Learning: The Case for Minimizing Irrelevant Sounds in the Design of Multimedia Messages. *Journal of Educational Psychology* 92:117-125.

———. (2004). Personalized Messages that Promote Science Learning in Virtual Environments. *Journal of Educational Psychology* 96:165-173.

Moreno, R., and L. Ortegano-Layne. (2008). Do Classroom Exemplars Promote the Application of Principles in Teacher Education? A Comparison of Videos, Animations, and Narratives. *Educational Technology Research & Development* 56:449-465.

Nievelstein, F., T. van Gog, G. van Dijck, and H.P.A. Boshuizen. (2011). Instructional Support for Novice Law Students; Reducing Search Processes and Explaining Concepts in Cases. *Applied Cognitive Psychology* 25:408-413.

———. (2013). The Worked Example and Expertise Reversal Effect in Less Structured Tasks: Learning to Reason About Legal Cases. *Contemporary Educational Psychology* 38(2): 118-125.

Noroozi, O., A. Weinberger, H.J.A. Biemans, M. Mulder, M. Chizari. (2012). Argumentation-Based Computer Supported Collaborative Learning (ABCSCL): A Synthesis of 15 Years of Research. *Educational Research Review* 7:79-106.

Ohlsson, S. (1992). The Learning Curve For Writing Books: Evidence From Professor Asimov. *Psychological Science* 3:380-382.

Paas, F., and J. Sweller. (2014). Implications of Cognitive Load Theory for Multimedia Learning. *The Cambridge Handbook of Multimedia Learning*, 2nd ed., ed. R.E. Mayer. New York: Cambridge University Press.

Pashler, H., M. McDaniel, D. Rohrer, and R. Bjork. (2008). Learning Styles Concepts and Evidence. *Psychological Science in the Public Interest* 9:105-119.

Peterson, S.E. (1992). The Cognitive Functions of Underlining as a Study Technique. *Reading Research and Instruction* 31:49-56.

Primack, B.A., M.V. Carroll, M. McNamare, M.L. Klem, B. King, M. Rich, C.W. Chan, and S. Nayak. (2012). Role of Video Games in Improving Health-Related Outcomes: A Systematic Review. *American Journal of Preventive Medicine* 42:630-638.

Quilici, J.L., and R.E. Mayer. (1996). Role of Examples in How Students Learn to Categorize Statistics Word Problems. *Journal of Educational Psychology* 88:144-161.

References

Renkl, A. (2014). The Worked Out Examples Principles in Multimedia Learning. In *The Cambridge Handbook of Multimedia Learning*, ed. R.E. Mayer. New York: Cambridge University Press.

Rey, G.D., and A. Fischer. (2013). The Expertise Reversal Effect Concerning Instructional Explanations. *Instructional Science* 41:407-429.

Rey, G.D., and N. Steib. (2013). The Personalization Effect in Multimedia Learning: The Influence of Dialect. *Computers in Human Behavior* 29:2022-2028.

Richey, J.E., and T.J. Nokes-Malach (2013). How Much Is Too Much? Learning and Motivation Effects of Adding Instructional Explanations to Worked Examples. *Learning and Instruction* 25:104-124.

Riener, C., and D. Willingham. (2010). The Myth of Learning Styles. *Change* 42:33-35.

Roelle, J., and K. Berthold. (2013). The Expertise Reversal Effect in Prompting Focused Processing of Instructional Explanations. *Instructional Science* 41:635-656.

Roelle, J., K. Berthold, and A. Renkl. (2014) Two Instructional Aids to Optimize Processing and Learning From Instructional Explanations. *Instructional Science* (Online): 1-22.

Rohrer, D. (2012). Interleaving Helps Students Distinguish Among Similar Concepts. *Educational Psychology Review* 24:355-367.

Rohrer, D., and K. Taylor. (2006). The Effects of Overlearning and Distributed Practice on the Retention of Mathematics Knowledge. *Applied Cognitive Psychology* 20:1209-1224.

———. (2007). The Shuffling of Mathematics Problems Improves Learning. *Instructional Science* 35:481-498.

Roseth, C.J., A.J. Saltarelli, and C.R. Glass. (2011). Effects of Face-To-Face and Computer-Mediated Constructive Controversy on Social Interdependence, Motivation, and Achievement. *Journal of Educational Psychology*, 103, 804-820.

Sackett, D.L., W.M. Rosenberg, J.A. Gray, R.B. Haynes, and W.S. Richardson. (1996). Evidence Based Medicine: What It Is and What It Isn't. *British Medical Journal* 312:71-72.

Sampayo-Vargas, S., et al. (2013). The Effectiveness of Adaptive Difficulty Adjustments on Students' Motivation and Learning in an Educational Computer Game. *Computers & Education* 69:452-462.

Scheiter, K., P. Gerjets, T. Huk, B. Imhof, and Y. Kammerer. (2009). The Effects of Realism in Learning With Dynamic Visualizations. *Learning and Instruction* 19(6): 481-494.

Schnackenberg, H.L., and H.J. Sullivan. (2000). Learner Control Over Full and Lean Computer-Based Instruction Under Differing Ability Levels. *Educational Technology Research and Development* 48:19-35.

Schuler, A., K. Scheiter, and P. Gerjets. (2013). Is Spoken Text Always Better? Investigating the Modality and Redundancy Effect With Longer Text Presentation. *Computers in Human Behavior* 29(4): 1500-1601.

Schwamborn, A., R.E. Mayer, H. Thillmann, C. Leopold, and D. Leutner. (2010). Drawing as a Generative Activity and Drawing as a Prognostic Activity. *Journal of Educational Psychology* 102(4): 872-879.

Schwartz, D.L., and J.D. Bransford. (1998). A Time For Telling. *Cognition and Instruction* 16:475-522.

Schworm, S., and A. Renkl. (2007). Learning Argumentation Skills Through the Use of Prompts for Self-Explaining Examples. *Journal of Educational Psychology* 99:285-296.

Sears, D.A., and J.M. Reagin. (2013). Individual Versus Collaborative Problem Solving: Divergent Outcomes Depending on Task Complexity. *Instructional Science* 41(6): 1153-1172.

Shapiro, A.M., and L.T. Gordon. (2012). A Controlled Study of Clicker-Assisted Memory Enhancement in College Classrooms. *Applied Cognitive Psychology* 26:635-643.

Sitzmann, T. (2011). A Meta-Analytic Examination of the Instructional Effectiveness of Computer-Based Simulation Games. *Personnel Psychology* 64:489-528.

Sitzmann, T., K.G. Brown, W.J. Casper, K. Ely, and R.D. Zimmerman. (2008). A Review and Meta-Analysis of the Nomological Network of Trainee Reactions. *Journal of Applied Psychology* 93:280-295.

Spanjers, I.A.E., P.I. Wouters, T. van Gog, and J.J.G. van Merrienboer. (2011). An Expertise Reversal Effect of Segmentation in Learning From Animated Worked-Out Examples. *Computers in Human Behavior* 27:46-52.

Strayer, D.L., D. Crouch, and F.A. Drews. (2006). A Comparison of the Cell-Phone Driver and the Drunk Driver. *Human Factors* 46:640-649.

Stull, A., and R.E. Mayer. (2007). Learning by Doing Versus Learning By Viewing: Three Experimental Comparisons of Learner-Generated Versus Author-Generated Graphic Organizers. *Journal of Educational Psychology* 99:808-820.

Sung, E., and R.E. Mayer. (2012a). Five Facets of Social Presence in Online Distance Education. *Computers in Human Behavior* 28:1738-1747.

———. (2012b). When Graphics Improve Liking but Not Learning From Online Lessons. *Computers in Human Behavior* 28:1618-1625.

Sweller, J. (2005). Implications of Cognitive Load Theory for Multimedia Learning. In *The Cambridge Handbook of Multimedia Learning*, ed. R.E. Mayer. New York: Cambridge University Press.

Sweller, J., and P. Chandler. (1994). Why Some Material Is Difficult to Learn. *Cognition and Instruction* 12:185-233.

Sweller, J., and G.A. Cooper. (1985). The Use of Worked Examples as a Substitute for Problem Solving in Learning Algebra. *Cognition and Instruction* 2.59-89.

Taylor, K., and D. Rohrer. (2010). The Effects of Interleaved Practice. *Applied Cognitive Psychology* 24:837-848.

Um, E.R., J.L. Plass, E.O. Hayward, and B.D. Homer. (2012). Emotional Design in Multimedia Learning. *Journal of Educational Psychology* 104:485-498.

U.S. Department of Education. (2002). Strategic Plan for 2002–2007. Cited in Burkhardt and Schoenfeld (2003).

———. (2010). Office of Planning, Evaluation, and Policy Development, Evaluation of Evidence-Based Practices in Online Learning: A Meta-analysis and Review of Online Learning Studies, Washington, D.C.

Van Gog, T., L. Kester, F. Paas. (2011). Effects of Worked Examples, Example-Problem, and Problem-Example Pairs on Novices' Learning. *Contemporary Educational Psychology* 96:212-218.

Van Gog, T., and K. Scheiter. (2010). Eye Tracking as a Tool to Study and Enhance Multimedia Learning. *Learning and Instruction* 20:95-99.

Van Meter, P., and J. Garner. (2005). The Promise and Practice of Learner-Generated Drawing: Literature Review and Synthesis. *Educational Psychology Review* 17:285-325.

Wang, N., W.L. Johnson, R.E. Mayer, P. Rizzo, E. Shaw, and H. Collins. (2008). The Politeness Effect: Pedagogical Agents and Learning Outcomes. *International Journal of Human Computer Studies* 66:96-112.

Watson, G., J. Butterfield, R. Curran, C. Craig. (2010). Do Dynamic Work Instructions Provide an Advantage Over Static Instructions in a Small Scale Assembly Task? *Learning and Instruction* 20:84-93.

Wittwer, J., and A. Renkl. (2008). Why Instructional Explanations Often Do Not Work: A Framework for Understanding the Effectiveness of Instructional Explanations. *Educational Psychologist* 43:49-64.

———. (2010). How Effective Are Instructional Explanations in Example-Based Learning? A Meta-Analytic Review. *Educational Psychology Review* 22:393-409.

Wouters, P., C. van Nimwegen, H. van Oostendrop, and E.D. van der Speck. (2013). A Meta-Analysis of the Cognitive and Motivational Effects of Serious Games. *Journal of Educational Psychology* 105:249-265.

Young, M., S. Slota, A.B. Cutter, G. Jalette, G. Mullin, B. Lai, Z. Simeoni, M. Tran, and M. Yukhymenko. (2012). Our Princess is in Another Castle: A Review of Trends in Serious Gaming for Education. *Review of Educational Research* 82:61-89.

Yue, C.L., E.L. Bjork, and R.A. Bjork. (2013). Reducing Verbal Redundancy in Multimedia Learning: An Undesired Desirable Difficulty? *Journal of Educational Psychology* 105:266-277.

About the Author

Ruth Colvin Clark has focused her career on bridging the gap between academic research and practitioner application in instructional methods. A specialist in instructional design and workforce learning, she holds a doctorate in instructional psychology and served as training manager for Southern California Edison before founding her own company, Clark Training & Consulting.

Clark was president of the International Society for Performance Improvement and received the Thomas Gilbert Distinguished Professional Achievement Award in 2006. She was selected as an ASTD Legend Speaker at the 2007 International Conference & Exposition. Her recent books include *Scenario-Based E-Learning* and *E-Learning and the Science of Instruction* coauthored with Richard Mayer. She resides in southwest Colorado and Phoenix, Arizona, and divides her time among speaking, teaching, and writing.

Index

with audio narration, 111
with text and audio, 113–117
visuals and words used in, 108–109, 253
visuals not used in, 247
words not used in, 109–110
in worked examples, 192
Explanatory visuals, 92–93
Expository text, details added to, 153
Extraneous cognitive load, 55–57, 322–323
Eye-tracking data, 39–41, 118–119

F

Facebook, 127, 142
Factoids, 154
Factorial experiments, of graphics, 32–34
Faded worked examples, 186–187, 196
Fading, 186, 192
Failure to connect, 279–280
Feedback
benefits of, 334
corrective, 220, 224
definition of, 219
directive lessons, 278
in directive tasks, 274
elaborate, 220
evidence on, 220
expert comparison as, 296
focus of, 220–221
frequency of, 221–222
from games, 318–319
goals of, 219
instructive, 295
intrinsic, 218, 295–296
peer, 222
practice with, 278
in scenario-based learning, 295–296, 302
worked examples and, 196
Focused explanations, 242–243

G

Games
action-adventure, 310

action-based, 310, 314
active engagement with, 316, 318–320
arcade, 310
cognitive skills and behaviors, 313–315, 327
collaborative play of, 324
competitive elements in, 326
definition of, 308
design of, for learning, 311–313
drill and practice using, 273
effectiveness of, 307, 317–327
entertainment-based, 327–328
evidence-based principles for, 346–347
extraneous cognitive load, 322–323
feedback from, 318–319
genres of, 310
goal setting features of, 308–309
health benefits of, 315
instructional methods used to supplement, 323–324
instructional support for, 324–325
interactive and responsive features of, 308
for learning, 16–19, 74, 311–313, 315–317
learning aids for, 328
multiple plays of, 324
narratives in, 327
personalization principles added to, 325
popularity of, 307
role-play, 310
rules and constraints of, 310
second-language learning uses of, 311
self-explanation questions added to, 320–322
simulation-based, 311, 316
simulations versus, 311
spatial ability affected by, 314
sports, 311
strategy-based, 311
training program application of, 328–329
types of, 310–311
Germane cognitive load, 57
Germane load, 205
Google, 127
Graphics. *See also* Visuals

M

W

Y

HOW TO PURCHASE ATD PRESS PUBLICATIONS

ATD Press publications are available worldwide in print and electronic format.

To place an order, please visit our online store: www.td.org/books.

Our publications are also available at select online and brick-and-mortar retailers.

Outside the United States, English-language ATD Press titles may be purchased through the following distributors:

United Kingdom, Continental Europe, the Middle East, North Africa, Central Asia, and Latin America
Eurospan Group
Phone: 44.1767.604.972
Fax: 44.1767.601.640
Email: eurospan@turpin-distribution.com
Website: www.eurospanbookstore.com

Asia
Cengage Learning Asia Pte. Ltd.
Email: asia.info@cengage.com
Website: www.cengageasia.com

Nigeria
Paradise Bookshops
Phone: 08033075133
Email: paradisebookshops@gmail.com
Website: www.paradisebookshops.com

South Africa
Knowledge Resources
Phone: 27(11)880.8540
Fax: 27(11)880.8700/9829
Email: mail@knowres.co.za
Website: www.kr.co.za

For all other territories, customers may place their orders at the ATD online store: **www.td.org/books**.

101417.62220